THE WORLD WAR TWO ERA

THE AMERICAN RETROSPECTIVE SERIES

THE

WORLD WAR TWO

ERA

*Perspectives on
All Fronts
from*
HARPER'S MAGAZINE

*With an introduction by Paul Fussell
Edited by Katharine Whittemore*

FRANKLIN
SQUARE
P·R·E·S·S

NEW YORK

Published by Franklin Square Press, a division of Harper's Magazine,
666 Broadway, New York, N.Y. 10012

First Edition.

First printing 1994.

Library of Congress Cataloging-in-Publication Data:
The World War Two era: perspectives on all fronts from Harper's Magazine/
edited by Katharine Whittemore/ with an introduction by Paul Fussell.
p. cm.—(The American retrospective series)
ISBN: 1-879957-15-9 $14.95 (pbk.)
1. World War, 1939–1945. I. Whittemore, Katharine. II. Harper's Magazine.
III. Title: World War II era. IV. Series.
D743.W667 1994
940.53—dc20
94-8004
CIP

Book design by Deborah Thomas.
Cover design by Louise Fili.

Manufactured in the United States of America.

This book has been produced on acid-free paper.

CONTENTS

INTRODUCTION

Paul Fussell

IF DURING THE World War Two era you were searching for some intelligent, freewheeling analysis and comment on public events, there weren't a lot of places you could look. *The Nation* and *The New Republic* were there, of course, but they were weeklies, allowing their writers little time for consideration and reconsideration or the sort of aesthetic distance from their causes that memorable essays seem to require. Among monthlies, there was *The Atlantic Monthly,* still resonant with overtones of puritan New England, given to highmindedness and conservative views. And then there was *Harper's Magazine,* the voice of New York just as *The Atlantic* was the voice of Boston. Some thought *Harper's* programmatically liberal, while others thought it simply clear-eyed and courageous. What the wartime tone of *Harper's* was can be determined by readers of these thirty-two articles the magazine published from 1936 to 1946. They constitute an implicit psychological profile of America in the Second World War, although because of censorship, both official and patriotic-voluntary, that profile must omit the unpleasant facts that would belong to a full, frank view of that decade.

In any highly bureaucratized state, wartime writing that conveys optimistic, morale-raising news compels the suspicion that the propaganda services, like the Office of War Information in the United States, have participated in its production. This is especially so at bad moments, like, say, the spring of 1942. The Allies were still shaken by such disasters as Pearl Harbor, the sinking of the British warships *Repulse* and *Prince of Wales*, and the surrender of Singapore, Hong Kong, and the Philippines. Although not known at the time, in Germany the Wannsee Conference had just consigned the bulk of European Jews to the gas chamber. In North Africa, the Afrika Korps was pushing the British back toward Cairo and humiliation. Readers of *Harper's* were exhorted by Bernard DeVoto (pages 69–71) to face facts and to resist the natural American assumption that victory would automatically attend the virtuous. Actually, he knew, victory would require sacrifice and sorrow unimaginable at the outset of the war. And even winning it was by no means certain. "We are perilously close," DeVoto warned in April 1942, "to being licked."

At that moment, Margaret Bourke-White was in Moscow, not as a private citizen but as an official visitor photographing and reporting on the Soviet war effort. Thank God, the reader of her copy is to understand, the news from Russia is uniformly encouraging, even ennobling. Indeed, Allied success there nicely counterbalances Allied disaster on the other side of the world, and all is well. Under German bombing, even Moscow's schoolboys are heroically pitching in to help put out fires, and evidently enjoying the work. Given an opportunity to photograph Stalin in his Kremlin office, Bourke-White actually got him laughing and shot that moment. "Then I knew I had the expression I wanted." Was this monster the mass murderer of more innocents than even Hitler? Forget that. Much must be whitewashed if morale and Allied solidarity are to be served, and if the high moral pretenses of the Allied side are to be protected from irony and ridicule.

An opportunity to tour the front presented Bourke-White with further encouraging images and implications. The Russian army's skill in camouflaging its positions with trees and greenery "made the war look like a back-to-nature movement." The front-line scenes are almost little versions of pastoral, thoroughly benign:

> As we traveled directly along the front lines, we proceeded from one grove to another. Each little wood, as we approached, looked uninhabited until we went in under the trees and our eyes grew accustomed to the dim green light. Then it revealed itself as a complete living community with field telephones, dug-in tanks, batteries shrouded with green boughs, and [of course] soldiers singing.

Such images of happiness and ability lead naturally to vignettes of triumph over evil. At the battlefield of Yelnya, she saw where 50,000 dead German soldiers had been "hastily shoveled into their own trenches." No Russian dead are mentioned, no hospitals are visited, no Solzhenitsyns are interviewed about how awful the Stalin dictatorship is. All is successful and even rather beautiful, and everywhere there are auguries of the ultimate triumph of decency, modesty, and domesticity over rude force and public wickedness. In a ruined town, she notes, "I saw a woman borrowing some hot charcoals from the fire of a neighbor. 'What is she carrying them in?' I wondered, as I watched her heading homeward. The shape was familiar. She was bringing home hot coals in a Nazi helmet."

Richard E. Lauterbach's article "How the Russians Try Nazi Criminals" (pages 245–256) continues the process of burnishing the morals of an indispensable ally. His article deals with the trial in Kharkov of some German officers and a Russian collaborator accused of atrocities. Convicted, they are publicly hanged. During the trial, Lauterbach lunches with the Soviet's Atrocity Commission. In the light of his report on this trial and its outcome, in the context of high moral partisanship that he's established, it would be impossible to accommodate the news that the Soviets themselves were masters of atrocities, one minor example being their systematic murder of the Polish officer corps, ordered by Stalin and known today as the Katyn Massacre. But this is wartime, and even *Harper's* must be exploited as an agent of noble fictions.

Since nothing derogatory about any of the Allies must see print,

C. J. Fernand-Laurent's "France from the Inside" (pages 133–139) must present Parisians as uniformly contemptuous of their German occupiers. Not to be noticed is a simultaneous phenomenon, the denouncing of Jews to German and Vichy authorities by Frenchmen anxious to obtain Jewish apartments and household goods.

In addition, American writers, William L. Shirer implies, should refrain from saying anything critical of the United States, lest it be picked up by the enemy and simply reprinted to demoralize Allied prisoners in their hands. In "What the Germans Told the Prisoners" (pages 183–194), he castigates journalist Louis Bromfield for his *Reader's Digest* article of August 1943, "We Aren't Going to Have Enough to Eat," a serious disclosure of bungling in the American rationing and food-distribution system. This piece, says Shirer, constituted a gift to German propagandists working on the sensibilities of the U.S. prisoners. That Bromfield's charges contained some useful truth is not the issue. What is, is his actually venturing to say something honest that might be useful to German propagandists, who, indeed, simply reprinted Bromfield's article word for word and set it before their captives. Shirer's moral for American writers is clear: don't criticize anything. Even mildly corrective comment must be watched closely, for fear it offend. This performance of Shirer's suggests the virtually seamless continuity between the Total Americanism demanded by the war effort and such subsequent phenomena as McCarthyism and the Total Anti-Communism obligatory during the Cold War. (Interestingly, in this same article Shirer reveals that he himself has fallen for the Soviet propaganda assertion that it was not they but the Germans who committed the atrocity in the Katyn Forest.)

One thing notable in some of the early chapters here, articles written in the war's earliest stages, is innocence about the kind of American brutality winning the war is going to entail. There is a lurking notion that wartime behavior can still be rational, controllable, "social" in an almost peacetime sense. Early on, people thought the war was about words and argument, eked out by armaments. They didn't know yet what unspeakable things we'd have to do to win: bombing guiltless non-combatants by the hundreds of thousands;

shooting adolescent boys rigged out as soldiers; devising and dropping the A-bombs; sinking merchant ships without warning. That is, imitating the Germans and the Japanese in every military way except maltreating prisoners and exterminating unwanted populations.

What this suggests is that at the outset no one was confronting the problem of evil, with the result that the facts of the Holocaust, when finally fully revealed at the end of the war, proved monstrously surprising. At the beginning, the man who insisted upon the total extermination of the Jews by the cruelest methods would be talked about in the terms invoked by John Gunther in his 1936 character sketch of Hitler (pages 1–14). Then, Gunther's assumption that Hitler was sort of like other European politicians could lead to jocose notice of his "Charlie-Chaplin" mustache and to such a well-meditated conclusion as: "by no stretch of generosity could he be called a person of genuine culture." It is not Gunther's fault, but innocent, like almost everyone, of the function of Eva Braun, he buys the fiction about the Führer's purity and declares: "He is totally uninterested in women from any personal sexual point of view." So well was Eva concealed that people still speculated that Hitler was homosexual. But this period of journalistic innocence could not last forever, and by 1938 Elmer Davis (pages 15–19) is finding that "Hitler's mustache is no longer a joke, nor is anything else about Hitler." And Davis earns credit for noticing how much of Hitler's total program involves the simple physical application to all of Europe of late-nineteenth-century obsessions about "eugenics" and improving the breed.

By 1943, experience was beginning to erode much of the initial innocence, but those who fought the war in 1945 will smile when the British journalist Patrick Maitland, in his article "Under Fire on Guadalcanal" (pages 117–131), observes, as if delivering an account of the most interesting primitive conditions, that "just behind our front line" he takes his meals at a "rough table." Two more years of war and there will be no tables at all, but, if one is lucky, a freezing hole in the ground, miles from the comforts of a field-kitchen, with the cold food eaten from cardboard boxes. The full viciousness of the Japanese way of war is still not entirely understood—the Japanese readiness to savage corpses, their lunatic tactics in assaults (rush forward screaming and get shot), and their officially sanctioned cruelty to prisoners.

One persisting indication of general innocence was the conviction that bombs could be aimed precisely and that even in "area bombing"— a handy euphemism for the intentional destruction of civilian morale, and of civilian bodies too—military targets could be hit, civilian avoided. This "dehousing" of the enemy population is one reason why in this war civilian casualties surpassed those suffered on the fighting fronts.

C. Lester Walker, in "How We Planned the Invasion of Europe" (pages 199–219), has sought to project an idyll of engineering efficiency. Censorship doubtless prevents his alluding to the disastrous sinking, one after the other upon launching, of the bulk of the highly touted Dual Drive swimming tanks, whose inflated collars were supposed to float them safely ashore at Normandy. Twenty-seven of them sank like stones, carrying their crews with them. It is probably not censorship, however, but actual conviction that prompts him to celebrate the proposed pinpoint bombing of "a particular wing of a particular precision tool plant." Planning was so precise, Walker asserts, that it was determined that "at exactly H-hour minus thirty minutes, 1,350 heavy bombers would . . . lay their eggs just so" to assist the ground troops. But actually, after a series of spectacular disasters arising from such confidence, Eisenhower finally forbade entirely the use of grossly inaccurate heavy bombing as a tactical aid to the ground forces.

As these articles often imply, the demand that the war be won quickly and efficiently required an implicit curb on traditional American individualism and orneriness in the interest of community, solidarity, and finally, conformity. Well-known satirists of American absurdities like H. L. Mencken fell silent, and such staples of American humor as exaggerated hostility to the government, in the Mark Twain and Will Rogers tradition, yielded to a common front of cheerful acceptance and satisfaction. We were all in this together, which tended to imply that it would be well if we were all alike.

Thus some thought the war an event almost to be welcomed because of its power to reduce American "discords." This is part of Bernard DeVoto's message in his Commencement Address of 1942 (pages

91–97). "We are here together," he observes, and that is taken to be a good thing, as now the "fellowship" of soldiers may remind us. DeVoto tells his young male audience (women are nowhere mentioned),

> You are suddenly members one of another . . .
> You are enlarged in a fraternity of things shared.

That his audience consists largely of future helpless conscripts who soon will be cruelly chewed out and humiliated by contemptuous drill instructors is something better not noticed. DeVoto's rhetorical world is one where death in battle is still "seemly." One gets the impression that neither he nor the graduates he's addressing are acquainted with Wilfred Owen's unforgettable rejection of Horace's conclusion that "it is sweet and seemly to die for one's country."

Virginia Snow Wilkinson (pages 141–148) is another who values highly the wartime "co-operative spirit" as a relief from individualism. Formerly "just a housewife," she now has found satisfaction working in a shipyard not by herself but with a team of women. As they have worked together, she testifies, those troublesome individual characteristics have faded away, until "we [have become] integrated persons working together. . . ." The wartime ideal of community, unthreatened by criticism, nay-saying, or personal oddity, is nicely encapsulated in her conclusion, "It was good, I thought, this working together on a ship."

The demand for solidarity, undisturbed by natural distinctions, interests, or competing concerns, impels even so acute an observer of facts and details as Frederick Lewis Allen, in "Notes on an English Visit" (pages 149–160), to participate in the wartime British myth of total social unity. Britons badly bombed in the city of Plymouth in 1941, he reports three years later,

> wonder now how they got through the exhaustion and sleeplessness and menacing suspense that dogged them week after week and month after month; and they feel too, one sometimes notes, a little yearning of regret for the exaltation that took hold of them then: the exaltation of discovering that all of them, rich and poor, were knit together by the sharing of labor and peril.

A reader who could swallow that whole would have trouble understanding why Churchill, visiting the bombed ruins of Bristol in April 1941, when the city was close to open rebellion, was welcomed by being soundly booed, or why, in the general election of 1945, the "poor," to some people's surprise, voted to throw out the wartime government they associated with "the rich." The unmentionable fact is that during the war there was widespread agreement with the traditional view expressed by one soldier fighting in North Africa who deposed that in Britain, "one class gets the sugar, and the other class gets the shit."

The war having been prosecuted successfully and brought to a triumphant moral conclusion, it's easy now to forget the long, strident, patriotic campaign against getting into it at all. In 1939, C. Hartley Grattan, to whom *Harper's* opened its hospitable pages, argued (pages 21–22) that the wreckage left by the First World War should be a sufficient warning against plunging into the Second. This last peacetime moment, he wrote, is the time to oppose "the men, emotions, opinions, drives which are pushing this country toward the charnel house once more." And a year later, as Elmer Davis reports (pages 27–29), Charles Lindbergh, still a hero grand enough to command attention, emphasized on the radio, "I do not believe this is a war for democracy; it is a war over the balance of power in Europe." *Harper's* deserves praise for calmly publicizing these inflammatory contributions to the life-or-death national debate, justifying its procedure by giving E. B. White an opportunity to say a little later: "The written word, unlike the spoken word, is something which every person examines privately and judges calmly by his own intellectual standards. . . ." *Harper's* deserves praise too for resisting the Office of Censorship's attempt to stifle public knowledge of General MacArthur's personal vanity and political ambition under the guise of necessary military censorship (pages 165–166). "This situation," said *Harper's*, "is intolerable in a free country." Thus the power of the First Amendment habit, weakened in wartime, but never entirely subdued.

In abeyance for so long, the American urge to rake the muck could not be silenced forever. Their being held under pressure for so long perhaps accounts for the vehemence with which John Bartlow Martin's home truths burst forth once the war was over. In "Anything Bothering You, Soldier?" (pages 263–272), he vents his anger at the behavior of the home-front civilians during the past four years, at their greed and ignoble materialism, their cowlike vulnerability to the lies of propagandists and ad agencies and the slick soporific voices on the radio. When they think about it at all, he says, "Civilians think war means battle." The boobs haven't enough imagination to realize that it means also the indignity of virtual slavery, with attendant shame, guilt, and self-hatred. Martin is angry because, as every soldier knows, the war was a sad mess, and no one is aware of it but him and his fellow victims. No matter how necessary, mass murder is not an enterprise to be proud of, even though manufacturers and advertisers make a lot of money from it. Aware of all this and letting it out for the first time, no wonder Martin is so angry that he has trouble holding his discourse within the currently expected genteel bounds. In a later comment on his article, he defends his anger and says, "Having been in the Army has done one thing of great value for me: it has convinced me that all of us have always got to do everything in our power to prevent this from ever happening again."

It is from Oscar Williams's "War and the Poets: A Symposium" (pages 221–225), published a month before the war's end in Europe, that one might draw a couple of conclusions. The British poet Geoffrey Grigson is quoted saying, "One must be self-deluded if one simplifies something so muddled as a twentieth-century complete war into causes, either good or bad. The only clear thing that I can see is that humanity has walked into a mess. . . ." And the words of John Berryman can serve as a finale: "War is an experience, worse than most. . . . those who 'have' it will be affected in different degrees, in different ways; some trained to speech will talk about it, others trained equally and affected strongly will have nothing to say; those affected most—the dead—will be most silent."

HITLER

(JANUARY 1936)

John Gunther

*The union of theorist, organizer, and leader in one man is the
rarest phenomenon on earth; therein lies greatness.*
—Adolf Hitler

ADOLF HITLER, SEEMINGLY so irrational and self-contradictory,
is a character of great complexity—not an easy nut to crack. To many
he is meager and insignificant; yet he holds sixty-five million
Germans, a fair share of whom adore him, in a thraldom compounded
of love, fear and nationalist ecstasy. Few men run so completely the
gamut from the sublime to the ridiculous. He is a mountebank, a
demagogue, a frustrated hysteric, a lucky misfit. He is also a figure of
extreme veneration to millions of honest and not-even-puzzled
Germans. What are the sources of his extraordinary powers?

This paunchy, Charlie Chaplin–mustached man, given to insomnia
and emotionalism, who is head of the Nazi Party, commander-in-chief
of the German army and navy, Leader of the German nation, creator,
president, and chancellor of the Third Reich, was born in Austria in
1889. He was not a German by birth. This was a highly important
fact inflaming his early nationalism. He developed the implacable

1

patriotism of the frontiersman, the exile. Only an Austrian could take Germanism so seriously.

His imagination is purely political. I have seen his early paintings, those which he submitted to the Vienna art academy as a boy. They are prosaic, utterly devoid of rhythm, color, feeling, or spiritual imagination. They are architect's sketches: painful and precise draftsmanship, nothing more. No wonder the Vienna professors told him to go to an architectural school and give up pure art as hopeless.

He went only to grade school, and by no stretch of generosity could he be called a person of genuine culture. He is not nearly so cultivated, so sophisticatedly interested in intellectual affairs as is, say, Mussolini. He reads almost nothing. The Treaty of Versailles was probably the most concrete single influence on his life; but it is doubtful if he ever read it in full. He dislikes intellectuals. He has never been outside Germany since his youth in Austria (if you except his war experiences in Flanders and the brief visit to Mussolini in Venice in 1934), and he speaks no foreign language except a few words of battered French.

To many who meet him Hitler seems awkward and ill-at-ease. This is because visitors, even among his subordinates, obtrude personal realities which interfere with his incessant fantasies. He has no poise. He finds it difficult to make quick decisions: capacity for quick decisions derives from inner harmony, which he lacks. He is no "strong, silent man."

Foreigners, especially interviewers from British or American newspapers, may find him cordial and even candid, but they seldom have opportunity to question him, to participate in a give-and-take discussion. Hitler rants. He is extremely emotional. He never answers questions. He talks to you as if you were a public meeting, and nothing can stop the gush of words.

One after another he eliminated those who helped him to his career: Drexler, Feder, Gregor Strasser. It is true that he has been loyal to some colleagues—those who never disagreed with him, who gave him absolute obedience. This loyalty is not an unmixed virtue, considering the unsavoriness of such men as Streicher, the Jew baiter of Nuremberg. Nothing can persuade Hitler to give Goering up, or Streicher, or Rosenberg.

Unsavoriness alone is not enough to provoke his draconian ingratitude.

His physical courage is a moot point. When his men were fired on in the Munich *Putsch* of 1923, he flung himself to the street with such violence that his shoulder was broken. Nazi explanations of this are two: (1) linked arm in arm with a man on his right who was shot and killed, he was jerked unwittingly to the pavement; (2) he behaved with the reflex action of the veteran front-line soldier, *viz.*, sensibly fell flat when the bullets came.

Hitler has told an acquaintance his own story of the somewhat mysterious circumstances in which he won the Iron Cross. He was a dispatch bearer. He was carrying messages across a part of No Man's Land which was believed to be clear of enemy troops when he heard French voices. He was alone, armed only with a revolver; so with great presence of mind he shouted imaginary orders to an imaginary column of men. The Frenchmen tumbled out of a deserted dugout, seven in all, hands up. Hitler alone delivered all seven to the German lines. Recounting this story privately, he told his interlocutor that he knew full well the feat would have been impossible had the seven men been American or English instead of French.

Like that of all fanatics, his capacity for self-belief, his ability to delude himself, is enormous. Thus he probably is perfectly "sincere" when in a preposterous interview with the *Daily Mail* he says that the Nazi revolution cost only twenty-six lives. He believes absolutely in what he says—at the moment.

But his lies have been notorious. Hitler promised the authorities of Bavaria not to make a *Putsch;* and promptly made one. He promised to tolerate the Papen government; then fought it. He promised not to change the composition of his first cabinet; then changed it. He promised to kill himself if the Munich coup failed; it failed, and he is still alive.

Hitler, at forty-six, is not in first-rate physical condition. He has gained about twelve pounds in the past year, and his neck and midriff show it. His physical presence has always been indifferent; the extreme sloppiness with which he salutes is, for instance, notorious. The forearm barely moves above the elbow. He had lung trouble as a boy, and was blinded by poison gas in the War.

In August, 1935, it was suddenly revealed that the Leader had suffered a minor operation some months before to remove a polyp on his vocal chords—penalty of years of tub-thumping. The operation was successful. The next month Hitler shocked his adherents at Nuremberg by alluding, in emotional and circumlocutory terms, to the possibility of his death. "I do not know when I shall finally close my eyes," he said, "but I do know that the party will continue and will rule. Leaders will come and Leaders will die, but Germany will live. . . . The army must preserve the power given to Germany and watch over it." This speech led to rumors (quite unconfirmed) that the growth in Hitler's throat was malignant, and that he had cancer.

He takes no exercise, and his only important relaxation (though recently he began to like battleship cruises in the Baltic or North Sea) is music. He is deeply musical. Wagner is one of the cardinal influences in his life; he is obsessed by Wagner. He goes to the opera as often as he can. Sessions of the Reichstag, which take place in the Kroll Opera House, sometimes end with whole performances of Wagner operas—to the boredom of non-musical deputies!

When he is fatigued at night then his friend and court jester Hanfstaengl may be summoned to play him to sleep, sometimes with Schumann or Verdi, more often with Beethoven and Wagner, for Hitler needs music as if it were a drug. Hanfstaengl is a demoniac pianist. I have heard him thump the keys at the Kaiserhof with such resonance that the walls shook. When Hanfstaengl plays he keeps time to his own music by puffing out his cheeks and bellowing like a trumpet. The effect is amazing. You cannot but believe that a trumpeter is hidden somewhere in the room. Hanfstaengl's popularity with Hitler is, however, believed to be waning.

Hitler cares nothing for books, nothing for clothes (he seldom wears anything but an ordinary brown-shirt uniform, or a double-breasted blue serge suit, with the inevitable raincoat and slouch hat), nothing for friends, and nothing for food and drink. He neither smokes nor drinks, and he will not allow anyone to smoke near him.

He is practically a vegetarian. At the banquet tendered him by Mussolini he would eat only a double portion of scrambled eggs. He drinks coffee occasionally, but not often. Once or twice a week he crosses from the Chancellery to the Kaiserhof Hotel (the G.H.Q. of the Nazi Party before he came to power), and sits there and sips—chocolate.

This has led many people to speak of Hitler's "asceticism," but asceticism is not quite the proper word. He is limited in aesthetic interests, but he is no flagellant or anchorite. There is very little of the *austere* in Hitler. He eats only vegetables—but they are prepared by an exquisitely competent chef. He lives "simply"—but his flat in Munich is the last word in courtly sumptuousness.

He works, when in Berlin, in the palace of the Reichskanzler on the Wilhelmstrasse. He seldom uses the President's palace a hundred yards away on the same street, because when Hindenburg died he wanted to eliminate as much as possible the memory of Presidential Germany. The building is new, furnished in modern glass and metal, and Hitler helped design it. Murals of the life of Wotan adorn the walls. An improvised balcony has been built over the street, from which on public occasions the Leader may review his men. Beneath the hall—according to reports—is a comfortable bombproof cellar.

Hitler dislikes Berlin. He leaves the capital at any opportunity, preferring Munich or Berchtesgaden, a village in southern Bavaria, where he has an alpine chalet, Haus Wachenfeld. Perched on the side of a mountain, this retreat, dear to his heart, is not far from the Austrian frontier, a psychological fact of great significance. From his front porch he can almost see the homeland which repudiated him, and for which he yearns.

By a man's friends may ye know him. But Hitler has none. For years his most intimate associate, beyond all doubt, was Captain Ernst Roehm, chief of staff of the S.A. (*Sturm Abteilung*—storm troops—brown shirts), whom he executed on June 30, 1934. From one of the half dozen men in Germany indisputably most qualified to know, I have heard it that Roehm was the *only* man in Germany, the single

German out of sixty-five million Germans, with whom Hitler was on *Du-fuss* (thee and thou) terms. Now that Roehm is dead there is no single German who calls Hitler "Adolf." Roehm was a notorious homosexual; but one should not deduce from this that Hitler is homosexual also.

The man who is closest to Hitler at present is his chief bodyguard, Lieutenant Brückner. The only two men who can see him at any time, without previous appointment, are Ribbentrop, his adviser in foreign affairs, and Schacht, the economics dictator. His chief permanent officials, like Dietrich, his press secretary, may see him daily, and so may Hess, the deputy leader of the party; but even Hess is not an *intimate* friend. Neither Goering nor Goebbels may see Hitler without previous appointment.

He is almost oblivious of ordinary personal contacts. A colleague of mine traveled with him in the same airplane, day after day, for two months during the 1932 electoral campaigns. Hitler never talked to a soul, not even to his secretaries, in the long hours in the air; never stirred, never smiled. My friend remembers most vividly that in order to sneak a cigarette when the plane stopped he had to run out of sight of the entourage. He says that he saw Hitler five or six hours a day during this trip, but that he is perfectly sure Hitler, meeting him by chance outside the airplane, would not have known his name or face.

He dams up his emotions to the bursting point, then is apt to break out in crying fits. A torrent of feminine tears compensates for the months of uneasy struggle not to give himself away. For instance, when he spent a whole night trying to persuade a dissident leader, Otto Strasser, from leaving the party, he broke into tears three times. In the early days he often wept when other methods to carry a point failed.

Hitler does not enjoy too great exposure of this weakness, and he tends to keep all subordinates at a distance. They worship him, but they do not know him well. They may see him every day, year in and year out; but they would never dare to be familiar. Hanfstaengl told me once that in all the years of their association he had never called Hitler anything except "Herr Hitler" (or "Herr Reichskanzler" after the Leader reached power); and that Hitler had never called him by first name or his diminutive (Putzi), but always "Hanfstaengl" or "Dr. Hanfstaengl." There is an inhumanity about the inner circle of the Nazi Party that is scarcely credible.

An old-time party member today would address Hitler as *"Mein Führer"*; others as "Herr Reichskanzler." When greeted with the Nazi salute and the words "Heil Hitler," Hitler himself replies with "Heil Hitler." Speechmaking, the Leader addresses his followers as "My" German people. In posters for the plebiscites he asks, "Dost thou, German man, and thou, German woman . . . etc." It is as if he feels closer to the German people in bulk than to any individual German, and this is indeed true. The German *people* are the chief emotional reality of his life.

Let us now examine Hitler's relation to the imperatives which dominate the lives of most men.

He is totally uninterested in women from any personal sexual point of view. He thinks of them as housewives and mothers or potential mothers, to provide sons for the battlefield—other people's sons.

"The life of our people must be freed from the asphyxiating perfume of modern eroticism," he says in *Mein Kampf*, his autobiography. His personal life embodies this precept to the fullest. He is not a woman-hater, but he avoids and evades women. His manners are those of the wary chevalier, given to hand-kissing—and nothing else. Many women are attracted to him sexually, but they have had to give up the chase. Frau Goebbels formerly had evening parties to which she asked pretty and distinguished women to meet him, but she was never able to arrange a match. The rumor was heard for a time that the coy Leader was engaged to the grand-daughter of Richard Wagner. It was nonsense. It is quite possible that Hitler has never had anything to do with a woman in his life.

Nor, as is so widely believed, is he homosexual. Several German journalists spent much time and energy, when such an investigation was possible, checking every lodging that Hitler in Munich days had slept in; they interviewed beer hall proprietors, coffee house waiters, landladies, porters. No evidence was discovered that Hitler had been intimate with anybody of any sex at any time. His sexual energies, at the beginning of his career, were obviously sublimated into oratory.

Hitler takes no salary from the state; rather he donates it to a fund which supports workmen who have suffered from labor accidents; but his private fortune could be considerable if he chose to save. He announced late in 1935 that he—alone among statesmen—had no bank account or stocks or shares. Previous to this it had been thought that he was part-owner of Franz Eher & Co., Munich, the publishers of the chief Nazi organs, *Völkischer Beobachter, Angriff,* etc., one of the biggest publishing houses in Europe. Its director, Max Amman, was Hitler's top-sergeant in the War, and later for many years his business manager.

If Hitler has no personal fortune, he must have turned all his earnings from his autobiography, *Mein Kampf,* to the party. This book is almost obligatory reading for Germans and, at a high price (RM 7.20, or about $2.88), it has sold 1,930,000 copies since its publication in 1925. If his royalty is 15 per cent, a moderate estimate, Hitler's total proceeds from this source at the end of 1935 should have been about $800,000.

Nothing is more difficult in Europe than to discover the facts of the private fortunes of leading men. This is forbidden ground to questioners in all countries. Does any dictator, Hitler or Mussolini or Stalin, carry cash in his pocket or make actual purchases in cash? It is unlikely.

He was born and brought up a Roman Catholic. But he lost faith early and he attends no religious services of any kind. His Catholicism means nothing to him; he is impervious even to the solace of confession. On being formed, his government almost immediately began a fierce religious war against Catholics, Protestants, and Jews alike.

Why? Perhaps the reason was not religion fundamentally, but politics. To Hitler the overwhelming first business of the Nazi revolution was the "unification," the *Gleichschaltung* (co-ordination) of Germany. He had one driving passion, the removal from the Reich of any competition, of whatever kind. Catholicism, like Judaism, was a profoundly international (thus non-German) organism. Therefore—out with it.

The basis of much of the madness of Hitlerism was his incredibly severe and drastic desire to purge Germany of non-German elements, to create a one hundred per cent Germany for one hundred per cent Germans only. He disliked bankers and department stores—as Dorothy Thompson pointed out—because they represented non-German, international, financial and commercial forces. He detested socialists and communists because they were affiliated with world groups aiming to internationalize labor. He loathed, above all, pacifists, because pacifists opposed war and were internationalist in basic views.

Catholicism he considered a particularly dangerous competitive force because it demands two allegiances of a man, and double allegiance was something Hitler could not countenance. Thus the campaign against the "black moles," as Nazis call priests. Thus the attacks on the Munich cardinal, Faulhauber; the anti-Catholic polemics of Rosenberg and Goebbels; the outrages of August, 1935.

Protestantism was—theoretically—a simple matter for Hitler to deal with because the Lutheran Church presumably was German and nationalist. Hitler thought that by the simple installation of an army chaplain, a ferocious Nazi named Mueller, as Reichsbishop, he could "co-ordinate" the Evangelical Church in Germany, and turn it to his service. The idea of a united Protestant church appealed to his neat architect's mind. He was wrong. The church question has been an itching pot of trouble ever since.

It was quite natural, following the confused failure to Nazify Protestantism, that some of Hitler's followers should have turned to Paganism. The Norse myths are a first-class nationalist substitute. Carried to its logical extreme, Naziism in fact demands the creation of a new and nationalist religion.

Heiden has quoted Hitler's remark, "We do not want any other God than Germany itself." This is a vital point. *Germany* is Hitler's religion.

Vividly in *Mein Kampf* Hitler tells the story of his first encounter with a Jew. He was a boy of seventeen, alone in Vienna, and he had never seen a Jew in his life. The Jew, a visitor from Poland or the Ukraine in native costume, outraged the tender susceptibilities of the youthful Hitler.

"Can this creature be a Jew?" he asked himself. Then bursting on him came a second question: "Can he possibly be a *German?*"

This early experience had a profound influence on him, forming the emotional base of his perfervid anti-Semitism. He was provincially mortified that any such creature could be one with himself, a sharer in Teuton nationality. Later he "rationalized" his fury on economic and political grounds. Jews, he said, took jobs away from "Germans"; Jews controlled the press of Berlin, the theater, the arts; there were too many Jewish lawyers, doctors, professors; the Jews were a "pestilence, worse than the Black Death."

No one can properly conceive the basic depth and breadth of Hitler's anti-Semitism who has not carefully read *Mein Kampf.* This book was written ten years ago. He changed it as edition followed edition, in minor particulars, and refuses to allow its publication—unexpurgated—abroad. Recently he sued a French publisher who tried to bring out an unabridged translation. In all editions the implacability of his anti-Jewish prejudice remains.

Any number of incidents outside the book may be mentioned. For instance, in the winter of 1934–35 he went four times to see a play called "Tovarish," recounting sympathetically the plight of aristocratic Russian emigrés and sneering at the Bolsheviks. Before he first attended it, it is said, his secretaries telegraphed to Paris to ascertain if the author, Jacques Deval, was Aryan as far back as his grandparents. It would have been unthinkable for Hitler to have witnessed a play by even a partly Jewish author.

Long before he became chancellor, Hitler would not allow himself to speak to a Jew even on the telephone. A publicist as well known as Walter Lippmann, a statesman as eminent as Lord Reading, would not be received at the Brown House. An interesting point arises. Has Hitler since his youth actually ever been in the company of a Jew, ever once talked to one? Probably not.

Now we may proceed to summarize what might be called Hitler's positive qualities.

First of all, consider his single-mindedness, his intent fixity of purpose. His tactics may change; his strategy may change; his *aim,* never. His aim is to create a strong national Germany, with himself atop it. No opportunistic device, no zigzag in polemics, is too great for him; but the aim, the goal, never varies.

Associated with his single-mindedness is the quality of stamina. All dictators have stamina; all need it. Despite Hitler's lack of vigorous gesture and essential flabbiness, his physical endurance is considerable. I know interviewers who have talked to him on the eve of an election, after he had made several speeches a day, all over Germany, week on end; they found him fresh and even calm. "When I have a mission to fulfil, I shall have the strength for it," he said.

Like all dictators, he has considerable capacity for hard work, for industry, though he is not the sloghorse for punishment that, for instance, Stalin is. He is not a good executive; his desk is usually high with documents requiring his decision which he neglects. He hates to make up his mind. His orders are often vague and contradictory. Yet he gets an immense amount of work done. "Industry" in a dictator or head of state means, as a rule, ability to read and listen. The major part of the work of Hitler or Mussolini is perusal of reports and attention to the advice of experts and subordinates. During half their working time they are receiving information. Therefore it is necessary for a dictator (a) to choose men intelligently (many of Hitler's best men he inherited from the old civil service); and (b) to instil faith in himself in them. Hitler has succeeded in this double task amply. And when his men fail him he murders them.

Hitler's political sense is highly developed and acute. His calculations are shrewd and penetrating to the smallest detail. For instance, his two major decisions on foreign policy—Germany's departure from the League of Nations and the introduction of conscription—were deliberately announced on Saturday afternoon to ease the shock to opinion from abroad. When he has something unpleasant to explain, the events of June 30th for instance, he usually speaks well after 8:00 P.M., so that foreign newspapers can carry only a hurried and perhaps garbled account of his words.

He made good practical use of his anti-Semitism. The Jewish terror was, indeed, an excellent campaign maneuver. The Nazis surged into power in March, 1933, with an immense and unrealizable series of electoral pledges. They promised to end unemployment, rescind the Versailles Treaty, regain the Polish corridor, assimilate Austria, abolish department stores, socialize industry, eliminate interest on capital, give the people land. These aims were more easily talked about than achieved. One thing the Nazis could do, one pledge they could redeem—beat the Jews.

Another source of Hitler's power is the impersonality I have already mentioned. His vanity is extreme, but in an odd way it is not personal. He has no peacockery. Mussolini must have given autographs and photographs to at least several thousand admirers since 1922. Those which Hitler has bestowed on friends may be counted on the fingers of two hands. His vanity is the more effective because it expresses itself in non-personal terms. He is the vessel, the instrument, of the will of the German people; or so he pretends. Thus his famous statement, after the June 30th murders, that for twenty-four hours he had been the supreme court of Germany.

Hitler is a man of passion, of instinct, not reason. His "intellect" is that of a chameleon who knows when to change his color, of a crab who knows when to dive into the sand; his "logic" that of a panther who is hungry, and thus seeks food.

His brain is small and vulgar, limited, narrow, suspicious, but behind it is the lamp of passion, and this passion has such quality that it is immediately discernible and recognizable, like a diamond in the sand. The range of his interests is so slight that any sort of stimulus provokes the identical reflex: music, religion, economics mean nothing to him except exercises in nationalism.

Then there is oratory. This is probably the chief external explanation of Hitler's rise. He talked himself to power. The strange thing is that Hitler is a bad speaker. He screeches; his mannerisms are awkward; his voice breaks at every peroration; he never knows when to stop. Goebbels is a far more subtle and accomplished orator. Yet Hitler, whose magnetism across the table is almost nil, can arouse an audience, especially a big audience, to frenzy.

He knows, of course, all the tricks. At one period he was accustomed to mention at great length the things that "we Germans" (*wir*) had or did not have or wanted to do or could not do. The word *"wir"* drove into the audience with the rhythmic savagery of a pneumatic drill. Then Hitler would pause dramatically. That, he would say, was the whole trouble. In Germany the word *"wir"* had no meaning; the country was disunited; there was no "we."

Recently Hitler told a French interviewer about an early oratorical trick and triumph, fifteen years ago in a communist stronghold in Bavaria. He was savagely heckled. "At any moment they might have thrown me out of the window, especially when they produced a blind War invalid who began to speak against all the things that are sacred to me. Fortunately I had also been blind as a result of the War. So I said to these people, 'I know what this man feels. I was even more bewildered than he at one moment—but *I* have recovered my sight!'"

Hitler's first followers were converts in the literal sense of the term. They hit the sawdust trail. Hitler might have been Aimee Semple McPherson or Billy Sunday. Men listened to him once and were his for life—for instance, Goebbels, Brückner, Goering, Hess.

Hitler never flinched from the use of terror, and terror played a powerful role in the creation of the Nazi state. From the beginning he encouraged terror. The only purely joyous passage in *Mein Kampf* is the description of his first big mass meeting, in which the newly organized SA pummelled hecklers bloody. The function of the SA was rough-house: first, rough-house with the aim of preserving "order" at public meetings; second, rough-house on the streets, to frighten, terrorize, and murder communists.

He gave jobs, big jobs, to confessed and admitted terrorists and murderers, like Killinger and Heines. When a communist was murdered at Potempa, in Silesia, in circumstances of peculiarly revolting brutality, Hitler announced publicly his spiritual unity with the murderers. When, in August, 1932, he thought that Hindenburg might appoint him chancellor, he asked for a three-day period during which the S.A. could run wild on the streets, and thus avenge themselves upon their enemies. And we cannot forget the 30th June, 1934.

Hitler's one contribution to political theory was the *Führer Prinzip* (Leader Principle). This means, briefly, authority from the top down, obedience from the bottom up, the reversal of the democratic theory of government. It was, as Heiden points out, a remarkably successful invention, since almost anybody could join the movement, no matter with what various aims, and yet feel spiritual cohesion through the personality of the leader. The Nazi movement gave wonderful play to diverse instincts and desires.

Then again, Germans love to be ruled. "The most blissful state a German can experience is that of being bossed," a friend of mine put it in Berlin. And Edgar Ansel Mowrer has recorded the shouts of Nazi youngsters on the streets, "We spit at freedom." A German feels undressed unless he is in uniform. The *Führer Prinzip* not only exploited this feeling by transforming the passive character of German docility, German obedience, into an active virtue; it gave expression also to the bipolar nature of obedience, namely that most men—even Germans—associate with a desire to be governed a hidden will to govern. The *Führer Prinzip* created hundreds, thousands, of sub-*Führers*, little leaders, down to the lowest storm-troop leader. It combined dignified submission with opportunity for leadership.

Mein Kampf, for all its impersonality, reveals over and over again Hitler's faith in "the man." After race and nation, personality is his main preoccupation. It is easy to see that the *Führer Prinzip* is simply a rationalization of his own ambition; the theory is announced on the implicit understanding that "the man" is Hitler himself. "A majority," he says, "can never be a substitute for the Man."

THE ROAD FROM MUNICH

(DECEMBER 1938)

Elmer Davis

A shrewd victor will, if possible, keep imposing his demands on the conquered by degrees. He can then, in dealing with a nation that has lost its character—and this means every one that submits voluntarily —count on its never finding in any particular act of oppression a sufficient excuse for taking up arms once more. On the contrary; the more the exactions that have been willingly endured, the less justifiable does it seem to resist at last on account of a new and apparently isolated (though to be sure constantly recurring) imposition.
                                             —Adolf Hitler, *Mein Kampf*

THERE, SET DOWN twelve years ago, is a preview of the history of Europe after Munich—a Europe which at the end of 1938 stands about where it stood at the end of 1811, with this difference: In 1811 England was not only the implacable but the impregnable enemy of the man who dominated the Continent. The England of 1938 is something else, strategically and morally.

Already as I write, Hitler is applying the policy outlined above to the Czechs; though they can hardly be accused of voluntary submission to an ultimatum not only from an enemy five times their size but

15

from their "friends" as well. The nations that lost their character, in the harsh practical sense that Hitler gives to that word, in the September crisis were the nations that not merely threw the Czechs to the wolves to save themselves but purchased immunity from German air raids by the surrender of their own voice in the affairs of Europe. It is hardly becoming for those who sit in safety overseas to criticize a bargain that suits the peoples involved; but few Englishmen, fewer Frenchmen, seem to realize that what they paid at Munich was only the first installment on the price. As Charles Merrill says, you can no longer buy peace; you can only rent it on short-term leases. A racketeer selling protection is not content with a single lump sum.

Comment on the ethics of the Munich agreement is irrelevant. We live now in a world of force; the point of importance to Americans is what new facts or new emphases, in the field that might better be called international physics than international politics, emerged from the recent hullabaloo. They seem to me to be the following:

(1) The substance of what half the world achieved by four years of war was undone in three weeks, without war, by the resolution of one man. So long as that man lives he is the principal fact in world politics.

(2) The dominant emotion of the peoples of Europe, Germans and Italians included if we can believe the news dispatches, is antipathy to war—at least to a general war, in which anybody might get hurt. In other circumstances this would be the happiest omen in human history. As things are, it can act as an effective deterrent only in the democracies; the dictators are still able to use the threat of war as an instrument of policy. It was above all the memory of the last war that made the world safe for Hitler.

(3) The only possible solution of the problem of intermingled races in Central Europe—if there is any solution at all—is that of which Masaryk was the chief proponent and his people, whatever their mistakes, gave the best example: The living together of different races, with equal rights, in the democratic states whose frontiers might gradually lose most of their significance. That solution was deliberately sabotaged, and is now discarded.

(4) Most important for Americans is Hitler's discovery that

Germany's biggest asset is London. London, head and heart of England, huge, rich, and appallingly vulnerable. The pressure of a threat against London is enough to swing the immense weight of England in support of German policy. For the September crisis proved that the English will ransom London at any price—so long as the price is paid by others. The Czechs paid it this time. Somebody else will pay it next time.

Hitler's mustache is no longer a joke, nor is anything else about Hitler. Only a few months ago, so astute an observer as Winston Churchill could set him down as inferior to Mussolini; which is not possible now. Mussolini may be better balanced, more of a realist in ordinary times; but Hitler has an incomparable instinct for the realities—ugly and distorted perhaps, but still real—of an age of crisis and revolution. Every one of his great strokes was undertaken against the judgment of the best-informed, the supposedly wisest, of his advisers; every one, so far, has succeeded. We had better stop calling that luck.

People have underestimated him because they do not like to believe that things are as he sees them. Certainly it is a bleak and hard-boiled Weltanschauung that underlies the doctrines of *Mein Kampf*—a world where race struggles against race for existence under the neutral chairmanship of a God who awards the prize to whatever people has proved its superior fitness by outfighting and outbreeding the rest. (Characteristic is Hitler's hostility to birth control, on the ground that it is better for the race to breed as many children as possible and let the tough survive.) But this is a true picture of what man's condition has been, except as it has been mitigated by certain human sentiments which Hitler despises; because he believes it is a true picture, it will come nearer being true, for our time, than anybody would have thought possible twenty-five years ago.

Major Attlee in the House of Commons debate said that the difference between the behavior of Beneš in the crisis and that of Hitler was the difference between a civilized man and a gangster; which by the canons of what we call civilization is true. But if Hitler keeps on winning, something else may be called civilization in the twenty-first century. Meanwhile it is apparent that much of the violence, the shrieking abuse of Beneš and the Czechs in general, was merely tactics, and successful tactics.

Many who heard those two broadcasts must have thought the man was crazy, especially when he came to that last hysterical passage about the "lonely unknown soldier." But if he feels messianic the evidence bears him out; he was a lonely unknown soldier, and he did conquer a Reich—indeed several Reichs; if anything is crazy it is the world we live in, not Hitler who is admirably adapted to it.

Mr. Winston Churchill, who has a far better sense of the realities of world physics than most of his fellow-countrymen, said in the House of Commons on October 3rd: "What I find unendurable is the sense of our country falling into the power, orbit, and influence of Nazi Germany, and our existence becoming dependent on their good will and pleasure. In a few years, perhaps in a few months, we shall be confronted with demands with which we shall be invited to comply." (A shrewd victor will always impose his demands on the conquered by degrees.) "But these demands may involve the surrender of territory or of liberty." (And the alternative, again, will be Goering's bombers over London.) If Hitler gave them another way out, let them ransom London by helping to force the surrender (as they did last September) of other people's territory and liberty, would they not take it? The business of any government is to look out for its own people, not others; and the English lost their last chance to say "No" and make it stick when they said, "Oh, very well if you insist" at Munich.

This is set down with regret, and apologies to my English friends, most of whom feel about Hitler (and perhaps by this time about Chamberlain) as I do. But it is a calculation of realities affecting American interests; the English who lately consulted what they consider, however mistakenly, their own interests, cannot be surprised if we look out for ours.

What to do about all this? That is beyond my competence; my only suggestion is that we had better stop thinking about the evils and ugliness of Hitler's Germany. It is ugly and evil enough; but the important thing for a nation which has to live in the world with Hitler's Germany and wants to go on standing on its own feet is to look at the things that make Germany strong, to see if there are not some of those qualities that we can emulate, without giving up our principles; to see if we cannot once more—as we have done once or twice in great crises of the past—rise to a sense of unity and resolution in the service of democracy and freedom, such as Hitler has created in his people in the service of autocracy and conquest.

And to remember, if, as, and when he bothers us, that the time to stop Hitler is the first time. A shrewd victor will always keep imposing his demands on the conquered by degrees; try to buy peace from Hitler and you find you have only rented it—on short-term leases, at an ever-increasing price.

NO MORE EXCURSIONS!

THE DEFENSE OF DEMOCRACY BEGINS AT HOME

(APRIL 1939)

C. Hartley Grattan

THE PROPER POLICY is clear: No American shall ever again be
sent to fight and die on the continent of Europe.

We are told that democracy is in danger. It is. We must defend it. It
is endangered by war. We must oppose war—unless forced upon us by
the absolute necessity of defending this continent.

In the First World War the emotions of the American people were
deeply stirred by President Wilson's eloquent glosses on the word
"democracy" and we went out, like the good democrats we are, to
implement our extremely liberal emotions with lethal weapons. We
did not do so because of "entangling alliances" (we became an "associated," not an "allied" power); we did it because we lost our heads,
failed in our job—which was to maintain neutrality. When it was too
late we found that while we had sincerely thought that everyone was
agreed upon the composition of the star to which we had hitched our
wagon, our failure to ask for a spectroscopic analysis of the star had
led to our undoing.

No candid reader of the literature of the First World War can fail to
recognize the deep sincerity of President Wilson and the American
people at large. One may regard them as misguided, stupid, bull-

headed, ignorant, or a variety of other things, but they had as large a measure of moral certainty about their position as usually gets involved in human affairs. The difficulty came in reconciling this profound sincerity with the conditions under which it had to be implemented, conditions which eventually led to its utter defeat both at home and abroad.

The slogans used to move us toward this unwonted end are being refurbished today, filled with a content only slightly different from that of 1914–1918, and obviously designed to lead toward a repetition on a more appalling scale of the débâcle of 1919. The alleged moral certainty is as fervent as that which misled us twenty-odd years ago. Don't forget that it wasn't the going to Europe and engaging in the fighting that disillusioned us with the First World War; rather it was our failure to solve Europe's problems.

Look at the wreckage which strewed the world after the First World War: gutted personalities, pale simulacra of once great men, vast reputations irretrievably tarnished, traitors all to their calling. This is no time to imitate the familiar story. It is rather the moment to take the aggressive against the men, emotions, opinions, drives which are pushing this country toward the charnel house once more. It is the exact moment to reaffirm the simple dogma: No American shall ever again be sent to fight and die on the continent of Europe.

WHERE ENGLAND STANDS

(MAY 1939)

J. B. Priestley

WHAT CANNOT BE endured any longer is this elaborately exploited, almost universal state of nerves and "jitters," in which the dictators, who keep it in existence, bluff their way from one dingy triumph to another.

We have a double task. We have to defend our democracy not only from outside aggression but also from internal collapse. For in one very important matter the dictators have an immense advantage over us. This new and horrible game is being played according to their rules, not ours. A condition of military preparedness, a country that is like an armed camp, a people permanently mobilized—all this suits dictatorship, which indeed cannot flourish in any other atmosphere. Not so democracy. It is terribly easy to lose your democracy by agreeing to defend it. In order to remain a free man, you find yourself submitting to conditions that finally take away your freedom. We can counteract this only by heightening the consciousness of democracy in the citizens we ask to defend it.

In short, the Britain we must defend will have to be more democratic, less tolerant of privilege, with a wider vision of its own destiny, than the Britain that has been muddling and messing about for the past few years. But let nobody, least of all any American, imagine that this second Britain, which has received so much attention in your press, really represents the mass of decent citizens here; for they have as yet shown no signs of hysteria and panic, have not willingly let other democracies go to their doom, and, I believe, are ready now to make a firm stand against the dictators. For they know—as we all must know—that at the heart of the Nazi and Fascist movements there is an evil principle, something that will have to be destroyed before humanity can go forward again into the sunlight.

ONE MAN'S MEAT:

ON "SECRET" INFORMATION

(SEPTEMBER 1939)

E. B. White

QUITE A LITTLE time elapses between writing a piece for *Harper's* and having it published. (I hasten to add that the same is true of any monthly.) For the writer it is a strange interval, full of all sorts of odd possibilities. Planes wing back and forth across the Atlantic depositing passengers and mail (safely, the writer hopes), wars wax and wane, Britons are stripped, submarines are lost, felons are tried and hung, people fall off horses and into fortunes, kings and queens arrive and depart. There is always the chance that between the date of writing and the date of publication some living character will die—or some dead one be reborn. There is always the chance that some country will be absorbed, or blown apart, or inundated, making what the writer said about it sound rather silly. (As well as discomfiting the populace.) This cloud which hangs over all typewriters used to bother me more than it does now; for I have recently been checking up on the newspapers, and it is astonishing how much which passes for news isn't news at all, and how many things which you would think were just on the point of coming to pass, never happen. I have here a clipping from the *World Telegram.* It is almost three months old—I've been saving it to let it ripen. It says:

HITLER WEIGHS QUICK BLOWS
AT GIBRALTAR, SUEZ, POLAND

"Secret information reaching London and Paris from Berlin indicates that Chancellor Hitler is now weighing his chances for a sudden, simultaneous move against Poland, Egypt, Suez, and Gibraltar." It went on to say that Goering favored a lightning war. There was another story right next to it (another "secret" source story) saying that the German General Staff had completed plans for a surprise landing of troops on English soil—in Kent, on the south coast, and on the shores of Wales in the southwest. This seemed like quite a program for Germany over the weekend: Poland, Egypt, Suez, Gibraltar, Kent, and Wales. It occurred to me that if events were moving as rapidly as that, I'd better abandon the news altogether and get a job telling stories to children on the radio. Events, however, didn't move rapidly; at the moment of writing, there has been no lightning war, no surprise landing of troops. Maybe I am being unusually innocent, but I believe that papers are publishing vast quantities of "secret" information which has a news content of zero and which contains no more startling information than does a recipe for gingerbread.

THE WAR AND AMERICA

(APRIL 1940)

Elmer Davis

There is a vast difference between keeping out of war, and pretending that this war is none of our business.
— President Roosevelt to Congress, January 3rd

WITH THE FOREGOING statement a considerable section of American opinion disagrees. Persistently during the debate on the Neutrality Bill, and sporadically since, some of our most respected and/or most vocal citizens have insisted that nothing about this war concerns us at all; that it is only a struggle between rival imperialisms, equally alien and obnoxious.

This point of view was ably expounded by the late Senator Borah on October 2nd, in his speech opening the neutrality debate. Denouncing "the hideous doctrines of the dominating power of Germany," he nevertheless contended that they were not an issue and seemed to see no ethical difference between the belligerents. "I look upon the present war as nothing more than another chapter in the bloody volume of European power politics." So said Lindbergh in his radio talks of September 15th and October 13th; "I do not believe this is a war for democracy; it is a war over the balance of power in Europe." So Phil

LaFollette was saying too: and the newspaper column of General Ironpants Johnson kept pounding away at the argument, and still comes back to it now and then, with a wealth of illustrative detail not always hampered by a quibbling regard for accuracy.

The effect of all this is to praise Hitler by faint damns, to imply that he is no worse than the rest of them. These men cited above are not pro-Nazi; most of them have denounced Nazi doctrine and practice as vigorously as anybody. But they are all convinced that it is imperatively necessary for us to keep out of the war; and since there is no danger of our going in on Hitler's side, they all concentrate on the faults and misdoings of the other side, with the zeal of lawyers arguing a case—contending, whether they really believe it or not, that this is only a war between the pot and the kettle.

As to the pot and the kettle. There are plenty of black spots on the past record of England, and France, and the United States; Nazi propagandists gleefully emphasize them, following the well-known tactics of "unmasking" the pretensions to virtue of those who criticize Nazi practices, and many of our isolationists give all their time to reiterating the sins of the Allies (and our own) as if no other nation had ever sinned comparably. You would have to go very far back indeed in British or French history to find anything comparable to the horrors of the German concentration camps; this country has never had anything like them (though we should have if our local Nazis had their way). In any case these things in our record, or England's, or France's, are in the past; and the overwhelming majority of Americans and Englishmen and Frenchmen are ashamed of them. What is the logical implication of the doctrine that we mustn't worry about what the Germans do because other people did something like it forty, or a hundred, or four hundred years ago? It is that there is no use in anybody's ever trying to reform; if the ex-criminal who is now behaving himself decently is still morally as reprehensible as the man who is doing the same things and even worse, then it is pointless to try to improve either the world or the individual. No doubt I shall be set down by some readers as a hireling of perfidious Albion if I dare cite any British opinion at all; but an editorial in *Time and Tide* of October 14th is worth quoting:

> Nobody pretends that our record is blameless. We have done things that we ought not to have done, but compared with the hands of the Nazis our hands are so clean that they positively blaze. Are we to allow men who know neither mercy nor decency to stop us from halting their disintegration of every standard we have slowly built up, just by pointing out that we ourselves have sometimes fallen short of these standards?

That is true, even though a resident of London wrote it. The process of unmasking, writes Hermann Rauschning (*The Revolution of Nihilism*), "is destroying the elements of every spiritual order, and preventing the creation of any new one." Its logic leads us straight back to the cannibal's cave.

GERMANY—THE VOICE
FROM WITHIN

(JUNE 1940)

Hans Schmidt

THE TRAGEDY OF Europe, as I witnessed it from within Germany during the critical August days of 1939 and into the spring of 1940, was an overwhelming experience.

When I found myself in the United States again, all of this seemed but a bizarre dream. The more I talked to American friends the more puzzled I became. They spoke of mediation and early peace; I thought in terms of twilight and world catastrophe. They listened to my stories of food rationing and rabble-rousing Joseph Goebbels as one listens to good college stories. I had come to think of the Nazi chieftains as half demons, as were Genghis Khan, Nero, and Ivan the Terrible. Most Americans appeared excellently informed as to facts and factors, and some of them had figured it all out—on paper. But few, if any, seemed capable of sensing the tremendous tension that is hovering over central Europe and of grasping the awesome gloom that has taken possession of millions of Europeans. Or was I wrong? Was I being carried away by personal emotions and disappointments? Had I become so spoiled during many years in America that the hardships of Europe at war appeared unbearable?

I had, after all, spent my childhood in Germany during the first world war, when there were turnips and watery milk and many air attacks. Turnips did not taste so very bad then—and in 1940 the food was distinctly better and more plentiful in Germany than in 1917. Watery milk and substitute coffee? Well, I never cared much for milk or coffee anyway. And as to the air attacks—there really were none in 1939–40; in 1917 they seemed "fun" to us children, as well as to many grown-ups. And yet—why were these last months in Europe so unbearable, so unforgettably bitter? Why was there nobody who did not envy me when I finally left for America—engulfed in utter gloom and sadness and a feeling of frustration?

In order to talk intelligently on events in Germany today and tomorrow it is imperative to eradicate one misconception widespread in America: This is no phony war! Events will probably have dissipated the phony-war concept by the time these lines go to press.* But even if the rulers of Europe should withhold, for the time being, the order for the most terrific ordeal of mankind to begin, one fact cannot be underscored heavily enough: This is a very real, a very grim, and a very destructive war, and it has been such from the beginning. I remember well the August days of 1914. We children were lifted up so that we could touch the golden buckles on the soldiers' helmets. There was an abundance of flowers, songs, marches, tears, and smiles. During the last days of August in 1939 I saw no smiles anywhere in Germany and I know there were no smiles. There was some hard nervous laughter; it broke out of faces that were pale, bitter, and determined. But it ceased as suddenly as it came. It hurt. There were few flowers. A horse-drawn artillery battery came dashing past us down a village street. A man with a steel helmet on a motorcycle cried: *"Bahn frei!—Bahn frei!"* and then came the horses in a furious gallop; they had red and yellow chrysanthemums behind their ears. It was the late afternoon of August 26, 1939. Many anxious faces looked westward, where the sun was setting over the Rhine Valley and France. The guns were to be in position at 8:00 P.M. on the Westwall. The red and

This article was finished before the German invasion of Scandinavia.

yellow chrysanthemums looked utterly out of place.

This is no phony war! Statistics on men under arms, on armaments, and on daily expenditures may not mean much to the distant onlooker. But if you had seen the faces of the men who stood guard at the bridgeheads; if you had heard the sighs of those evacuated from a border city at a few hours' notice; if you had walked through the empty ghostlike streets of the evacuated towns; if you had stood up, night after night, swaying in overcrowded trains; if you had been compelled to sit in your home evening after evening in your overcoat because there was no coal—you would not think this is a phony war! True, the slaughter of millions and the bombing of cities have not yet started. But there are few who think that it will not start. Everybody in Europe knows: the second great war is on and it will be decided. When and how? These are interesting questions for the bystander to discuss over a cup of tea. But for millions in Europe these questions mean life or death, and these millions forget it not for *one* moment. They think and speak of nothing else. Or do they? Yes, their thoughts mill about one other question, though they rarely mention it. This question is: "Why?" In the minds of some this question hovers, only dimly veiled, behind the official Nazi slogans (*"Dieser uns von England aufgezwungenen Krieg"*—"this war forced upon us by England"); in the minds of others it has attained a cruel clarity. This question is a constant companion; more than anything else, it lies at the root of suffering in Germany. I heard dozens of people say: "We would gladly do without butter; we would not mind giving up our Sunday excursions; we would give up our silver, our savings, our homes, our sons if there were only some sense, some meaning to it all." "Don't you think this senseless war will be over by Christmas?" was the final sentence in most of the conversations I had last autumn, even with intelligent and "informed" Germans. "But it will be over by next Christmas, at least—if we are still alive." With this remark a soldier friend took leave of me at the station, just a short while ago.

ONE MAN'S MEAT:

FOLLOWING FASHION

(SEPTEMBER 1940)

E. B. White

I HAVE OFTEN noticed on my trips up to the city that people have recut their clothes to follow the fashion. On my last trip, however, it seemed to me that people had remodeled their ideas too—taken in their convictions a little at the waist, shortened the sleeves of their resolve, and fitted themselves out in a new intellectual ensemble copied from a smart design out of the very latest page of history. It seemed to me they had strung along with Paris a little too long.

I confess to a disturbed stomach. I feel sick when I find anyone adjusting his mind to the new tyranny which is succeeding abroad. Because of its fundamental strictures, fascism does not seem to me to admit of any compromise or any rationalization, and I resent the patronizing air of persons who find in my plain belief in freedom a sign of immaturity. If it is boyish to believe that a human being should live free, then I'll gladly arrest my development and let the rest of the world grow up.

I shall report some of the strange remarks I heard in New York. One man told me that he thought perhaps the Nazi ideal was a sounder ideal than our constitutional system "because have you ever noticed what fine alert young faces the young German soldiers have in the newsreel?" He added: "Our American youngsters spend all their time at the movies—they're a mess." That was his summation of the case, his interpretation of the new Europe. Such a remark leaves me pale and shaken. If it represents the peak of our intelligence, then the steady march of despotism will not receive any considerable setback at our shores.

Another man informed me that our democratic notion of popular government was decadent and not worth bothering about—"because England is really rotten and the industrial towns there are a disgrace." That was the only reason he gave for the hopelessness of democracy; and he seemed mightily pleased with himself, as though he were more familiar than most with the anatomy of decadence, and had detected subtler aspects of the situation than were discernible to the rest of us.

Another man assured me that anyone who took *any* kind of government seriously was a gullible fool. You could be sure, he said, that there is nothing but corruption "because of the way Clemenceau acted at Versailles." He said it didn't make any difference really about this war. It was just another war. Having relieved himself of this majestic bit of reasoning, he subsided.

Another individual, discovering signs of zeal creeping into my blood, berated me for having lost my detachment, my pure skeptical point of view. He announced that he wasn't going to be swept away by all this nonsense, but would prefer to remain in the role of innocent bystander, which he said was the duty of any intelligent person. (I noticed, however, that he phoned later to qualify his remark, as though he had lost some of his innocence in the cab on the way home.)

Those are just a few samples of the sort of talk that seemed to be going round—talk which was full of defeatism and disillusion and sometimes of a too studied innocence. Men are not merely annihilating themselves at a great rate these days, but they are telling one another enormous lies, grandiose fibs. Such remarks as I heard are fearfully disturbing in their cumulative effect. They are more destructive than dive bombers and mine fields, for they challenge not merely one's immediate position but one's main defenses. They seemed to me to issue either from persons who could never have really come to grips with freedom, so as to understand her, or from renegades. Where I expected to find indignation, I found paralysis, or a sort of dim acquiescence, as in a child who is dully swallowing a distasteful pill. I was advised of the growing anti-Jewish sentiment by a man who seemed to be watching the phenomenon of intolerance not through tears of shame but with a clear intellectual gaze, as through a well-ground lens.

The least a man can do at such a time is to declare himself and tell where he stands. I believe in freedom with the same burning delight, the same faith, the same intense abandon which attended its birth on this continent more than a century and a half ago. Since my attitude is regarded in some circles as a youthful one, I shall address my declaration to the young men and women of America, the upcropping generation. I've always wanted to tell them what I love anyway—ever since I discovered America in a Model T Ford and saw, in every town, the high school building so much bigger and newer than the other buildings, and wondered what was going on behind those walls. My declaration is built on plain lines—nothing fancy. When you know what you love, when you know where you stand, the business of making a declaration is easy and goes along without a hitch. I want to tell something to all the young men and the young women in all the forty-eight States and in the territory of Alaska, the ones that are cropping up and getting going, looking for the jobs, casting the brand new votes, shining up the new guns in the old armories, looking for the answers, reading the ads in the papers, and listening to the bulletins from London. I want to make an affidavit before the generation that is making America go round—the girls getting their first jobs writing the letters that begin "Yours of the fifth instant," the boys showing up at the factory in the early morning, punching the time-clock and taking their places on the assembly line for the first time, the fellows swinging a racquet or a scythe or holding a drill, boys and girls on the banks of the Hudson and the Columbia and the Snake and the Kanawha, sons and daughters of cowhands on the dude ranches in the big States where the bigness is something you can cut with a knife, young fellows and girls in the tank towns and in the cities that make all the noise, boys rafting on ponds and translating Caesar's Gallic Wars to the thunder of the new wars, playing the slot machines in the drugstores, swimming in the pool below the falls everywhere in America, skiers on the winter hills returning in the twilight down the white lanes to the New England farmhouses, boys in camp and on the trails between lakes, carrying their canoes, American boys hunting jobs and finding them and not finding them, boys on the sand truck sanding the tarred roads in the slippery weather in the country places, fellows and girls in the Bluegrass where the big oaks stand on the beautiful lawns where the thoroughbred horses graze, young fishermen in the smelt houses along the frozen Kennebec, boys and girls in Westchester who can hear the foghorn from the Sound when the wind is right, fellows working on lake steamers or walking in the Shenandoah in the soft spring months when the scent of mayflowers searches the heart, in the filling station at the pump checking the oil, working in the big hotels—in Miami, in Atlantic City, in the Adirondacks, hopping the bells and carrying the ice water and on the golf course handing the mashie to the man who wants to make an approach shot, young people who are taking the secretarial courses and the night-school training and who are writing to the manufacturers for the samples and saving the coupons and saving the stamps and writing the new poems and the love letters and the bills of sale all over America from the Atlantic to the Pacific, from the Canadian border to the Gulf of Mexico. There are millions of them; and I think their faces are good alert faces too, and their faces have an inquiring look, which I like, because they haven't been told the answer—haven't been told how to do, with precision, the audacious deed.

I am writing my declaration rapidly, much as though I were shaving to catch a train. Events abroad give a man a feeling of being pressed for time. Actually I do not believe I am pressed for time, and I apologize to the reader for a false impression that may be created. I just want to tell, before I get slowed down, that I am in love with freedom and that it is an affair of long standing and that it is a fine state to be in, and that I am deeply suspicious of people who are beginning to adjust to fascism and dictators merely because they are succeeding in war. From such adaptable natures a smell rises. I pinch my nose.

For as long as I can remember I have had a sense of living somewhat freely in a natural world. I don't mean I enjoyed freedom of action, but my existence seemed to have the quality of free-ness. I traveled with secret papers pertaining to a divine conspiracy. Intuitively I've always been aware of the vitally important pact which a man has with himself, to be all things to himself, and to be identified with all things, to stand self-reliant, taking advantage of his haphazard connection with a planet, riding his luck, and following his bent with the tenacity of a hound. My first and greatest love affair was with this thing we call freedom, this lady of infinite allure, this dangerous and beautiful and sublime being who restores and supplies us all.

It began with the haunting intimation (which I presume every child receives) of his mystical inner life; of God in man; of nature publishing herself through the "I." This elusive sensation is moving and memorable. It comes early in life: a boy, we'll say, sitting on the front steps on a summer night, thinking of nothing in particular, suddenly hearing as with a new perception and as though for the first time the pulsing sound of crickets, overwhelmed with the novel sense of identification with the natural company of insects and grass and night, conscious of a faint answering cry to the universal perplexing question: "What is 'I'?" Or a little girl, returning from the grave of a pet bird, leaning with her elbows on the windowsill, inhaling the unfamiliar draught of death, suddenly seeing herself as part of the complete story. Or to an older youth, encountering for the first time a great teacher who by some chance word or mood awakens something and the youth beginning to breathe as an individual and conscious of strength in his vitals. I think the sensation must develop in many men as a feeling of identity with God—an eruption of the spirit caused by allergies and the sense of divine existence as distinct from mere animal existence. This is the beginning of the affair with freedom.

But a man's free condition is of two parts: the instinctive free-ness he experiences as an animal dweller on a planet, and the practical liberties he enjoys as a privileged member of human society. The latter is, of the two, more generally understood, more widely admired, more violently challenged and discussed. It is the practical and apparent side of freedom. The United States, almost alone today, offers the liberties and the privileges and the tools of freedom. In this land the citizens are still invited to write their plays and books, to paint their pictures, to meet for discussion, to dissent as well as to agree, to mount soapboxes in the public square, to enjoy education in all subjects without censorship, to hold court and judge one another, to compose music, to talk politics with their neighbors without wondering whether the secret police are listening, to exchange ideas as well as goods, to kid the government when it needs kidding, and to read real news of real events instead of phony news manufactured by a paid agent of the state. This is a fact and should give every person pause.

To be free, in a planetary sense, is to feel that you belong to the earth. To be free, in a social sense, is to feel at home in a democratic framework. In Adolf Hitler, although he is a freely flowering individual, we do not detect either type of sensibility. From reading his book I gather that his feeling for earth is not a sense of communion but a driving urge to prevail. His feeling for men is not that they co-exist but that they are capable of being arranged and standardized by a superior intellect—that their existence suggests not a fulfillment of their personalities but a submersion of their personalities in the common racial destiny. His very great absorption in the destiny of the German people somehow loses some of its effect when you discover, from his writings, in what vast contempt he holds *all* people. "I learned," he wrote, ". . . to gain an insight into the unbelievably primitive opinions and arguments of the people." To him the ordinary man is a primitive, capable only of being used and led. He speaks continually of people as sheep, halfwits, and impudent fools—the same people from whom he asks the utmost in loyalty, and to whom he promises the ultimate in prizes.

Here in America, where our society is based on belief in the individual, not contempt for him, the free principle of life has a chance of surviving. I believe that it must and will survive. To understand freedom is an accomplishment which all men may acquire who set their minds in that direction; and to love freedom is a tendency which many Americans are born with. To live in the same room with freedom, or in the same hemisphere, is still a profoundly shaking experience for me, so that I can't rest till I have tried to tell young men and women about it.

One of the earliest truths (and to him most valuable) that the author of *Mein Kampf* discovered was that it is not the written word but the spoken word which in heated moments moves great masses of people to noble or ignoble action. The written word, unlike the spoken word, is something which every person examines privately and judges calmly by his own intellectual standards, not by what the man standing next to him thinks. "I know," wrote Hitler, "that one is able to win people far more by the spoken than by the written word. . . . " Later he adds contemptuously: "For let it be said to all knights of the pen and to all the political dandies, especially of today: the greatest changes in this world have never yet been brought about by a goose quill! No, the pen has always been reserved to motivate these changes theoretically."

Luckily I am not out to change the world—that's being done for me, and at a great clip. But I know that the free spirit of man is persistent in nature; it recurs, and has never successfully been wiped out, by fire or flood. I set down the above remarks merely (in the words of Mr. Hitler) to motivate that spirit, theoretically. Being myself a knight of the goose quill, I am under no misapprehension about "winning people"; but I am inordinately proud these days of the quill, for it has shown itself, historically, to be the hypodermic which inoculates men and keeps the germ of freedom always in circulation, so that there are individuals in every time in every land who are the carriers, the Typhoid Mary's, capable of infecting others by mere contact and example. These persons are feared by every tyrant—who shows his fear by burning the books and destroying the individuals. A writer goes about his task today with the extra satisfaction which comes from knowing that he will be the first to have his head lopped off—even before the political dandies. In my own case this is a double satisfaction, for if freedom were denied me by force of earthly circumstance, I am the same as dead and would infinitely prefer to go into fascism without my head than with it, having no use for it any more and not wishing to be saddled with so heavy an encumbrance.

MEETING HITLER'S ARMY

(APRIL 1941)

Ida Treat

Ida Treat is the German-speaking American wife of a French naval officer. After being penned up on an island off the coast of Brittany for months, she was finally extricated through the efforts of the State Department and reached the United States late in 1940. Here she found news of her husband—she had heard nothing from him since the preceding May—and discovered that he was with the de Gaulle forces at Port Said. In this account, she talks of the occupation of the island by German troops.

THE NEWS OF the bombing of Berlin upset Müller even more than the others. His wife and boy were there. He told me of a soldier who had received a letter saying his family had been killed in a bombardment and who had shot himself. There was a rumor that the German censor intended to hold up letters to keep bad news from leaking out. If so it was *"gemein"* (a dirty trick). "First they said no British planes could ever get through to Germany. Then they said they'd never fly over Berlin. Now they say British bombs aren't worth anything—they don't do any harm." All that was nothing but lies—and it too was *"gemein."*

He told me the soldiers had started a petition asking to be informed what places had been bombed and who had been killed. He said later it had been refused. "They say it would be giving information to the enemy. As if the British didn't know what they had bombed and where!"

In the meantime the war showed no signs of ending. The soldiers grew depressed. Hitler had promised it would all be over by Christmas, but no one believed it any longer. Even the French were better off than the German soldiers. The French were conquered but many had come home to their families, whereas the Germans had not seen theirs for months— and who knew when they would see them again? They were fed up with the war. Hans the Rheinländer put the general feeling into words.

"Only ten thousand people at most, in all the world, ever want war—the people high up." Of course the British were to blame and the Jews. Germany never wanted war, Germany wanted justice and a new order in Europe.

Talk about the war grew increasingly bitter. Why should Britain stand always in the way of German hopes and plans? "What made her interfere when we went into Poland? Someone had to clean up Poland." That experience in Poland had been a nightmare. All the soldiers said the same thing about it—it wasn't war, but sheer butchery. Guerrilla warfare is no warfare, it isn't "honorable." That was the way the Poles fought—they all took part, even the women and children. "They shot at us from windows and trees and behind walls; you never knew where they were. We waded through bogs. I lost my gun four times—all I had left was a knife. I was all covered with blood like a butcher. A barber cut the throat of one of my comrades he was shaving. We tied the man to his chair and threw a grenade under it. The women were the worst of all. We had to do dreadful things, but the Poles were to blame. They fought like savages. War is for soldiers, not civilians. A German is an *edler Mensch*. He fights in uniform."

Now they were in France. They had beaten the French, but the French didn't seem to know they were beaten. They were a funny people.

"I guess you don't realize how nice we've been. We could have done what we did in Poland. You ought to be grateful. You don't know what war is. Your women run a mile when they see us, the children too, though you know how fond we are of children. Why don't you like us?"

I was asked that question many times. For it was true, ever increasingly true, the French population had no love for the invaders. French and Germans were two parallel and hostile worlds. There was almost no interpenetration. Sailors who had come home from England after the first shock of the Armistice regretted their return openly. I had to explain and explain again to the neighbors my own contact with the German soldiers. Their continued visits were embarrassing. Madame Lebras, who from the first had done what she could to help me—dropping in with her knitting every time she saw a green uniform enter the garden—defended me with energy.

"What can she do? They just keep coming, and she can't throw them out. They are the conquerors."

By this time summer had gone. Since July a wall of silence had shut off occupied France from the rest of the world. Still no news from my husband—already five months. No news from my sisters or friends in America. No hope of mail except from rare friends who had not fled to the south and "family post cards" which the Germans had at last allowed us to exchange with unoccupied France. The cards were printed forms like the ones I used to receive from André, "somewhere" with the Fleet. ("Health . . . Send me . . . Sentiments . . .") For these "family post cards" the careful Germans had thought out all the details of our correspondence in advance and specified even the greetings.

They ran as follows:

CARTE POSTALE	
. . . . . . in good health	We are without news of . . . . .
. . . . . . tired	since . . . . . .
. . . . . . sick	. . . . is sick
. . . . . . very sick	. . . . very sick
The family . . . . is	. . . . died . . . . . .
. . . . . . is leaving	
on	I need { baggage / funds / provisions
. . . . . . has started	
school at	
Affectionate greetings	
Kisses	*Signed* . . . .

WHO GOES NAZI?

(AUGUST 1941)

Dorothy Thompson

IT IS AN interesting and somewhat macabre parlor game to play at a large gathering of one's acquaintances: to speculate who in a show-down would go Nazi. By now, I think I know. I have gone through the experience many times—in Germany, in Austria, and in France. I have come to know the types: the born Nazis, the Nazis whom democracy itself has created, the certain-to-be fellow-travelers. And I also know those who never, under any conceivable circumstances, would become Nazis.

It is preposterous to think that they are divided by any racial characteristics. Germans may be more susceptible to Nazism than most people, but I doubt it. Jews are barred out, but it is an arbitrary ruling. I know lots of Jews who are born Nazis and many others who would heil Hitler tomorrow morning if given a chance. There are Jews who have repudiated their own ancestors in order to become "Honorary Aryans and Nazis"; there are full-blooded Jews who have enthusiastically entered Hitler's secret service. Nazism has nothing to do with race and nationality. It appeals to a certain type of mind.

It is also, to an immense extent, the disease of a generation—the generation which was either young or unborn at the end of the last war. This is as true of Englishmen, Frenchmen, and Americans as of Germans. It is the disease of the so-called "lost generation."

Sometimes I think there are direct biological factors at work—a type of education, feeding, and physical training which has produced a new kind of human being with an imbalance in his nature. He has been fed vitamins and filled with energies that are beyond the capacity of his intellect to discipline. He has been treated to forms of education which have released him from inhibitions. His body is vigorous. His mind is childish. His soul has been almost completely neglected.

At any rate, let us look round the room.

The gentleman standing beside the fireplace with an almost untouched glass of whiskey beside him on the mantelpiece is Mr. A, a descendant of one of the great American families. There has never been an American Blue Book without several persons of his surname in it. He is poor and earns his living as an editor. He has had a classical education, has a sound and cultivated taste in literature, painting, and music; has not a touch of snobbery in him; is full of humor, courtesy, and wit. He was a lieutenant in the World War, is a Republican in politics, but voted twice for Roosevelt, last time for Willkie. He is modest, not particularly brilliant, a staunch friend, and a man who greatly enjoys the company of pretty and witty women. His wife, whom he adored, is dead, and he will never remarry.

He has never attracted any attention because of outstanding bravery. But I will put my hand in the fire that nothing on earth could ever make him a Nazi. He would greatly dislike fighting them, but they could never convert him. . . . Why not?

Beside him stands Mr. B, a man of his own class, graduate of the same preparatory school and university, rich, a sportsman, owner of a famous racing stable, vice-president of a bank, married to a well-known society belle. He is a good fellow and extremely popular. But if America were going Nazi he would certainly join up, and early.

Why? . . . Why the one and not the other?

Mr. A has a life that is established according to a certain form of personal behavior. Although he has no money, his unostentatious distinction and education have always assured him a position. He has never been engaged in sharp competition. He is a free man. I doubt whether ever in his life he has done anything he did not want to do or anything that was against his code. Nazism wouldn't fit in with his standards and he has never become accustomed to making concessions.

Mr. B has risen beyond his real abilities by virtue of health, good looks, and being a good mixer. He married for money and he has done lots of other things for money. His code is not his own; it is that of his class—no worse, no better. He fits easily into whatever pattern is successful. That is his sole measure of value—success. Nazism as a minority movement would not attract him. As a movement likely to attain power, it would.

The saturnine man over there talking with a lovely French émigrée is already a Nazi. Mr. C is a brilliant and embittered intellectual. He was a poor white-trash Southern boy, a scholarship student at two universities where he took all the scholastic honors but was never invited to join a fraternity. His brilliant gifts won for him successively government positions, partnership in a prominent law firm, and eventually a highly paid job as a Wall Street adviser. He has always moved among important people and always been socially on the periphery. His colleagues have admired his brains and exploited them, but they have seldom invited him—or his wife—to dinner.

He is a snob, loathing his own snobbery. He despises the men about him—he despises, for instance, Mr. B—because he knows that what he has had to achieve by relentless work men like B have won by knowing the right people. But his contempt is inextricably mingled with envy. Even more than he hates the class into which he has insecurely risen does he hate the people from whom he came. He hates his mother and his father for *being* his parents. He loathes everything that reminds him of his origins and his humiliations. He is bitterly anti-Semitic because the social insecurity of the Jews reminds him of his own psychological insecurity.

Pity he has utterly erased from his nature, and joy he has never known. He has an ambition, bitter and burning. It is to rise to such an eminence that no one can ever again humiliate him. Not to rule but to be the secret ruler, pulling the strings of puppets created by his brains. Already some of them are talking his language—though they have never met him.

There he sits: he talks awkwardly rather than glibly; he is courteous. He commands a distant and cold respect. But he is a very dangerous man. Were he primitive and brutal he would be a criminal—a murderer. But he is subtle and cruel. He would rise high in a Nazi regime. It would need men just like him—intellectual and ruthless.

But Mr. C is not a born Nazi. He is the product of a democracy hypocritically preaching social equality and practicing a carelessly brutal snobbery. He is a sensitive, gifted man who has been humiliated into nihilism. He would laugh to see heads roll.

I think young D over there is the only *born* Nazi in the room. Young D is the spoiled only son of a doting mother. He has never been crossed in his life. He spends his time at the game of seeing what he can get away with. He is constantly arrested for speeding and his mother pays the fines. He has been ruthless toward two wives and his mother pays the alimony. His life is spent in sensation-seeking and theatricality. He is utterly inconsiderate of everybody. He is very good-looking, in a vacuous, cavalier way, and inordinately vain. He would certainly fancy himself in a uniform that gave him a chance to swagger and lord it over others.

Mrs. E would go Nazi as sure as you are born. That statement surprises you? Mrs. E seems so sweet, so clinging, so cowed. She is. She is a masochist. She is married to a man who never ceases to humiliate her, to lord it over her, to treat her with less consideration than he does his dogs. He is a prominent scientist, and Mrs. E, who married him very young, has persuaded herself that he is a genius, and that there is something of superior womanliness in her utter lack of pride, in her doglike devotion. She speaks disapprovingly of other "masculine" or insufficiently devoted wives. Her husband, however, is bored to death with her. He neglects her completely and she is looking for someone else before whom to pour her ecstatic self-abasement. She will titillate with pleased excitement to the first popular hero who proclaims the basic subordination of women.

On the other hand, Mrs. F would never go Nazi. She is the most popular woman in the room, handsome, gay, witty, and full of the warmest emotion. She was a popular actress ten years ago; married very happily; promptly had four children in a row; has a charming house, is not rich but has no money cares, has never cut herself off from her own happy-go-lucky profession, and is full of sound health and sound common sense. All men try to make love to her; she laughs at them all, and her husband is amused. She has stood on her own feet since she was a child, she has enormously helped her husband's career (he is a lawyer), she would ornament any drawing room in any capital, and she is as American as ice cream and cake.

How about the butler who is passing the drinks? I look at James with amused eyes. James is safe. James has been butler to the 'ighest aristocracy, considers all Nazis parvenus and communists, and has a very good sense for "people of quality." He serves the quiet editor with that friendly air of equality which good servants always show toward those they consider good enough to serve, and he serves the horsy gent stiffly and coldly.

Bill, the grandson of the chauffeur, is helping serve tonight. He is a product of a Bronx public school and high school, and works at night like this to help himself through City College, where he is studying engineering. He is a "proletarian," though you'd never guess it if you saw him without that white coat. He plays a crack game of tennis—has been a tennis tutor in summer resorts—swims superbly, gets straight A's in his classes, and thinks America is okay and don't let anybody say it isn't. He had a brief period of Youth Congress communism, but it was like the measles. He was not taken in the draft because his eyes are not good enough, but he wants to design airplanes, "like Sikorsky." He thinks Lindbergh is "just another pilot with a build-up and a rich wife" and that he is "always talking down America, like how we couldn't lick Hitler if we wanted to." At this point Bill snorts.

Mr. G is a *very* intellectual young man who was an infant prodigy. He has been concerned with general ideas since the age of ten and has one of those minds that can scintillatingly rationalize everything. I have known him for ten years and in that time have heard him enthu-

51

siastically explain Marx, social credit, technocracy, Keynesian economics, Chestertonian distribution, and everything else one can imagine. Mr. G will never be a Nazi, because he will never be anything. His brain operates quite apart from the rest of his apparatus. He will certainly be able, however, fully to explain and apologize for Nazism if it ever comes along. But Mr. G is always a "deviationist." When he played with communism he was a Trotskyist; when he talked of Keynes it was to suggest improvement; Chesterton's economic ideas were all right but he was too bound to Catholic philosophy. So we may be sure that Mr. G would be a Nazi with purse-lipped qualifications. He would certainly be purged.

H is an historian and biographer. He is American of Dutch ancestry born and reared in the Middle West. He has been in love with America all his life. He can recite whole chapters of Thoreau and volumes of American poetry, from Emerson to Steve Benét. He knows Jefferson's letters, Hamilton's papers, Lincoln's speeches. He is a collector of early American furniture, lives in New England, runs a farm for a hobby and doesn't lose much money on it, and loathes parties like this one. He has a ribald and manly sense of humor, is unconventional and lost a college professorship because of a love affair. Afterward he married the lady and has lived happily ever afterward as the wages of sin.

H has never doubted his own authentic Americanism for one instant. This is his country, and he knows it from Acadia to Zenith. His ancestors fought in the Revolutionary War and in all the wars since. He is certainly an intellectual, but an intellectual smelling slightly of cow barns and damp tweeds. He is the most good-natured and genial man alive, but if anyone ever tries to make this country over into an imitation of Hitler's, Mussolini's, or Petain's systems H will grab a gun and fight. Though H's liberalism will not permit him to say it, it is his secret conviction that nobody whose ancestors have not been in this country since before the Civil War really understands America or would really fight for it against Nazism or any other foreign ism in a showdown.

But H is wrong. There is one other person in the room who would fight alongside H and he is not even an American citizen. He is a young German émigré, whom I brought along to the party. The people in the room look at him rather askance because he is so Germanic, so very blond-haired, so very blue-eyed, so tanned that somehow you expect him to be wearing shorts. He looks like the model of a Nazi. His English is flawed—he learned it only five years ago. He comes from an old East Prussian family; he was a member of the post-war Youth Movement and afterward of the Republican "Reichsbanner." All his German friends went Nazi—without exception. He hiked to Switzerland penniless, there pursued his studies in New Testament Greek, sat under the great Protestant theologian Karl Barth, came to America through the assistance of an American friend whom he had met in a university, got a job teaching the classics in a fashionable private school; quit, and is working now in an airplane factory—working on the night shift to make planes to send to Britain to defeat Germany. He has devoured volumes of American history, knows Whitman by heart, wonders why so few Americans have ever read the Federalist papers, believes in the United States of Europe, the Union of the English-speaking world, and the coming democratic revolution all over the earth. He believes that America is the country of Creative Evolution once it shakes off its middle-class complacency, its bureaucratized industry, its tentacle-like and spreading government, and sets itself innerly free.

The people in the room think he is not an American, but he is more American than almost any of them. He has discovered America and his spirit is the spirit of the pioneers. He is furious with America because it does not realize its strength and beauty and power. He talks about the workmen in the factory where he is employed. . . . He took the job "in order to understand the real America." He thinks the men are wonderful. "Why don't you American intellectuals ever get to them; talk to them?"

I grin bitterly to myself, thinking that if we ever got into war with the Nazis he would probably be interned, while Mr. B and Mr. G and Mrs. E would be spreading defeatism at all such parties as this one. "Of course I don't like Hitler but . . ."

Mr. J over there is a Jew. Mr. J is a very important man. He is immensely rich—he has made a fortune through a dozen directorates in various companies, through a fabulous marriage, through a speculative flair, and through a native gift for money and a native love of power. He is intelligent and arrogant. He seldom associates with Jews. He deplores any mention of the "Jewish question." He believes that Hitler "should not be judged from the standpoint of anti-Semitism." He thinks that "the Jews should be reserved on all political questions." He considers Roosevelt "an enemy of business." He thinks "It was a serious blow to the Jews that Frankfurter should have been appointed to the Supreme Court."

The saturnine Mr. C—the real Nazi in the room—engages him in a flatteringly attentive conversation. Mr. J agrees with Mr. C wholly. Mr. J is definitely attracted by Mr. C. He goes out of his way to ask his name—they have never met before. "A very intelligent man."

Mr. K contemplates the scene with a sad humor in his expressive eyes. Mr. K is also a Jew. Mr. K is a Jew from the South. He speaks with a Southern drawl. He tells inimitable stories. Ten years ago he owned a very successful business that he had built up from scratch. He sold it for a handsome price, settled his indigent relatives in business, and now enjoys an income for himself of about fifty dollars a week. At forty he began to write articles about odd and out-of-the-way places in American life. A bachelor, and a sad man who makes everybody laugh, he travels continually, knows America from a thousand different facets, and loves it in a quiet, deep, unostentatious way. He is a great friend of H, the biographer. Like H, his ancestors have been in this country since long before the Civil War. He is attracted to the young German. By and by they are together in the drawing-room. The impeccable gentleman of New England, the country-man-intellectual of the Middle West, the happy woman whom the gods love, the young German, the quiet, poised Jew from the South. And over on the other side are the others.

Mr. L has just come in. Mr. L is a lion these days. My hostess was all of a dither when she told me on the telephone, " . . . and L is coming. You know it's *dreadfully* hard to get him." L is a *very* powerful labor leader. "My dear, he is a man of the people, but really *fascinating*."

L is a man of the people and just exactly as fascinating as my horsy, bank vice-president, on-the-make acquaintance over there, and for the same reasons and in the same way. L makes speeches about the "third of the nation," and L has made a darned good thing for himself out of championing the oppressed. He has the best car out of anyone in this room; salary means nothing to him because he lives on an expense account. He agrees with the very largest and most powerful industrialists in the country that it is the business of the strong to boss the weak, and he has made collective bargaining into a legal compulsion to appoint him or his henchmen as "labor's" agents, with the power to tax pay envelopes and do what they please with the money. L is the strongest natural-born Nazi in the room. Mr. B regards him with contempt tempered with hatred. Mr. B will use him. L is already parroting B's speeches. He has the brains of Neanderthal man, but he has an infallible instinct for power. In private conversations he denounces the Jews as "parasites." No one has ever asked him what are the creative functions of a highly paid agent, who takes a percentage off the labor of millions of men, and distributes it where and as it may add to his own political power.

It's fun—a macabre sort of fun—this parlor game of "Who Goes Nazi?"

And it simplifies things—asking the question in regard to specific personalities.

Kind, good, happy, gentlemanly, secure people never go Nazi. They may be the gentle philosopher whose name is in the Blue Book, or Bill from City College to whom democracy gave a chance to design airplanes—you'll never make Nazis out of them. But the frustrated and humiliated intellectual, the rich and scared speculator, the spoiled son, the labor tyrant, the fellow who has achieved success by smelling out the wind of success—they would all go Nazi in a crisis.

Believe me, nice people don't go Nazi. Their race, color, creed, or social condition is not the criterion. It is something in them.

Those who haven't anything in them to tell them what they like and what they don't—whether it is breeding, or happiness, or wisdom, or a code, however old-fashioned or however modern, go Nazi.

It's an amusing game. Try it at the next big party you go to.

A PHOTOGRAPHER IN MOSCOW

(MARCH 1942)

Margaret Bourke-White

WHEN GERMAN PLANES began dropping bombs on a chain of Russian cities and the Soviet Union entered the war, one of the first military regulations to be passed was a law providing that anyone seen with a camera would be shot on sight. Here was I already in Moscow, facing the greatest scoop of my life, the kind of an opportunity that would seem possible to a photographer only in an opium dream: the biggest country enters the biggest war in the world, and I was the only foreign photographer of any nationality to be present.

The anti-camera law was inconvenient, but I had only to reflect on the supreme convenience of being within Russian borders at all, at a time when all other photographers attempting to enter were being refused visas, to be willing to meet any difficulty. I did think, however, that to have to face German bombing planes and Russian firing squads on the same side of the same war was rather a lot for even a photographer to do.

The first two weeks of the war were probably the hardest for the Russians, for they had to set their armies against unpredictable advances along the world's longest front. That first fortnight was certainly the hardest for me. My advances were confined to the short home front, a distance of seven blocks between the Commissariat of

Foreign Affairs, its little cousin, the Press Bureau, and my hotel; but in the end a determined frontal attack conquered, as it does in most wars. I was given several precious bits of pasteboard bearing my picture along with decorative stamps and signatures, variously affixed in purple and red, and my status as Amerikanski photo-correspondent was established. These documents were so unusual, however, that militiamen to whom they were shown almost invariably put me in temporary custody in the nearest police station to give them ample time to telephone to higher authorities for verification. Moscow sunlight is a shifting thing at best, so it was a foregone conclusion that the sun would be behind the clouds by the time I was returned with apologies and a courteous military escort to the place where I had started out to work; and I would have to come back and repeat the identification procedure to a new patrol on the next sunny day.

The balcony of our hotel suite, however, provided one of the best photographic view-points in the whole city, and without benefit of documents. It overlooked the Kremlin and faced the Red Square, and it possessed certain elements of history. Trotsky had stood on this balcony addressing the unheeding Trade Unions at the time of his fall from power. Lindbergh had stayed in our suite during his visit to Moscow. When we moved out of it, Lord Beaverbrook moved in, while attending sessions of the American-British Economic Conference. But during our occupancy it furnished a camera view-point whose value was beyond measure.

Every night there was something to photograph because, whether it was a light raid or a heavy one, the Germans always managed to aim at least one bomb at the Kremlin.

They didn't always hit it, although one night I watched a whole palace rise up in a plumelike formation against a moonlit sky. Frequently missiles aimed at the Kremlin landed on various buildings across the street. Why our hotel managed to stay erect so successfully I do not know, for it was so old that it trembled every time a streetcar passed. Perhaps its very flexibility helped.

During the first weeks of the war every citizen of Moscow received thorough training in home defense, with emphasis on the habits and treatment of the fire bomb. This was made possible by the extraordinary amount of organization which existed in Moscow civilian life, even in peacetime. Apartment-house groups in Moscow are social units, with little movie theaters, playgrounds, house committees. The discipline which in recent years has been a feature of Soviet home life came into play with the beginning of the war. The same House Committee which used to decide on when to put a new swing in the children's playground and when to repaint the house and repair the stove began directing the work of home defense.

On alternate nights the committee members went to large central schools, and on the nights in between they taught the folks at home such subjects as first aid, how to behave in case of gas attack, how to treat incendiary bombs.

Children took an important part in this. It was their duty to keep water pails constantly filled, sandbags always ready.

Each night of bombing was a demonstration of how thoroughly this job of home defense was being done. Every doorway, every alley, every roof top had its watchers, who worked on four-hour shifts and then were relieved by others. As more and more men went off to the front, the ranks of these watchers were filled largely by women and boys and girls of school age. All the children that I knew dreamed of having their watch on a night with plenty of fire bombs, for they were all ready to be heroes.

After utilizing my splendid balcony to the utmost—to photograph the centuries-old silhouette of the Kremlin towers against a strictly modern fire-spangled sky, which lighted up each night into new and unexpected patterns—I began to search for new view-points. The British Embassy faced the opposite side of the Kremlin from our hotel, and was situated at the edge of a mass of roofs which became alive with activity when bombing started; and big, bluff General Mason-MacFarlane, who headed the British Military Mission, gave us a standing invitation to drop in for air raids.

When the alarm began sounding we would jump into our car and make a dash for the British Embassy, some eight blocks away from our hotel. We had this procedure so perfectly timed that we could make the trip before the siren stopped blowing, at which time all but official cars must be off the street.

One night gave me more usable negatives than all my past nights' work put together, for it was a night in which the Germans tried to burn down Moscow.

When I arrived at the Embassy so much was happening in all corners of the heavens that I decided to try to work four cameras at once, instead of one as heretofore.

The General lead me to the attic, where we buckled on our helmets. Mine was the regulation Russian army type which had been lent to me by the Mayor of Moscow. It was shaped like a mushroom, and so heavy that I had to develop a whole new set of neck muscles before I learned to keep it on for more than a quarter of an hour at a time. The General held a guarded flashlight while I picked out the lenses and filmpack-holders I expected to need, and then we climbed up a little ladder through a trap door in the roof.

There is something unearthly about being on an open roof in a raid. My first feeling was one of extreme loneliness. The sky was so startlingly big with its probing spears of searchlights and flaming onions hurtling their way through space that man seemed too small to count at all. But as the raid got under way I had so much to do that I could not think of anything except the four cameras that I was trying to operate at once.

There are no rules for exposure on a subject like this—at least none that I know of. The most I could do was to guess, by the mounting action, which points of the horizon would be the most interesting to photograph and then, after the spurts of firing had taken place, to try to estimate whether the illumination had been correct for the exposure of each of the four negatives in process. The exposure varied from a few seconds to several minutes, depending on the fire pattern that had etched their way meanwhile over the field of each plate.

Once I became so engrossed in calculations as I focused on a group of cathedral towers with anti-aircraft guns sending up decorative spurts behind their onion-shaped domes that the General reproved me. "You can't hesitate over your decisions in war, you know."

"But I'm not a general, only a photographer," I said, so apologetically that when I completed my focussing arrangements he added kindly, "Are you sure you are quite happy about that camera now?"

As we started on all fours down the slope of the roof he suddenly called out, "Get behind that chimney. Those things will be hot when they come down." I did not realize what "those things" were, as I heard a swish like satin through the air; but within less than a minute, a hundred fire bombs had fallen within eye-range over the city.

At the back of the embassy was a cluster of roofs and I could hear the fire-watchers calling out to one another. Some of the voices had such a youthful quality that I could tell that these were schoolboys who had recently taken to serving as fireguards. Suddenly I realized that on a neighboring roof an astonishing thing was happening: a group of youngsters were actually arguing with one another for the privilege of putting out the next fire bomb. At the drone of each German plane that passed overhead I could hear the youthful voices calling out; each boy wanted the next one, for each wanted to make a record.

A garage building somewhere off to the side caught into a blaze, and a fire-truck rushed up and pulled into the drive. By now the grounds were illuminated with red light and I could plainly distinguish the fire engine's crew. It consisted not of men but of girls, wearing firemen's helmets and asbestos suits and mitts.

"May we take a short cut through your driveway?" asked a pleasant woman's voice. "We have come to liquidate the fire."

The blaze was still confined to the corner of the garage, and the "liquidation" was rapidly effected, whereupon the truck of firewomen took off toward the Lenin Library, near which another spurt of flames was mounting toward the sky.

By this time another phase of the raid had begun. A second wave of the Luftwaffe was coming with demolition bombs, hoping, I suppose, to take advantage of the light from the fires that had been set. I wondered how the city looked to them up there, and whether the amount of "liquidation" accomplished between waves of planes would annoy them. The peculiar whoosh-like whistle of bombs began—that sound which means that a quarter of a ton of finely turned steel is rushing down through the resisting atmosphere—and at regular intervals we could hear the shrapnel tinkle on the roofs and streets about us. The General said, "It's getting too thick to stay out here. Come inside for a while."

We climbed through the attic window, and there on the ladder, hanging like a furry bat, was Sir Stafford Cripps, in pajamas and a fuzzy bathrobe, watching the raid. It takes a spectacular raid to rouse the interest of an Englishman, for they have been through so many; but this one was enough to bring the British Ambassador out of bed.

Periodically I would have to go out to change the films in my four cameras, and as the General helped me out of the trap door he would say, "Do it as quickly as possible, and if you hear something little coming, stand up, because you're less of a target, but if you hear something coming that sounds big, lie down." I was never able to analyze whether the various descending articles were big or little, so I buckled my wabbly helmet on tighter, made the rounds, changed films, checked the focus, and then returned for a short breather on the ladder.

His Excellency had gone off finally, and his place at the trap door had been taken by the British Vice Admiral. Then something was dropped that was so spectacular that we all crawled out on the roof and crouched along a railing by a drainpipe to watch it. A flare had been dropped directly overhead, and was drifting down toward the Kremlin so close that we could count the ribs in the enormous parachute that held it. Suspended from the giant umbrella was a ball of blazing magnesium, so bright that it hurt our eyes to look at it.

"They're certainly looking for something very specific in this neighborhood," said the General, "when they burn up as much magnesium as that. That stuff costs plenty."

"It's not just the cost," said the Vice Admiral. "There's only just so much of that stuff in the world."

It took half an hour for the mammoth parasol to drift to earth, and it was a fruitful working time for me. Photographers have taken pictures by the light of magnesium flares for years, but I had never expected to have the help of a fleet of German pilots dropping flares from the sky to light up my night pictures of the Kremlin.

At last from the square near us we could hear the loud speaker blaring out, "The raid is over. Go to your rest," and we went downstairs and had whiskey and soda with the Ambassador, who was sitting very comfortably in his pajamas and bathrobe, with his dog Joe at his slippered feet.

Lady Cripps had once told me how she had ended a cable to her husband with the message "REGARDS TO JOE," and then, afraid that the Ambassador might think that she referred to Stalin, she had revised it to read "REGARDS TO JOE AIREDALE." On various occasions I had photographed Joe Airedale, but what I wished more than anything else was to have the opportunity to take a portrait of Joseph Stalin.

Arranging for that portrait was my hardest single job in the Soviet Union, but at last a day came when Molotov had been induced to recommend it, and a government car whirled me through the Kremlin gates. I was conducted by an escort of soldiers into the old Tzarist palace in which leading government officials have their offices, taken up to the second floor in a little gilt, red-carpeted elevator, and led down the long winding hall toward Stalin's office. On the way I kept making little speeches to myself. Nothing could be accomplished by being nervous, I told myself reasonably. Just treat Uncle Joe the way I would anyone else. Ask him to sit down and chat and act natural.

But when his office door was opened and I caught sight of his face, I said to myself, "That is not the way you talk to a dictator."

Ordering Joseph Stalin round would be like giving directions to a statue made of Vermont granite. As I began to focus on that immobile profile I thought he had the strongest face that I had ever seen.

But as soon as I sank to my knees and began shooting, the fact that he was the most mysterious and inaccessible figure in two continents faded away, and his last name might have been Doakes, instead of what it was, or Ivan Ivanovitch, as Joe Doakes is called in his country.

Whoever is unfortunate enough to be within reach of my right arm when I have my head under a camera cloth is apt to find himself a camera assistant. This time it was "Young Litvinov," as he is known in diplomatic circles. He is not related to the present Soviet Ambassador in Washington, but he happens to have the same name and he acts as Kremlin interpreter. As I kept automatically handing out reflectors and flashbulbs he began holding them for me, first on the far side of Stalin's face, and then above his head, for toplighting, which the interpreter accomplished easily, for Stalin is a very short man. Soon Tovarisch Litvinov was changing flashbulbs with a single twist of the wrist as though he had done it all his life. This amused Stalin and he began to laugh, and then I knew I had the expression I wanted.

When I left and walked back through the endless corridor, a little question began forming in my mind. In the Soviet Union there is a custom that appears unshakable. Elevators are made for the apparent purpose of carrying people upward, but not of carrying them down. As we approached the little gilt conveyance I thought, "Surely in the Kremlin itself it is possible to ride down in the elevator." I turned toward it. But no—the colonel accompanying me took me courteously by the arm and I found that even when one has come from an audience with Joseph Stalin it is still necessary to walk down the stairs.

It was almost half-past nine when I left the Kremlin, and the Luftwaffe had been calling regularly at ten o'clock each night. I couldn't risk developing my precious films at the hotel. I had been doing my developing in the bathtub, but there was too much danger of being interrupted by the hotel wardens, whose strict duty it was to put all guests in the cellar shelter when the alarm sounded. To have an air raid warden break into my bathroom and tear me away from a partially developed negative of Stalin was more than I cared to risk.

Our chauffeur helped me carry my developing tanks and trays of solutions down the stairs and place them on the floor of the car. We drove to the American Embassy, arriving just as the alarm sounded, and I set up a laboratory in the servants' bathroom in the cellar. Sandbags stacked against the cellar windows helped to insure that my darkroom would be light-tight.

The negatives of Stalin were so irreplaceable should anything go wrong that I did not have the courage to plunge them in, sink or swim, a whole filmpack at a time, as I usually do. I began processing them one at a time. It was a busy night outside, and I could hear the rhythmic booming of the guns as I worked, and when finally long descending shrieks began sounding through the air, I was glad that there was that bank of sandbags outside the cellar window.

Wouldn't it be fantastic to have a negative fogged by a fire bomb, I reflected, as I dipped Joe's face thoughtfully into the hypo.

As the night wore on I grew hungry. I had entirely forgotten about supper in the excitement of the appointment. But it should be easy to get something to eat in your own Embassy, I thought.

I came out and found several Embassy clerks sleeping in the inner part of the cellar, which had been designated as a shelter. One of them sat up on his cot, and when I whispered that I was hungry he got up and started on a hunt. But the steward, it seemed, had gone off to the big shelter in the subway with all the pantry keys in his pocket. One rarely used icebox had been left unlocked, but it contained only a bowl of rice of doubtful date.

While I rested, eating cautious spoonfuls of the cold boiled rice, the clerk searched out other articles to speed my work: an extension cord, so that a Mazda bulb could be draped over the radiator; a box of pins for hanging up wet negatives; an electric fan to shorten their drying time; a couple of soup plates for print developer.

I wanted to be prepared for the possibility that I might have to radio-photo the pictures to America, which meant that I had to have a set of prints made by morning.

I had no regular printing apparatus, but an old type of clamp-back printing frame which I had borrowed from the chauffeur would serve. It could be held up to the Mazda lamp on the radiator, to expose the prints, but I must conjure up a red safe-light to develop them.

The most valuable contribution of the United States Diplomatic Service that night, from my point of view, was a piece of red muslin. At least it was a dustcloth of a reddish color. With a hand-held flash-light wrapped in the dustcloth, it was possible to control the developing time of the prints in the soup plate, and by dawn I had a full set of Stalin prints.

After finishing the Stalin portrait there was one thing more that I wanted greatly to do, and that was to go to the front. This was difficult to arrange, for the Russians were too busy fighting the Germans to want to be bothered with photographers and reporters on their front lines, but finally I was granted permission.

We went to the front over a succession of rivers of mud which had once been called roads. "General Mud has been reduced to the rank of Colonel in modern warfare," was a favorite Red Army quip, but I believe that during the fall months, when the Germans were pushing their drive toward Moscow, the Russians managed to promote him to the rank of Generalissimo.

Sometimes while negotiating these almost liquid highways, small units of the Luftwaffe would appear and begin their work on the roads. The first time this happened we dashed out of our cars and slithered across the slippery surface to the edge of a meadow, where we threw ourselves down in the low shrubbery. It is odd what images become engraved on one's mind. I remember noticing that we were lying in the largest patch of fringed gentians that I had ever seen. The gentians were at a level with my eyes, and over this blue border I watched three great curtains of mud rise into the air and hang there shimmering, as though suspended on invisible curtain poles in the sky. When these heavenly draperies descended to earth again there were three large sludgy pits, perfectly round in shape, in the road behind us; but our cars were undamaged, though they glistened with a coat of mud laid on thick, like maple icing on a cake.

I began gathering fringed gentians, but the soldiers who were driving our cars had something much more practical to gather. They began pulling boughs off the shrubs and trees and tucking them around the fenders and tying them on the tops of the cars, and when we moved again we looked like a nursery on wheels.

From then on, during my whole trip along the front lines, almost everything I saw was either covered with a tree or tucked under one.

This made things difficult for a photographer, because it made the war look like a back-to-nature movement, which in a way it is. When we visited an emergency airport we found that it had been laid out on a level stretch, suitable for takeoffs, but that clusters of fir trees had been cut down from the adjoining woods and stuck up along the runways to mask the planes and the pilots' tents. At night this greenery was conveniently removed, and at dawn it was realistically set back again.

As we traveled directly along the front lines, we proceeded from one grove to another. Each little wood, as we approached, looked uninhabited until we went in under the trees and our eyes grew accustomed to the dim green light. Then it revealed itself as a complete living community with field telephones, dug-in tanks, batteries shrouded with green boughs, and soldiers singing in their off moments, even when the Germans were only a mile away.

Photography in the daytime was difficult because everything was camouflaged so thickly in green leaves that there was nothing but verdure to be seen; and at night, when the woods were a hive of activity, I could use flashbulbs only with the greatest caution.

Once we were led to the edge of our grove after dark and allowed to run through an open meadow to an "action point" a quarter of a mile distant. We were told to run single file, three meters apart, and when we were halfway across the meadow, suddenly the landscape was ringed with light and a loud roar sounded above us. It was one of the Soviet batteries firing over our heads, and the Germans began answering with machine-gun fire.

When we reached the "action point"—where we had to go on tiptoe and talk in whispers because the Germans were only a stone's throw away—we found the guns set in the midst of a delightful little wood of birch and fir. Even with the white trunks of birch lighted periodically by star shells, the grove looked more as though it had been designed for picnic baskets than for cartridge cases.

But there was nothing of this sylvan character about the great battlefield of Yelnya, for that, when we reached it, looked like the end of the world. Here were the ghosts of blasted trees—great trunks split and smashed as though a giant hand had picked them up in bundles and dropped them broken back to earth.

Instead of fields we saw wastelands, as far as the eye could reach, channeled with trenches and littered with the remains of war which had swept in concentrated fury back and forth across it. We had to be careful where we stepped because the ground was full of unexploded shells and mines; sometimes their noses could be seen poking out of the earth.

Fifty thousand German dead had been hastily shoveled into their own trenches. Everywhere lay the paraphernalia of life. A torn sleeve, the piece of a boot, a tattered raincoat, a fragment of rain-soaked German newspaper, a broken sword. Like hundreds of empty turtle-shells lay the German helmets, some decorated with little swastikas painted in white, many cracked viciously through the top where the metal had given way during battle.

The town of Yelnya, situated between Vyasma and Smolensk, had passed so frequently from Russian to German hands, and from German back to Russian again, that most of its houses had been reduced to skeletons. Sometimes the central ovens, typical of Russian peasant houses, remained partially intact with their tile chimneys, like sentinels, rising out of the wreckage. Here and there was part of a wall, a corner of a roof. And where two or three beams held together, people were creeping back into their homes, so resilient is the human race. Sometimes they were welcomed back by their cats, which have a way of lingering around the house even after bombing, although dogs turn wild and run away.

Often I saw the people cooking, over what remained of their brick and plaster ovens, with strange utensils. I examined these utensils more closely. They were not mere pots and pans bent out of shape from bombing. They were pieces of downed German planes and portions of metal sheeting from captured enemy tanks, which when bent into shallow shapes could serve well as baking tins or broiling pans. Once I saw a woman borrowing some hot charcoals from the fire of a neighbor. "What is she carrying them in?" I wondered, as I watched her heading homeward. The shape was familiar. She was bringing home hot coals in a Nazi helmet.

THE EASY CHAIR:

TOWARD CHANCELLORSVILLE

(APRIL 1942)

Bernard DeVoto

AT THIS WRITING the phantasy of victory is dominant, dangerously so. Pearl Harbor has been our Bull Run. It has, that is, shocked the nation into an awareness of war; it has not shocked it into a realization of the intensity, duration, and currently disastrous outlook of the war. There is too much talk, in the newspapers, on the radio, in private, and by officials about the statistical war. We are anesthetized by figures about the potential productive capacity of the United States, the overwhelming weight of metal we are going to throw into the war eventually, the victories we are certain to win provided only the enemy will wait for us to begin. The most minor local success is magnified as a great victory and accepted as an earnest of things to come. The most alarming enemy success is shrugged off as something to be paid back later when our graphs get going properly. Presumably the military know that wars are won by battles, not figures, and that a battle lost in the field cannot be made good on paper. But that the United States stands defeated in the Pacific today, that our allies are likewise in both oceans, that the only offensive success won against the Axis has been won on the conquered soil of Russia—those facts have little public recognition. They may be perceived; they are not appreciated. The Japanese go on winning the islands but we seem to be winning the statistics, so we maintain a high-hearted belief in victory and so far have shown little will. It looks as though we are going to need a Second Bull Run to arouse it, perhaps a Fredericksburg and a Chancellorsville as well.

We find defeat, as an experience, unimaginable. Few of us are old enough to remember what it is like when the national existence is threatened by the defeat of American armies. Such eye-opening experiences as the South's loss of Vicksburg and Gettysburg and the North's loss of Fredericksburg and Chancellorsville go back eighty-one years. None of us can remember an earlier time when foreign military power was a menace to our immediate existence. Actually, the threat that is now renewed was a determining condition of our national life from the beginning of the republic down to the middle of the 1840's. Actually, we have resumed the strongest fear our ancestors knew and the effort that had to be instinctive with them. But there has been too long a period when even a slight disturbance of our security was inconceivable. The inertia of an impregnability, now ended, still restrains the public from appreciating that we are perilously close to being licked before we get fairly started. We are all in the mood of the coastal cities preparing for air raids. Nothing can reasonably be expected to happen to us but we might as well go through the motions—at a walk.

All this was probably inevitable, but there is no point in letting it get as far as Chancellorsville if it can be stopped short of there. We need an increased dosage of reports like the one on Pearl Harbor. Specifically, we need instruction—with the authority of the President behind it—in the military realities. We can dispense with glory-stories from the Office of Facts and Figures which read like the prospectus of a wildcat mining company and prove that by October, 1943, we shall be producing so many bombers that the Axis might as well submit today to the equations of eventual manufacture. We can dispense with Mr. Churchill's predictions of what we are going to do in 1943. It would be a good idea to dispense with 1943 entirely and produce some present public understanding of the beatings we are taking in 1942 and the calculated chances of surviving them. Someone in authority should induce us to understand that the Axis is going to have something to say about what we do in 1943—and is saying it. We need education, we need it from the horse's mouth, and we need it now. The public mood is utopian. Official instruction in the realities is the only force that can work on it from without in time to prevent the reaction of despair when the catastrophes break over us.

There is no way of forestalling those shocks, there are only ways of limiting them. We are on our way to Chancellorsville. Whether we shall have to travel every bitter step of it depends on how realistically the authorities are willing to confide in us and how rapidly the leaven can work within. The statistics that promise us eventual victory are conclusive but they have the troublesome defect of being open at one end. They will win the war for us all right but, unless they are assisted by an aroused common will, it will take them something like twenty-five years.

AMERICA'S ENEMY NO. 2: YAMAMOTO

(APRIL 1942)

Willard Price

PERHAPS OUR CHIEF individual enemy, next to Adolf Hitler, is leather-faced, bullet-headed, bitter-hearted Isoroku Yamamoto.

We have recently read in the newspapers an extract from his letter to a friend: "When war comes between Japan and the United States I shall not be content merely to occupy Guam, the Philippines, Hawaii, and San Francisco. I look forward to dictating peace to the United States in the White House at Washington."

Admiral Yamamoto is commander-in-chief of the Japanese combined fleets. He is Japan's first man against America and Britain, the spearhead of Japanese ambition to rule Asia and, later, the world. Not only ability makes him our great antagonist, but hate. There has been no heat in his hate, only a cold, implacable fury, and the complete dedication of his life to the crushing of white superiority.

I met Isoroku Yamamoto long before he had become an admiral and unapproachable. But he was already hating, icily. It was in 1915. Fellow-passengers with my wife and myself on the *Awa Maru* from Seattle to Yokohama had been Baron and Baroness Uriu. They were good friends of America. The Baron, who could also lay claim to the title of admiral, had received his training at the United States Naval Academy in Annapolis. His wife was a graduate of an American university—which one, I forget. She was a woman of charm and stamina. During the eighteen days of typhoon weather, as our snow-covered ship heaved and bucked along the stormy Great Circle route close to the Aleutians, she was the only woman to eat in the dining saloon.

Shipboard friendship led to an invitation to visit the Urius at their home in Tokyo—rather, their two homes. One was strictly foreign, the other strictly Japanese. They stood in a grove on the summit of a hill overlooking the city. We were stiffly entertained in the foreign house, then walked through the garden sprinkled with April blossoms to the Japanese house where the family did its real living. There our host and hostess visibly relaxed as they slipped the *geta* from their feet and stepped on to the familiar mats.

A previous guest who had been playing *go* with a young man of the family rose to take his leave. He was a solid, square, rather grim fellow, evidently in his thirties.

"Don't go," said the Baron, and he introduced Isoroku Yamamoto. "This is an American editor," he told him. "He will probably want your views concerning his country."

"I don't mind telling him if he doesn't mind the truth," said Yamamoto gruffly. His English was curiously pronounced but grammatically perfect.

I secretly resented his manner and turned my attention to the Baron. I had no desire to hear this sprig's opinions of America, but I had been trying for three weeks now to draw out the Baron's reminiscences. Here was the man who had fired the first shots of the Russo-Japanese War. Japan, using the pattern with which we are now bitterly familiar, struck first, declared war later. The first jubilation processions in the streets of Tokyo were in honor of Admiral Uriu's triumph at Chemulpo. But he would not talk. After an hour of pleasant nothings, he turned to me seriously with, "I wish to be of service to you. And I can think of no better way than to have you talk with young Yamamoto. I am—what you call—a goner. He is a comer." He gestured to Yamamoto. "Go, both of you, to the tea house. While you are gone we will show Mrs. Price some brocades."

Yamamoto and I walked down the path to the tea-ceremony pavilion. It would have been hard to say which of us was the more sulky. We sat on the green *tatami,* the scent of past pourings of ceremonial tea mingling with the perfume of cherry blossoms.

Well, I had to make the best of it. I began asking questions. Yamamoto answered them, always directly, sometimes brutally. That night I wrote it all down in my notebook and dismissed it. Who was Yamamoto? Why should anyone care about his story?

But when Pearl Harbor was blasted, Wake, Guam, and the Philippines attacked, the *Repulse* and the *Prince of Wales* unbelievably sunk by aerial torpedoes, and the Emperor Hirohito wired congratulations to a certain Admiral Isoroku Yamamoto, the life purpose of this man began to mean something to us. I dug up my notes.

Young Yamamoto began to hate America when his father told him tales of the hairy barbarians, creatures with an animal odor owing to their habit of eating flesh, who had come in their black ships, broken down the doors of Japan, threatened the Son of Heaven, trampled upon ancient customs, demanded indemnities, blown their long noses on cloths which they then put in their pockets instead of throwing away.

For many years the boy saw no foreigners—he could only imagine them. And he was, and is, a person of great imagination. His boyhood home was in Nagaoka in the bleak northwest of Japan, far across the Kiso range from the foreign ports of Yokohama and Kobe. The name of the province is Echigo, which means "behind the mountains." It was so isolated that in feudal days it was used as a place of exile for political malcontents. It became a brewing pot of strong minds and bitter determinations, a breeding place of heretics.

Yamamoto described his home town with a fondness that seemed scarcely appropriate to this place of wind and snow and solitude. The mountain roads to the rest of Japan became nearly impassable early in autumn. The winter snows literally buried the town for four months.

The small thatch-roofed houses disappeared. From above, an airman would have seen no town—only an unbroken white blanket. But underneath this blanket life went on. The wide eaves of the houses protected the sidewalks. The outer edge of each walk had been walled, before the snow came, with upright boards. In this wall were inserted at intervals windows of oiled paper. Against these windows lay the snow, but an uncertain light filtered through into the long corridor that flanked the fronts of the homes and shops. Down this dimly lighted hall it was possible to move in safety even in the worst weather. At street corners, tunnels were dug across the streets. In these passages, many feet below the surface of the snow, large characters could be read with ease, and children studied their lessons as they walked home from school by tunnel and corridor and tunnel. Except for the burrowings from one sidewalk to another, the snow that lay house-high down the middle of the street was not disturbed from autumn to spring.

Deep in these snowy catacombs there was protection for women and children—but men must still emerge through apertures in the surface, blinking in the strong light, and go on broad straw snowshoes after wood, or carry goods from town to town, or hunt, or fish in the icy waters of the Sea of Japan many miles away. There the boy got his first strong taste of the sea and liked it.

He spoke with a kind of sour satisfaction of the typhoons and blizzards, of the roping down of boathouses to prevent them from being blown away, of the capsizing of a fishing boat and his cold swim to a cavern in the cliff where he had to stay two days until the sea had quieted and he could swim to a beach. He learned how to fish for bream, sole, mackerel, octopus, and swordfish. He learned secrets of cloud, wind, and wave—and made up his mind either to be a fisherman when he grew up or to join the navy.

"Why did you choose the navy?" I asked him.

He smiled his frostbitten smile. "I wanted to return Commodore Perry's visit."

His barbarian-hating father was named Teikichi Takano, a rather grim man, I gathered, and very poor. But after he died the boy was adopted into the more prosperous Yamamoto family. Such adoptions are common in Japan. A family without a male heir will adopt a son to perpetuate the line.

Young Isoroku found himself in a home that boasted the largest and most sumptuously gilded Buddhist shrine in any house in the town. Also there was a very plain *kamidana,* or god-shelf, bearing a simple miniature of a Shinto temple. Display is not congenial to Shinto. While Buddhism embodies the flowering effulgence of the rich Orient, Shinto expresses a samurai severity that is not essentially Oriental at all, but only Japanese.

The army, dreaming already of world conquest, had sensed the value of Shinto in their plans. They had revived the ancient faith, given it new points of emphasis, made it a rallying point for Japanese patriotism, emperor-worship, and the mission of divine Japan to dispel the darkness that enveloped a godless globe.

All this suited Isoroku. He bowed only perfunctorily before the golden Buddha and the Yamamoto ancestral tablets—but he placed daily offerings on the god-shelf.

Not only was Shinto twisted to mean Japan-worship during Isoroku's impressionable years, but *bushido* was born at the same time. Of course both he and the West were taught to think *bushido* as old as the Japanese race. But you cannot find the word in any dictionary, Japanese or Western, published before the year 1900. Loyalty itself was nothing new, although it was no more common in Japan than elsewhere—but loyalty's code of rules called *bushido* was an invention of the Japanese army. If the militarists and their Emperor were to remain in the saddle, the unquestioning obedience of the masses was necessary. *Bushido* was the answer. By giving it the whiskers of great age, they insured that it would be venerated as no contemporary contrivance would be. A heavenly glow was cast over feudal days. Then every samurai was true to his daimio and every daimio would lay down his life for his Emperor. How ridiculously untrue such a picture was, Professor Basil Hall Chamberlain, one of the closest students of old Japan, has pointed out:

"An analysis of medieval Japanese history shows that the great feudal houses, so far from displaying an excessive idealism in the matter of fealty to one emperor, one lord, or one party, had evolved the eminently practical plan of letting their different members take different sides, so that the family as a whole might come out as winner in any event, and thus avoid the confiscation of its lands."

But Japanese history, as Isoroku studied it in school, had been rewritten to suit the requirements of the new expansionist policy of Japan. To go forth and conquer, Young Japan must have fanatical faith in itself and contempt for the rest of the human race. This was accomplished by teaching myths that made gods of the Nipponese people, "Seed of the Sun," and cast a dubious light over the origin of all other human beings.

"Were you ever taught the Darwinian theory of evolution?" I asked Yamamoto.

"Yes—as a Western idea—and perhaps applying to the West. But our teachers always made clear the special place of the people of Yamato."

"You don't mean," I questioned, "the story of the gods Izanagi and Izanami who gave birth to the Japanese islands and the people who inhabit them? No modern, educated Japanese would actually take such a legend seriously?"

Yamamoto stiffened. "Were there any other questions you wished to ask?"

I had a vision of a certain fundamentalist friend of mine who had once stiffened in just this fashion when I questioned her belief in the creation of the world in seven twenty-four-hour days and the shaping of Adam from the dust of the earth. In matters of religion questions are not safe. Faith plays too large a part.

And the Japanese self-exaltation is distinctly a religion—taught in childhood, thoroughly ingrained, soberly supported by scholars such as Hirata, who says, "From the fact of the divine descent of the Japanese people proceeds their immeasurable superiority to the natives of other countries in courage and intelligence." And the *History for Middle Schools* reminds student Japan that "Such a national character is without a parallel throughout the world."

I went on to the safer ground of questions regarding school routine. "Was school excused during bad weather?"

"On the contrary. During the midwinter month, supposed to be the coldest, our hours were longer and our tasks were made much harder."

"What was the purpose of that?"

"To build endurance. The room was heated only by *hibachi* [braziers]. The temperature was half of what would be considered necessary in a foreign home. On the ninth day of the midwinter month, thought to be the coldest day of the entire year, no fire whatever was allowed. We were given a hundred ideographs to write. We must keep at the task until it was finished, no matter if the brush-fingers became purple and frozen and there was no feeling from the wrist down. When the work was done we thawed our hands by rubbing them in snow."

"A good preparation for pneumonia," I suggested.

"What does that matter?" he flashed. "The lioness pushes her cub over the cliff and leaves it to climb back alone. It is a Japanese proverb."

"What did you like best in school?"

"Drill."

I remembered my own schooldays in Toronto and the weekly drill when we dressed front in the schoolyard, shouldered arms, presented arms, made right turns, left turns, and about turns. But it soon appeared that the drill Yamamoto was thinking of was nothing like this.

"We made long marches in the snow or rain. The worst weather was always chosen for these marches. We sometimes spent the night in the open. We stormed imaginary forts. We were taught maneuvers suited to various types of terrain: how to fight in the hills, on the plains, in the woods, in marshes, how to cross rivers, how to invade seacoasts."

"When did this training begin?"

"When school began, at the age of six. But we didn't get rifles and uniforms with brass buttons until we entered middle school at twelve.

The greatest sport was the annual military maneuvers of about ten thousand boys drawn from schools all over the western provinces and divided into two armies, the one taking its position in strong entrenchments, the other attacking an hour before dawn. Regular army officers commanded us. Of course we fired only blanks, but our rifles, grenades, machine guns, and field guns were all the real thing—not dummies. It was good practice."

A trained militarist at seventeen, Yamamoto entered the Naval Academy at Yetajima on the Inland Sea near Hiroshima. Here he studied for three years and then spent another year on the training ships. The first of these training ships was an old-fashioned square-rigged sailing vessel.

"But why train on a windjammer for a navy that contains nothing but steamers?"

"Because a sailor's first duty is to learn the sea, not the ship. And you are on closer terms with the sea in a square-rigger. You learn the habits of currents, waves, winds, storms. Besides, it's a hard life. It makes sailors."

Later I had an opportunity to go aboard a square-rigged training ship of the mercantile marine, similar to those used by the navy. On the Kyoto-Tokyo train the young man in blue uniform sitting next to me had suddenly asked if I had ever been in "Seedonay." I finally made out that he meant Sydney, Australia. He had gone there, he said, on a cruise of his training ship. I indulged his desire to practice English and was rewarded by an invitation to visit his ship. A few days later I met young Okawara at Shinagawa and we went by sampan out of the mouth of the Meguro River and over shallow Tokyo Bay to board the handsome white four-masted barque *Taisei Maru*.

I soon saw what Yamamoto had meant. The lads perched high on the yards furling sails knew where the wind was coming from. They and their officers studied the sky with an earnestness unknown to men of steam. And the toughening process was obvious. Barefoot cadets, who would be ships' captains some day, curled their toes round foot ropes from which one of their number had been blown into the sea during the last storm. They struggled with wet canvas that whipped back and forth in the grip of a strong breeze. The ship carried, when full-rigged, twenty-seven sails. That means plenty of exercise. Add to this the scrubbing down of the decks with sand and coconuts at 5:00 A.M., the long lessons in navigation, and the lifeboat drills which are staged when the sea is particularly bad. And I understood the claim of the nautical schools: "There is nothing to equal work on a deep-water square-rigger to harden and toughen a youngster. Training on a wind-jammer brings out qualities of iron nerve, quickness to act in emergencies, physical toughness, all of which are necessary to the future steamship commander."

Such training of course is not peculiarly Japanese. In fact Japan learned it from the seafaring English, and we have had it in America too.

But Yamamoto, when I talked to him, did not give much credit to the English—who taught Japan most of what she knows about how to fight the English! He briefly traced the growth of the Imperial Navy. The edict of the Shogun Iyemitsu forbidding the construction of any ships large enough to leave the shelter of the coasts isolated Japan for more than two centuries. It was not until Commodore Perry's squadron arrived with demands backed with force that Japan saw the need of ships and guns. The ban on shipbuilding was removed. A dockyard was constructed at Nagasaki and a naval school started with the aid of the Dutch. The Imperial Navy began with two presents, one a six-gun paddle-wheel steamer from the Dutch, the other a four-gun yacht from the Queen of England.

The first ironclad in the new navy was the *Stonewall Jackson,* purchased from the United States. Other ships were bought and some built. The Powers seem to have taken a most benevolent interest in the budding navy which was much too small and weak to be regarded seriously.

French engineers founded a dockyard at Yokosuka and taught all that the West knew about the construction of warships. Great Britain made the most significant contribution. She sent her naval officers as instructors to conduct a naval school at Yokohama and, later, a great naval college at Tokyo where Admiral Douglas and thirty-three picked English officers and seamen labored to create an expert personnel for the navy.

But Yamamoto principally emphasized the progress made since these outsiders had been dismissed and sent home. The Japanese, he pointed out, have a peculiar aptitude for the life of the sea and show remarkable technical ability. He did not mention the early warships of Japanese construction that turned turtle because too many clever ideas had been incorporated in them.

Doubtless the foreign fathers of the Nipponese fleet were very proud of their infant prodigy's performance in the war with China in 1894. They had even more reason for satisfaction at the outbreak of the Russo-Japanese War in 1904. Now Japan had seventy-six warships including battleships, destroyers, and torpedo boats.

Yamamoto, twenty years old, took part in this war as an ensign on the *Mikasa,* flagship of the great Togo. The war was begun, as I have said, by the gentleman in whose tea pavilion we now sat. Admiral Uriu challenged the Russian ship *Variag,* which should have been safe since it lay in the neutral Korean port, Chemulpo. The commander of the *Variag* appealed to the captains of other foreign warships in the harbor to make joint resistance to the proposed violation of neutral waters. Some were willing, but the most important, the commander of the United States cruiser *Vicksburg,* was not. His refusal reflected the pro-Japanese American attitude of that time. In effect, he opened Korea to the Japanese and gave Nippon a start in the conquest of Asia. The *Variag* was sunk. Admiral Uriu landed troops which took over Korea and made it the land base for the attack upon Port Arthur.

The sea attack upon Port Arthur was begun by Admiral Togo. For many months he blockaded the port, trying in vain to tempt the Russian fleet to come out and fight. Ships that did venture out were sunk. Young Ensign Yamamoto had a perfect opportunity to observe at close range the tactics of one of the greatest naval strategists. "There will never be another Togo," he said.

On May 27, 1905, the ensign was a participant, at least to the extent of two fingers, in what Hector C. Bywater has described as "the most decisive naval action in history." The main Russian fleet had taken seven months to come from the Baltic. It was wiped out in one day. The meeting took place in the Straits of Tsushima. Why there? Yamamoto had heard Admiral Togo several days previously explain the reason for the selection of this spot. It was here that the attempted invasion of Japan by Kublai Khan had been turned back seven centuries before. The souls of Japan's defenders who had died in that engagement would, Togo believed, fight beside him in this one.

With battleships and cruisers Togo steamed in ahead of the dog-tired Russian fleet, while ships commanded by Admiral Uriu and others closed in behind it. Above the head of Ensign Yamamoto where he stood on the deck of the flagship *Mikasa* rose Togo's famous signal, "The fate of the Empire depends upon this battle. Let every man do his utmost."

After only ten minutes of firing, the turret of the Russian flagship *Suvaroff* was blown away and other Russian vessels were in flames. Within three-quarters of an hour the issue was decided. The Russian fleet, bogged down with store ships and colliers and blocked by sinking battleships, was in complete confusion. At nightfall Togo withdrew his large ships and left his torpedo boats to pick the bones—which they did so effectively that by morning only four of the original Russian fleet of twenty-seven remained. These were allowed to surrender.

Yamamoto came out of this epic fight minus two fingers but plus the knowledge that the yellow man could whip the white. He had been a spectator of the first great triumph of the Asiatic over the Aryan. That seems to have set his life pattern. Now that he knew it could be done it must be done. The white man must be driven from Asia.

When he began to think of the airplane rather than the battleship as the means by which this would be accomplished, I do not know. He had been raised on deck. He had seen battleships, cruisers, destroyers, and torpedo boats turn the tide of history. And yet when I asked him which of these he believed would be the important war vessel of the future, he said:

"None of these. The most important ship of the future will be a ship to carry aeroplanes."

At that time, 1915, the "aeroplane" was as clumsy as its name and the aircraft carrier remained in the womb of imagination. There had been a few experiments. America had been the pioneer. The first plane to take off from a ship's deck left a temporary platform on the forward part of the *U.S.S. Birmingham*. The year was 1910 and the pilot, Eugene Ely. The first plane to land on a ship's deck was brought down by the same pilot on the stern of the *U.S.S. Pennsylvania* in 1911.

There was a tendency to regard these experiments as mere stunts. Four years had now passed and nothing more had been done with the idea. But it was fermenting in Yamamoto's brain. His superiors evidently gave it no attention.

Oddly enough, conservative Britain was the first to develop the fantastic scheme. The First World War brought home to her the need for a floating airdrome and she completed the world's first aircraft carrier in 1918. America commissioned the *Langley* in 1922, the *Lexington* and *Saratoga* in 1928. All navies were now alive to the idea. As Yamamoto and other air-minded men rose to power in the Nipponese navy, Japan took the lead, and she has today more aircraft carriers than any other nation.

But we are ahead of our story. The brown, brusque man in the tea pavilion who had suggested that the greatest surface ship of the future would be a mere handmaiden to the ship of the air ended the interview on a sour note. I asked him the usual question about Japanese-American relations and expected the usual guff.

"They cannot mend until they break," he snapped.

I looked for some trace of melancholy in his manner but found none. He evidently looked forward to the break with the liveliest anticipation.

A few days later I had a before-breakfast interview with Count Okuma, then Premier. He had been limping about his garden since dawn. He always said that his best thoughts came early in the morning.

His early thought for me was, "I believe the entire East is to be bound together in one heart and one mind. And I believe that Japan has a mission in helping to bring this about."

Could there have been a more suave proposal of the most stupendous program of aggression the world has yet known?

I spoke of my talk with Yamamoto.

"That young man," smiled Count Okuma, "will, I prophesy, be one of the instruments in the policy I have just mentioned."

But I found no one else who regarded Yamamoto seriously, and few who even knew of him. Certainly he meant nothing to American readers. Yet as the years ticked by I noted his activities.

His name was always associated with planes and airfields. He became Chief Instructor in the Kasumigaura Naval Air Corps. Some caustic remarks came from him when the Washington Conference put the United States, Britain, and Japan on a 5-5-3 naval ratio, Japan accepting the little end. He and other young radicals made life uneasy for Japanese representatives who had thus "humiliated" Japan.

He was Naval Attaché in the Japanese Embassy at Washington in 1925. He had much to do with United States naval officers and they had reason to feel flattered by the keen interest he took in American naval technic. He learned English thoroughly and improved his game of poker.

He returned to Japan and was appointed commander of the *Isuzu*, then of the *Akagi*. But while he trod the deck he turned his eyes aloft. His voice was increasingly heard arguing for aircraft and aircraft carriers.

He also talked oil. Japan had passed through the palanquin era and the ricksha interlude and as yet hardly realized that she was in the oil age. But Yamamoto had been raised on oil. Every summer at Nagaoka he had spent much of his time in the oilfields just outside the town. Here were the richest oil wells in Japan. For two hundred years oil had been known to exist here—but nothing much was done about it until 1876, when the Japanese government engaged an American geologist to survey the possibilities. His report was favorable. Wells were feverishly dug, Nagaoka talked oil, smelled oil, lived oil, and when Isoroku was six years old Echigo province was supplying ninety-nine per cent of the oil consumed in Japan.

The boy very naturally grew up oil-minded. He saw a civilization run on oil and by oil. He realized that oil was the lifeblood of mechanized warfare. His home province did not have enough for that, Japan did not have enough—but there was enough in the East Indies. Therefore the Japanese navy was destined to sail southward.

But it would never dare to do so if it were only a 3 navy as compared to America's 5 and Britain's 5. He so bitterly attacked this "degradation" that he was chosen as the right man to go to London in 1934 and upset the 5-5-3 ratio.

Rear Admiral Isoroku Yamamoto, Special Envoy to the London Naval Parley, declared when he left Japan that he would read no newspapers on his way to England. He knew the subtle wiles of Westerners and feared that his obduracy might be weakened by their arguments. He was determined to keep himself vacuum-fresh for London.

As he crossed the American continent he refused to see reporters. They were stopped by an interpreter who blandly brushed them off with the explanation that the Admiral did not speak English. Those who believed it must have been considerably surprised when the envoy, upon stepping off the *Berengaria* on English soil, immediately broke into voluble English. He did not wait to be subjected to the persuasions of the conference table. Between gangplank and taxicab he struck the blow that wrecked the London Naval Parley.

"Japan will not submit to the continuance of the ratio system. There is no possibility of any compromise by my government on that point."

After two months of talk the situation remained exactly where it had been when Yamamoto stepped off the boat. He stood for a "common upper limit." He assured his rivals that this was a matter of honor for Japan and that his nation probably would not actually build up to that limit.

"If we grant paper parity," suggested Prime Minister MacDonald, "will Japan promise not to build up to it?"

"Very sorry, but no," answered the Japanese envoy. "Very sorry, but no."

He was entertained at many dinners and always ate and drank heartily, but it never mellowed him. On one such occasion a British guest, when the atmosphere seemed particularly congenial, leaned over to say to the Admiral, "Now, tell me just why you won't agree to the ratio."

The Admiral consumed the last particles of roast and vegetables on his plate, then laid down his knife and fork.

"I believe I am shorter than you are," he said.

"Yes."

"But you don't tell me that I ought to eat only three-fifths of the food on my plate. I eat as much as I need."

Even if he had desired to yield he would not have dared. If he had yielded he would not be alive today. When it was rumored in Japan that the ratio might win, the Black Dragon Society met and vowed that if this happened the Japanese envoy and all his aides should be assassinated.

The British suggested that if the ratio were abandoned the three powers should at least agree to an interchange of information so that each should always know the building programs of the others.

"But it would be of value to Japan to know at all times what the others are building."

"We can find out," said Yamamoto bluntly. "But you can't find out what we're doing. So such an arrangement would be of no advantage to Japan."

His respect for aircraft carriers was shown in his suggestion that if Japan were given free rein in Asia she might agree to a world program of disarmament, beginning with the aircraft carrier.

"We consider the aircraft carrier the most offensive of all armament. Now that we are all concerned with reducing the menace that any one country may be to any other, it would seem logical to get rid of the most menacing weapon first of all."

Whether his expressed willingness to disarm was genuine or was made to test his opponents who can say? Certain it is that he showed no regret when the Washington Naval Treaty of 1922, first great venture of the human race to do away with armaments, lay in ruins in London, broken on the rock that he had provided for it. He went back to Japan and I happened to be in Tokyo when he arrived. A parade of admirals and two thousand members of reservist and patriotic associations, including the Black Dragons who had pledged his death if he failed, welcomed him. He went to the palace to receive the congratulations of the Emperor.

Time having been turned backward and the world plunged toward certain war, Japan rejoiced.

"A naval construction race," gloated the Navy Ministry in an official pamphlet, "may be regarded as a stage in the rapid expansion of our national strength. We therefore must be firmly resolved to overcome any difficulties that may arise ahead of us so that the glorious position in which our Empire now finds itself may increase in glory."

Since that time Japan has swiftly increased, if not in glory, at least in armament. The race has been made in secret, and any published figures of Japan's naval strength should be taken as a very mild approach to the truth. For example, the number of Japan's aircraft carriers is usually estimated at from seven to nine. But Brigadier General Sewell, military expert attached to the British Library of Information, has told us that a private report establishes the number at fifteen. The United States, according to pre-war Senate figures, has six, of which some may be in the Atlantic. This would give Japan a very heavy superiority in the Pacific. The Dutch have had no aircraft carriers, and at this writing no British aircraft carrier has been reported in the Pacific.

Japan is also far ahead in airplane strength. When it comes to battleships, cruisers, destroyers, and submarines she at least rivals our combined Pacific and Asiatic fleets; but both Admiral Yamamoto and Admiral Suetsugu have been criticized in Japan for their emphasis upon aircraft to the neglect of battleships.

"How," someone asked, "can you expect to destroy a battleship except with a battleship?"

"With torpedo planes," replied Yamamoto, and he quoted a Japanese proverb: "The fiercest serpent may be overcome by a swarm of ants."

The sinking of the *Repulse* and *Prince of Wales* made his meaning clear.

While Japan's army has been depleted in China, Japan's navy has had nothing to do but to grow and prosper. Today even in air power, which is usually an army prerogative, the navy is superior. Six hundred miles from the sea, navy planes have been bombing Chungking. If Japan is "exhausted," the navy does not know it. During the ten war years from the invasion of Manchuria in 1931 to the beginning of the present conflict the Japanese navy went unscathed.

The disastrous defeat of the Japanese army in 1939 at Nomonhan on the Russian-Manchurian border brought Japan to her senses so far as fooling with Russia was concerned. The Japanese war lords lost interest in Siberia and began to listen to the insistent demand of the navy for "southward expansion." Yamamoto had his chance.

He is now fifty-eight. No hampering system of seniority has prevented him from attaining power before he was too old to do anything with it. He is a hard chunk of a man, hair cropped as short as the bristles on a beaver-tail cactus, lips thick, jowl heavy, chin prominent. He is, I hear, as surly and abrupt as he was in Admiral Urin's tea pavilion. I have never met him again and never wanted to. But I have seen him occasionally and his house in Kamakura. It is a small place. He lives simply. This simplicity does not extend to his smoking, drinking, and eating, which are all on quite a grand scale. He takes pride in the fact that they do not hurt him. He dissipates hard, works hard. He plays hard too. He has the conquest complex, enjoys having opponents, plays games to win. For many years he has been navy champion in poker, bridge, chess, and *go*.

He is a man of tremendous conceit with the brains and stomach to back his bluff. He was in Washington once. He plans to be there again. If he gets there it will be because of Japan's superior air power.

If he doesn't get there it will be because of America's superior air power.

THE EASY CHAIR:

COMMENCEMENT ADDRESS

(JULY 1942)

Bernard DeVoto

THE CEREMONIES WE perform today embody one of the deepest American faiths—the faith that to grow in knowledge is to grow in personality and citizenship. They have a complex symbolism. They formally receive the Class of 1942 in a continuity which reaches as far back as the human spirit has sought to know the nature of things. And they formally proclaim that the Class of 1942 have completed an apprenticeship in learning and may now begin the lives for which, according to our enduring faith, their education has prepared them.

Twenty-five years ago these same ceremonies invoked this same symbolism on behalf of the Class of 1917. Then, as now, some members of the graduating class were already absent when the ritual was fulfilled. Then, as now, that ritual had an irony hardly to be borne. For young men are educated in order to live their lives in function, develop what is in them, and achieve their expectation. Education, if our faith is not merely frivolous, is education for peace. And in 1917, as in 1942, the graduating class was called upon to relinquish its preparation for peace and assume instead the obligation of war.

I conceive that it is as soldiers you should be addressed, and that any member of the Class of 1917 who ventures to speak to the Class of 1942 on Commencement Day should speak as a soldier. What could a man who was a soldier in 1917 say to his son who is a soldier in 1942? He would avoid the pitfall of rhetoric, he would say no more than he has found true in his own experience as a veteran of war and also of peace. He would try to phrase what the Class of 1917 found out.

They went off to war, they prepared to fight, some of them fought, some of them served without fighting, and the war reached its end— or its twenty-five years' armistice. When it ended some of the Class of '17 were dead, some were crippled in body or in soul, some were unaffected, some were diminished, some increased. Those who were left took up the interrupted expectation. They began the completion of their individual experience, which has included the begetting of sons and the hope that their sons might live out their lives in peace.

Decent reticences fence off a soldier's privacies. He can no more speak of love of country than any man can truly find words for love of a woman. Yet the inestimable experience is there, and a soldier has had his moment of dedication. It is, in his full consciousness, hardly more than a moment—a brief exaltation soon crusted over by the human habit of being shamefaced about consummate emotion and by the routine of war. It is remembered only in oblique associations, precisely as the privacies of love are remembered. But in that moment the soldier has achieved a knowledge otherwise altogether beyond his attainment. What were mere words have become a living truth for him, he has found the reality in experience deep in the bitter grief of mankind and knows that the function of those who must live for a country may also be to die for it and that to die for it truly is seemly. . . . That moment will overtake you suddenly at some point of the path you now start out on. In that moment you will seem to yourself already dead in your country's defense and already fulfilled by dying. It will pass swiftly, you will allude to it only with a grin or a cheap joke, you will deny it many times, it will lie covered over with the dreariness and the manifold boredoms of soldiering. Nevertheless at the depths an immutable change will have occurred, for you have been touched by something eternal.

Other knowledge comes to a soldier. It is not that he has looked on the unspeakable and survived, or seen the dignity of the human body made a mere blasphemy by wounds and filth and dismemberment, but has nevertheless endured. He has felt the deepest affirmation. No man has ever known that death must be faced—death in peace or in war—without fearing that his fear of death would betray the fundamental honor of life. For his God has promised him, and man's conception of himself has promised him, that at the extremity he will behave with dignity and fortitude. All men fear that fear may break this honor. What a soldier learns is that, at the extremity, he will rule his fear and do whatever it is his part to do. He will see it through. So that, whether he lives or dies, the knowledge will not fail him that when the simplest but most rigorous test of manhood was upon him he met it.

There is also the fellowship of soldiers. It may come to you quite suddenly and by way of only an eight-man squad marching down a road or resting under trees. You are suddenly members one of another, in daily boredom and labor, in the risk of death, in the necessity of the nation. You are enlarged in a fraternity of things shared, and the awareness widens out to the company, the regiment, the army, to a knowledge too often slurred or denied or scorned in times of safety, a knowledge that the Americans are members one of another. . . . During your college years you have seen the world break up. And in your senior year you have seen the nation form, as it always forms in times of danger. You have seen the discords lessen, the phantasms fade, the will harden, and the purpose take shape. You have felt your own doubts go. Some of you, I do not doubt, were long troubled by ignorance: you thought that you had no faith, that America had found for you no belief real enough and precious enough to make you will to live for it, still less to die for it. You have now come to know that it had been there all along, too plain to be seen, too mighty to be realized. You have seen it waken all around you. They say that in the Naval Hospital at Pearl Harbor on December 7th a young sailor with half his body shot away held out his hand to no one in particular, to someone unnamed and unseen, and said, "We were there together." In five months you have seen America wake to the knowledge of a soldier, that we are here together. While we meet in a college hall other Americans face death in all the oceans and continents. A year ago no one could have communicated to you the fellowship you now feel with the men who died and those who lived at Pearl Harbor and on the Bataan Peninsula.

As you go to war some private symbol will mean that faith to you. It may be one of those names which embody the poetry of the American land—Susquehanna, Yemassee, Kaskaskia, Niobrara. It may be a glimpse of some familiar landscape, the swell of a prairie, the edge of a woods, a hayfield or orchard, the curve of a highway, some effect of rain or cloud or sunlight over your own place. It may be the verse of a song, something from Stephen Foster, from some idle, ephemeral song, or from one of the songs sung on this campus last night. It may be a memory of some college hour, the sun on the lawns, or voices over the tennis courts, or friends talking together after midnight. Whatever it may prove to be, it will mean America in you. It will mean that you were nurtured to the expectation of peace and that on you also has fallen the necessity of war. On you also has been put the challenge which Abraham Lincoln put on other Americans long ago, to "nobly save or meanly lose the last, best hope of earth."

A few weeks ago America called on the Class of 1917 to register for the second time in universal liability to serve. Chance had me registering in a building of my own college, one which was erected as a memorial to the men of that college who died in the Civil War. Our line of registrants moved through a long hall where names of no meaning to us personally are recorded in marble with names of places where they died—Bull Run, Antietam, Chancellorsville, Shiloh, Chickamauga, Gettysburg, the Wilderness. We never knew them, but on them as on us had fallen the summons and the necessity. And every man who moved down that line beside those names could remember other men, members of the Class of 1917, who had been our friends and who had sat with us in that same building during the college years. Their names mean nothing to you, but on you has fallen the summons and the necessity. We were all there together.

I will not speak their names but only say that they were my friends. One would have been a lawyer in a small, obscure town. He married a girl in September, 1917; he was killed at Saint Mihiel. He begot no sons, he died, so we say, without issue, he never lived to be a lawyer. One would have been a chemist. He fought the war through, was in a number of battles, was wounded several times, survived, came home, studied chemistry for another year, and died. He also begot no sons. One served through the war, came home, lived according to his light, and died ten years ago. Another, a bacteriologist, served through the war and came home and took up the career that had been broken off, and died two years ago. He died triumphant, we should say, since when he died the terror of one disease that has afflicted mankind was ended forever because he had lived to do his work.

That bacteriologist nobly fulfilled the promise of his generation, after honorably fighting in its war. He married and begot children, worked out as much as might be of his expectation, lived fully, and when he rounded out his years had added to man's knowledge and power. Therein, we believe, is the implied contract which life makes with us and which is ratified by the college years: that every man shall have his chance. It would have been sweet and seemly if those others had had their chance. If the young lawyer had been able to come back to his wife, live in his little town, beget children, rear them to maturity, and round out his years. If the young chemist had been able to find his place, make his talent fruitful, and marry and beget children. But the past five months have taught you, as the years have taught me, that the phrase which you and I both have sometimes mocked is true—that their death was sweet and seemly, that their life was sweet and seemly in their death. They did not die without issue or without function. You are their issue, and their function was not to work out their personal promise but to die maintaining the continuity in which you have lived.

Now on the Class of 1942 has fallen the necessity they faced in 1917. No old soldier would dare in the slightest to mitigate for any young soldier the horror of what must be faced. Hell is real and you must go into hell and run your chance. No father can mitigate to himself or to his son the ruth of a young man's dying in war. It may be that your name will yet be carved in marble when this college lists her sons who died in the service of America. Your very dog may outlive you, and your father, who survived his war, be left to make what he can of hearing someone else whistling to that dog. All anyone can say is: good luck, God give you courage, may you do your parts as men and soldiers. Your cause is the last, best hope of earth, and in you the American people, all people who accept decency and practice freedom and believe that mankind has dignity, are working out their destiny. Moreover, in the knowledge you have discovered in yourselves during the past five months exists the certainty of triumph. When you felt the common will asserted in you, the fixed universe on which our enemy has staked his destiny was shattered. In that moment the underlying fear that has besotted the modern world was proved unreal; for you knew that the spirit of man is truly free and that its contemners, who have staked everything on the guess that it was bound, must go down defeated.

Living or dying, you have found your function and will have your issue: to do the common job, at the summons of your country, in the need of your kind. Your fathers, the Class of 1917, won their war. They lost their peace. I will not say that they meanly lost it but they did not do all that peace required of them. The disease that overspread the earth after the last war had many causes. In part we were ignorant, in part careless, in part weak. We were too timid or too stupid to assume for the United States in peace the responsibility of power we had asserted for it in war. We were too easily discouraged, too easily cynical, too superficial, too untrue to the knowledge and faith we have proved in ourselves. We were too Utopian, we asked too much of fallible men and so were too readily disheartened. Twenty-five years ago it was in our power to advance more than a little the solutions of the unsolved problems of giving order to the societies of the world. We failed, and so the disease spread, hope died, and you have grown up in an era abandoned to despair. You have the knowledge that we failed. But you have the knowledge that your generation, though it faces the result of our failure, also faces the possibility of repairing it.

So the summons has now fallen on you. You will win your war. You have a chance to win your peace.

There is no certainty that you will win it. With death and life, as with steel and explosives, men may either build or destroy. But if it is true, and it is true, that in my generation hope went out of the world, it is true that in your generation hope has come back to the world. If when you have ceased fighting you do not deal more successfully than your fathers with the problems of giving order to the societies of the world, then indeed the world will be more full of sorrow than anyone can understand and your sons will grow up to unmitigated and absolute despair. But before your eyes the wild and inconceivable has happened, the thing itself. Meaning has come back to men's effort and men's desire. When you recognized the will in yourselves, determinism was refuted and the monstrous nightmare of our time was broken. In you the world of free men again has a chance to bring itself to be. There is no more than a chance, a fighting chance. But need you, or the lives fulfilled in you, ask for more than a fighting chance? You have a chance to win the fight your predecessors lost. In the inexorable working out of man's fate, that has come to be the meaning of your lives.

BLOOD AND BANQUETS

(OCTOBER 1942)

Bella Fromm

In the nineteen-twenties Mrs. Fromm, member of a substantial Bavarian-Jewish family, became society reporter for the great German newspaper Vossische Zeitung. *Her acquaintance and friendship with members of the diplomatic set gave her an assured position in Berlin until the advent of the Nazis. Later she was forced out of her newspaper job, but she remained in Germany because her connections with French, American, and other diplomats enabled her to help many victims of the Nazis to get out of the country. This month we publish excerpts from her diary, beginning in 1936, at the time when Italy had completed its conquest of Ethiopia and the Olympic Games were about to be held in Berlin.*

—The Editors

JUNE 7, 1936:

Gala soiree at invitation of Italian Ambassador and Mrs. Bernardo Attolico. He doesn't look much like a diplomat. She's beautiful and exotic, but ice-cold, vain, and inordinately ambitious. Countess Edda Ciano was guest of honor. Mussolini's daughter is in her lower thirties, neither pretty nor plain, not too feminine. Looks a lot like her father with the same features and poses, and falls for nobility. Her hair is violently blond without any warmth: it doesn't seem natural to me. Also, like her father, she is quite immoderate in her consumption of lovers.

Attolico said that Count Ciano is dubbed *"Il cervo volante"* (the flying stag) in Rome. "Because flying is his passion and antlers are his adornment."

She is said to direct her father politically and to settle his private affairs, getting rid of the women for him. Throughout the evening Edda was surrounded by six or eight dashing flyers in snappy uniforms, especially selected by Goering and under special instructions to please.

Magda Goebbels has been very intimate with Edda ever since they spent vacations together in Switzerland. Edda taught her that there was no reason to be miserable about a faithless husband and that wedlock was only one of the states of man. Magda was most demonstrative about her friendship with Edda and has carefully maneuvered to keep "those climbers," the Ribbentrops, as far away from her as possible.

There was lots of clamor about the victory of Addis Ababa.

Edda is something to watch, and to listen to, at a party. Seeing Chief of Staff Lutze strutting around wearing white cotton gloves, she asked Prince Christian of Hessen loudly: "Since when do waiters wear the S.A. uniform?"

The evening was interesting. Goebbels had one of his fits of rage. It appeared that one of the Italian ladies, boasting of how well she was learning German, said that she had read a wonderful book by Erich Maria Remarque.

Goebbels began to foam. "That Communist!" he barked. "He writes about the war and has never been in the trenches."

"I don't see what difference that makes," argued Helena von Buelow, who is a convinced Nazi. "Schiller never participated in the Thirty Years' War."

"Well, who the hell was Schiller?" demanded Goebbels.

Leni Riefenstahl was there, though nobody knew in whose honor she was invited. Goebbels snubbed her. Neither Hitler nor Streicher was present.

"So pale!" I said to Leni. "And no lipstick."

"The Führer detests make-up," she shrugged. "You can never tell when he's going to show up, so I've quit using the stuff altogether."

July 3, 1936:

Talked with Dr. Esser, of the Ministry of National Economy. "I envy the Jews," he sighed. "They can emigrate. All a German can do is stick around here and be sickened by it, and finally end up as a so-called volunteer in Spain in the 'Condor' regiment. You have to volunteer if they ask you."

There's been a notable improvement in our streets. They've taken away the *Stürmer* showcases so as not to shock the Olympics visitors with the pornographic weekly. Up to now this has been on exhibition every few blocks for the benefit of those who could not afford the luxury of a private copy.

Hitler has a new hate, Count Henri de Baillet-Latour, president of the Olympic Games. Difficulties had arisen during the winter games, when the Count told Hitler that these games must be held free of all racial prejudice. If not, he would cancel the games. Hitler gave in, but it hurt.

July 26, 1936:

On Friday Mrs. Dodd gave a cocktail party in honor of the American aviator Colonel Charles A. Lindbergh. The Lindberghs are here as guests of the government. As a special privilege they were permitted to land at the military airfield in Staaken.

Lindbergh seems spellbound. He appeared overwhelmed when Secretary of State Milch, the unspeakable rat who disgraced his mother's name by inventing the story that he is the son of his Aryan mother by an Aryan lover, patted him on the shoulder; and when a genuine prince, Louis Ferdinand, linked arms with him his cup apparently ran over. I heard him say to Captain Udet: "German aviation ranks higher than that in any other country. It is invincible."

Mrs. Lindbergh is a gentle woman, one of the most feminine I have ever seen. She appears devoted to her tall, handsome, boyish husband, who is the ideal of the "Nordic" type that the Nazis rave about.

Axel von Blomberg, son of the Minister of the Reichswehr, and Colonel von Hanesse, Air Attaché at the "Foreign Armies" Department of the Ministry of Defense, scoffed at his pretended shyness, saying that it was a cloak to cover his avidity for the limelight.

"He's going to be the best promotion campaign we could possibly have invested in," said Blomberg.

It was an early hour of the day, but Loerzer, as usual, was already slightly tight.

"Wonder what the hell is the matter with that American?" he remarked. "He'll scare the wits out of the Yankees with his talk about the invincible Luftwaffe. That's exactly what the boys here want him to do. He's been saying that the Russian air force is not worth worrying about, and that the English have very few machines, and those few inferior. They were pretty nice to him in England, I hear. They praise, and he eats it up."

I heard the same thing at Mammi's. She's in mourning, so her friends drop in on her. Frau von Widkum had been at the gala dinner Duke Adolf Friedrich von Mecklenburg gave in honor of the Lindberghs.

"He seems incredibly naïve, this North American Colonel," she said, with a trace of disgust in her tone.

August 15, 1936:

Olympic Games. I attended a couple of times. Everything is colossal. The Swastika is everywhere, and so are the black and brown uniforms.

The lack of sportsmanship of Germany's First Man is disgusting and at the same time fascinating. He behaved like a madman, jumping from his seat and roaring when the Swastika was hoisted or when the Japs or Finns won a victory. Other champions left him cold and personally offended at their victories over their Nordic opponents.

The manner in which Hitler applauds German winners, in a frenzy of shrieks, clappings, and contortions, is painful proof that the whole idea of the Olympic Games is far too broad for his single-track mind. This is *his* show, and *his* Germans are supermen. That the whole world must admit. He has said some remarkable things.

"The American Negroes are not entitled to compete," he said for example. "It was unfair of the United States to send these flatfooted specimens to compete with the noble products of Germany. I am going to vote against Negro participation in the future."

He means it too. Although it is his policy to bid every winner to his box, to congratulate him and shake hands, he has repeatedly snubbed and ignored the colored American representatives. Whenever one of the tall, graceful, perfectly built, dark-skinned athletes scored a triumph Hitler left his seat hurriedly and returned only when the signal for the next event was sounded.

Leni Riefenstahl, official photographer, wearing gray flannel slacks and a kind of jockey cap, is obtrusively in evidence everywhere, pretending an untiring and exhaustive efficiency and importance. Meanwhile her assistants quietly, expertly, do the work, which Leni signs.

On and off she sits down beside her Führer, a magazine-cover grin on her face and a halo of importance fixed firmly above her head. She has priority rights, and cannot bear to have anyone else take a shot that she has overlooked. Page boys dash constantly from photographer to photographer, handing them the dreaded slip: "Leni Riefenstahl warns you to stay at your present position while taking pictures. Do not move around. In case of disobedience press permission will be confiscated."

August 16, 1936:

A glittering swirl of Olympic receptions. The foreigners are spoiled, pampered, flattered, and beguiled. Using the pretext of the Olympics, the propaganda machine has gone to work on the visitors to create a good impression of the Third Reich. The entertainment varies. Warm-hearted, friendly gatherings of the international set, showy and spectacular parties at German official houses.

At the Greek reception I met the good-looking Crown Prince Paul, husband of Emperor Wilhelm II's grand-daughter. He seemed vastly impressed by the sight of his royal relatives, Group Leader August Wilhelm and Prince von Hanover, in S.S. uniform.

Ribbentrop and Goering sizzled with activity and gave tremendous public parties in their private parks. It's amusing to watch them trying to keep up with each other. "Rib" had an ox roasted whole over a roaring fire. Goering presented his guests with the spectacle of Ernst Udet looping the loop over the startled heads of the foreigners. Ambassador Dodd told me they sat there in their overcoats, trying to extract some heat from the round-bellied little stoves that had been distributed here and there in the park. He said it was almost pitiful to see the dancers of the opera ballet doing their pastoral stuff with almost no clothes on, trying to keep the warmth of life in their bodies, which were turning blue with cold.

Goebbels outdid the two of them, running a party with two thousand guests at the Pfauen Island near Potsdam. For generations this island has been the scene of royal Prussian hospitality and splendor. Here the wonderful Barberina danced for the first time before Frederick the Great.

August 18, 1936:

Gonny's been here on a visit from America. *[Gonny is Mrs. Fromm's daughter.]* I was a little nervous about her coming back because I was afraid she might not be able to get away again, so I spoke to a friend high up in the Party. He said he would keep an eye on her for me, and that it might not be a bad idea for her to come as it would prove that it was perfectly safe for people to attend the Olympic Games. That would be in the nature of a protection for the child. He gave me the name, home and office telephones of one of his trusted assistants.

"If you get into trouble telephone him," he said.

It was breathtakingly wonderful to have my girl again. But she has changed. She looks well and her eye is clear and cynical.

"I could not breathe here any more," she said; that was all.

Last week my Nazi friend telephoned that it would be advisable for Gonny to leave before the termination of the games, because after the Olympics there would be no more leniency shown toward people who had left Germany to become citizens of another country.

August 23, 1936:

Argentina and Germany have raised their legations to embassies. The Argentines at the same time were *presented* by the Germans with one of the most gorgeous palaces of the Tiergartenstrasse.

The palace had been occupied by Consul Wilhelm Staudt's widow. She owns, together with her son, an important export firm. It so happened that mother and son had not been quick enough to enter the Party. Therefore Junior deemed it necessary to demonstrate their devotion to the great cause, and donated his mother's house to the government—*i.e.,* Party. Mrs. Staudt raged.

"Here I spent unforgettable hours with the Emperor and Empress. I lived through the most beautiful days of my life. I gave the most wonderful parties at this house. My son donates not his, but my house! Just to obtain the good graces of the Nazis!" she complained bitterly some time ago when I saw her. Today, at the Argentine housewarming, she was compounded of sweetness and honey.

"Imagine, I attended a soiree the Führer gave this week."

"How much did you pledge?" I asked dryly.

"Pledge! Just the palace," she said with a shrug.

August 28, 1936:

Soiree at the American Embassy. The Papens had stayed on in Berlin for a while after the Olympic Games. They were also invited and "very happy to see me."

"You could find a great many more of your old friends," I said to Martha von Papen, "if you cared to make a round of the more exclusive concentration camps."

On the scene also were the Schachts. Frau Schacht wanted to know why my column had vanished from the papers. I told her it had happened two years ago. It seems, according to her story, that she never knows what's going on because her husband, a frugal soul, always takes the paper to the office with him. After he comes home she cannot find the time to read it.

Schacht seems very anxious to please the Ambassador.

"If there is ever a chance to lend Frau Bella a helping hand, Dr. Schacht, please do," said Dodd.

"Any time," said the old fox. "I would be only too happy."

I'll keep it in mind.

March 9, 1937:

Gay party at the house of Dr. Keils, a nephew of Fritz Thyssen and related to the Krupps. They had invited a cross section of Nazi and anti-Nazi, Aryan and non-Aryan, pre- and post-war society.

Met Marga Richter there, the assistant to Eva von Schroeder at the Nazi People's Welfare. Marga's husband, a physician, has come to sudden Nazi power. She is so anxious to show her loyalty to the Nazis that she has even gone to the trouble to change her naturally dark hair to an approved Nordic hue. She likes to drink but can't take it.

She was quite high, and suddenly remembered that she was fond of me. She began to cry, blubbering in my lap, drenching me with her salty grief. She swore me to secrecy, but what I got out of her had its interest.

"My husband left for Japan this morning, with a staff of physicians and army officers. He is in charge of the commission to check on the effect of the new poison gas which Germany sold to Japan for her war with China. For God's sake, darling, don't tell anybody!" The latest barbarism Nazi culture has adopted made me shiver.

July 10, 1937:

Yesterday I saw "Broadway Melody" at a small theater in the Olivaer Platz under "well guarded" circumstances, which did not prevent me from enjoying it thoroughly. After I had parked and was scouting the street for the friends with whom I had an appointment, I suddenly felt that I had aroused the keen interest of two S.S. men. They jotted down my license number and scrutinized me surreptitiously. One of them raised his camera and took a quick snapshot. I always take an awful picture, so I was quite sure nobody would recognize me.

My friends turned up and we bought our tickets. Seeing that I was a mere cinema fan obviously reassured the two men, but now my curiosity had been aroused and I waited to see what would happen. The arrival of Heinrich Himmler, complete with his insipid, fat wife and grim bodyguard, confirmed my suspicions about the presence of the black guards.

Just a Nazi leader sneaking into a tiny cinema to revel in outlandish glamour. The two uniformed detectives on duty had taken my searching glances for political plotting. Thank heavens, once again the ever-looming threat of Gestapo "justice" was dissipated. With a sigh of relief I plunged into the rhythmic tunes of "Broadway Melody."

Frau Himmler has grown latitudinously since I last saw her. Of course, when you make whipped cream your favorite dish you can't expect anything else. The pleasures of the table are apparently about all the pleasures she gets, since Himmler keeps her at home, mostly with Gudrun, their only daughter, known as "Puppi."

July 15, 1937:

Professor Latz came to say good-by. I asked him why he was leaving so abruptly. He said it was due to Emmy Goering. She had telephoned him to meet her at an obscure little Grunewald café.

"Nobody must know I talked to you, doctor," she told him. "But you and your wife have been so loyal in your friendship to me for so many years that I felt I had to warn you. It is time for you and your wife to leave the country. As soon as you possibly can. Things are getting bad here and I can no longer protect my old friends."

I always had a feeling about Emmy Goering, a feeling that her character had its sound spots, in spite of the sincerity of her love for the rotund Hermann. Her first husband, a well-known Communist, was a man of fine attainments and culture. He undoubtedly had much influence in the development of Emmy Goering's character.

September 29, 1937:

Mussolini is here. He was received with Augustan pomp at the Heerstrasse Station—a little suburban railway stop. The reception was grandiose and included a complete upholstering of walls and ceilings in shining white silk, to soften the dreary impact of an ordinary railway station.

The remote station had been chosen to give the Roman conqueror an initial treat. He was to enjoy Berlin's finest boulevard rolling along through Charlottenburg, through the Tiergarten, the triumphant Brandenburger Tor, to the "Linden."

Friends of mine who have a house at the *Knie,* in the most convenient position to watch the road for miles ahead, had asked me to come to see with them the spectacle of the procession to an open-air play in honor of the Duce. They had sent me a permit without which no mortal could approach the vicinity of the boulevard or any house in the neighboring streets. The slip was issued by the superintendent of the building and marked "Be sure to be here not later than three o'clock." You couldn't enter or leave any building within a wide radius of the road for three solid hours before the actual procession was to pass by!

S.S. guards crouched on roofs, behind machine guns. Streets and side lanes were barred.

I had parked miles away from the tabooed section and pushed my way patiently through the roped-off neighborhood. Holding my pass in front of me, I followed instructions meekly, making a detour here, crossing through a side street there, having endless hands grab for my pass, and receiving clipped "O.K.'s."

There were very few voluntary onlookers. The German people have grown tired of waiting hours for a passing glimpse of important personages. They are tired out by the time they have to wave their flags and shout their welcome. Of course shops and schools and factories were closed for the occasion. Order was given to attend in "spontaneous rapture." But the "volunteers" were small in number. The excuse of illness was largely used. The usual chains of S.S. and S.A. stood there, lining both sides of the road. I was amused to see the "pushing crowd" consisted mainly of a mob of disguised Storm Troopers in mufti.

I heard a man cursing in Berlin slang: "Now we can wait here until our knees are way up in our bellies."

It was after six o'clock when the first cars began to roll by. Always a Nazi coupled with a Fascist. In front a driver and footman. Then the "Roman Imperator" and the "German Imitator" passed. They sat in gloomy silence side by side. Tense and uneasy. Mussolini's bulging black eyes, with the shimmering white of the eyeballs, darted rapid glances left, right, front, back. His brutal chin stuck out in theatrical defiance. He was obviously displeased with the ride in the open Mercedes. His complexion is swarthy. There is nothing noble about his features. He seemed bored, even annoyed. Probably he is just fed up to find so many scenes in the Nazi picture book borrowed from his own displays. I just had time to see that the Duce had donned no special uniform, as Goering would have done on such an occasion. He wore a dark uniform, with the Fascist insignia and the ugly black headgear of the Fascists. The great men drove out of sight. We left the balcony and went inside for dinner.

Meanwhile the show at the Sport Field had been drenched by torrents of rain. When, three hours later, the cars came rolling back, the whole show looked even drearier. The flags were soaked, the flowers wilted. The Nazis and Italians in their drenched clothes looked miserable and uncomfortable. Still the spartan Nazi tradition scoffs at closed cars! The "cheering crowd" stood shivering behind the S.S. and S.A. chains.

October 1, 1937:

The Japanese Ambassadress, Countess Mushakoji, entertained with a musicale. Mammi had a lot of gossip about the festival in honor of Mussolini. She had been at the Sport Field, where she got the sniffles in the pouring rain and her new hat was ruined.

Mussolini, it appears, was furious. During the banquet after the festival he sneezed and shivered. Soon after dinner he retired to bed with hot-water bottles and aspirin.

"In Italy," he is reported to have protested, "we have sense enough to put up our tops when it rains."

He fell hard for Emmy Goering. His passion is such that poor Emmy is afraid to remain alone with him in a room.

December 24, 1937:

The offensive has been resumed on a large scale in the embattled Goebbels ménage, this time because of a charming interlude the Don Juan had with Lydia Baarova, the wife of the operetta tenor Gustav Froehlich.

Tenors, as everyone knows, are unpredictable, and Froehlich did the most unpredictable thing he could have done. He lay in ambush for Goebbels and gave him a thorough trouncing. Goebbels, somewhat annoyed, found a pretext to have Himmler take Froehlich into "custody." This irritated Froehlich's friends, who caught up with Goebbels and gave him another—worse—beating.

Goebbels claimed an automobile accident had spoiled his beauty. Magda, however, in an endeavor to find out what was happening inside Germany, had tuned in Radio Moscow, which gave her the full story about her gay Lothario.

January 1, 1938:

Upon my return to Berlin from a trip up to the Bavarian Mountains, it did not surprise me that my apartment had been searched. They did a careful job, but it did not avail them much. Since I learned that I was under supervision I have had no secrets of any kind in the house. I had put such entries in my diary as were still in this country into the care of Louis P. Lochner.

June 18, 1938:

Helped free another twenty-one people from Buchenwald, that awful concentration camp near Weimar. I feel guilty about leaving so long as there is any chance to help.

June 28, 1938:

Another wave of Jew baiting. Scenes of ferocity and misery are carved in my mind. My friend Mia, a member of the Diplomatic Corps, had warned me about it in one of our cryptic telephone conversations. We met and covered the town from end to end in my car. Mia had a very cleverly camouflaged camera for obtaining evidence to be smuggled out of Germany.

The renowned old linen house of Grünfeld was the first place we saw surrounded by a howling mob of S.A. men. Mia took a picture of them "working" on an old gentleman who had insisted on entering the shop.

We proceeded, finding the same thing going on everywhere, varying only in violence and ignominy. The entire Kurfürstendamm was plastered with scrawls and cartoons. "Jew" was smeared all over doors, windows, and walls in waterproof colors. It grew worse as we came to the part of town where poor little Jewish retail shops were to be found. The S.A. had created havoc. Everywhere were revolting and bloodthirsty pictures of Jews beheaded, hanged, tortured, and maimed, accompanied by obscene inscriptions. Windows were smashed, and loot from the miserable little shops was strewn over the sidewalk and floating in the gutter.

We were just about to enter a tiny jewelry shop when a gang of ten youngsters in Hitler Youth uniforms smashed the shop window and stormed into the shop, brandishing butcher knives and yelling: "To hell with the Jewish rabble! Room for the Sudeten-Germans!"

I was worried about two old protégés of mine whom I had helped with little sums of money and food during the past two years. They had lost their two sons during the World War. Killed for Germany! We went to find out whether they had suffered.

Their shop was in ruins, their goods, paper, and stationery trampled into the gutter. Three S.A. men, roaring with obscene laughter, forced the trembling old man to pick up the broken glass with hands that were covered with blood. We stood there, choking with rage, trembling in helpless horror.

Next day, when we returned to bring them food and see what else we could do to help them, we found two coffins surrounded by silent neighbors. The faces of the old couple seemed peaceful and serene amid the broken glass and destruction. As we put down our basket and stood there wretchedly, a young woman spoke to me. "It is better for them. They took poison last night."

July 4, 1938:

What a contrast! Garden party at the American Embassy, in the tradition of Sackett's time. The Wilsons are fine hosts. One of the French diplomats said tartly: "The beautiful Ambassadress will undoubtedly be the next objective of Ribbentrop's efforts to worm himself into the good graces of the Americans." We were in a group with Otto Tolischus, Sigrid Schulz, and the Louis P. Lochners.

The Lochner's seventeen-year-old son is back on vacation from the States. "At first Bobby could not adjust himself to America," said Hilde Lochner. "Now he can scarcely wait to return."

"Have you been in the north of Berlin lately?" whispered Rolf. *[Rolf was a close friend of Mrs. Fromm's who held on to an important post in the German Home Office while secretly opposing the Hitler regime.]* "There's something going on. The concentration camps are being enlarged. Better get out, Bella. We're all with you. But you can't help much any more. Nobody can. If we don't stop interfering for your 'public enemies,' we'll all land in concentration camps ourselves. Outside Germany you may be of greater help than within these walls."

I am waiting for my papers.

July 20, 1938:

So far I have gathered a collection of twenty-three of the necessary documents. I have made a thorough study of the employees and furniture in fifteen official bureaus, down to the most humble clerk and the smallest inkwell, during the hours I have waited for another of my precious scraps of paper.

Today I had to see an important official at the Home Office. He received me with a lusty "Heil Hitler." His parting words, however, were illuminating.

"I hope to get the hell out of here before the war breaks out," he said. "I'll call on you in New York."

Maybe he can be trusted. It's doubtful. I've heard too much of the careful supervision the Third Reich gives to German citizens in foreign countries.

August 10, 1938:

Rolf has found devious short cuts, and sent me to comparatively decent officials. I simply can't imagine how other emigrants without any wires to pull ever manage to overcome the abyss of deliberate difficulties. One of the things I had to do was to pay all taxes for one year ahead, that is for a period when I should not be in Germany at all.

Only a few days are left before the final date given me at the American Consulate, and I haven't yet gathered all the papers and permissions I need. Luckily I remembered Schacht's promise to Ambassador Dodd. I sent him an S.O.S. Today I got the reply. Schacht has ordered my case to be rushed at the Foreign Exchange Office.

August 11, 1938:

Went with Schacht's letter to the Foreign Exchange Office yesterday. Today everything was settled. Tomorrow I am to receive the final confirmation.

The doors of the American Consulate General are opened at 9:00 A.M. This I know because I stood in line from seven o'clock on. My turn came at about ten minutes to one.

I was ushered in to my good friends, DeWitt Warner and Cybe Follmer, who regarded me in astonishment. "For heaven's sake, Bella! Why didn't you have someone announce you?"

"Two reasons," I said. "I didn't want any special privileges, and I enjoyed waiting in anticipation of the moment when I was at last to see you sign the visa."

There was a whirlwind of good wishes, hugs, farewell kisses, and back-slapping. When I found myself outside, the American visa in my hand, I had to sit down on the stone steps and cry in my grateful happiness. Again and again I looked at the document. I caressed the red silk cord that secured the pages. I actually kissed the golden seal. I mentally pledged my true and loyal adherence to my future homeland.

August 28, 1938:

[French Ambassador] François-Poncet seems hypnotized by Hitler and, at the same time, scared and impressed. I went to Wannsee to say good-by to him and his wife. He wished me a clipped good luck, and disappeared.

Jacqueline was apologetic. She started to unburden herself: "I am frightened. Everything is so obscure. André is jittery about politics. He's nervous. Don't blame him. He's afraid he might be accused of conspiring with the Jews. Please don't tell anyone that our courier took your trunks and furs to Paris. We want to help you—you know that. But we had better keep out of trouble if we can."

I did not stay long. It was not the good-by that I had expected. I am very fond of Jacqueline François-Poncet. But these times do strange things to people and to friendships.

September 2, 1938:

An enormous shipping van drove up to the front of the house. It is like a big room without windows. It is hauled on a truck, driven directly to the harbor, and put on the boat. Besides costing me twenty-five hundred marks, it was very difficult to get—until I found the right person to bribe.

Three officials of the Foreign Exchange Office are checking and rechecking every item that goes in, down to the smallest and most trivial ash-tray. Everything I had bought during the past six months had to be paid for with a two hundred per cent ransom to the Third Reich.

For nearly three days this packing, checking, and rechecking has gone on. Officials from departments I never heard of, departments that must have been invented only for their nuisance value, came pestering me every hour of the day. I am continually being cross-examined.

September 4, 1938:

The van is downstairs sealed and fastened. They will come and take it any minute now. "Berlin–New York" is painted in big letters on its sides. It makes me feel blue and happy at the same time.

Paris, September 6, 1938:

The last two days were a nightmare. At the last minute I discovered that I needed a Belgian visa, because of the one hour's ride at night through that country. I could not get it without photographs. It took a great deal of scurrying around, but it was all finally arranged.

At nine o'clock the night express came thundering into the station. Farewells and tears. At the far end of the platform, in civilian clothes, was Rolf. We had agreed that he was not to run the risk of being seen with me at the train. Blurred by my tears, I could hardly see his face. The train had already started. Good-by, Rolf. . . . God bless you. . . .

Four and a half years ago my child, Gonny, had left on the same train, from the same station, in her adventure in search of freedom and a new life. And now, I too was going on the same quest.

The heavy luggage was booked, sealed, and stamped. My few suitcases were in the rack above me. The passport was in order. I traveled luxuriously in a Pullman sleeper. Perhaps for the last time. I had not spared money, because I had to leave the rest in Germany anyway. Exhausted, I went to bed.

About 2:00 A.M. I was badly frightened by the sudden apparition of two uniformed figures. Drugged by my first sound sleep in weeks, my senses momentarily reeled with terror.

"Frontier pass control," one of them announced gruffly.

I asked them to let me put on some clothes, but they made me leave the door open while I dressed.

"Emigrant's passport!" announced one. "Jewish bitch! Trying to smuggle out her valuables, I suppose."

I kept my mouth shut. They turned everything inside out. They took the soles from my bedroom slippers. They squeezed the toothpaste from the tube.

"Have you anything that should not be taken out of the country?" demanded one.

"You've seen for yourself everything I have," I said.

"You Jewish whore!" one shouted at me. "Trying to smuggle out all that jewelry." He pointed to the little heap that had been emptied on the bed.

"I am not trying to smuggle anything out," I said. "All that has been the property of my family for generations. Here is the permit issued by the Foreign Exchange Office."

"We'll have to check on that with Berlin," said he. "We reach the frontier in half an hour. You'll have to get off the train."

My protests were futile. I said I should miss the boat.

"Then take the next one."

They seemed deliberately unaware of how hard it was to obtain passage. Cancellation or even delay was impossible, with so many hundreds eagerly awaiting their turn. I had a vision of being sent back to Germany and having to go through the business of laboriously collecting my exit papers all over again. My heart almost stopped.

The two went outside for a whispered consultation. When they returned, they submitted a statement for me to sign:

"I am a Jewish thief and have tried to rob Germany by taking German wealth out of the country. I hereby confess that the jewels found on me do not belong to me and that in trying to take them out I was eager to inflict injury on Germany. Furthermore, I promise never to try to reenter Germany."

I signed. I had to get out of this country. This was a country to get out of if you had to do it naked.

Half an hour later the train crossed the border. I was in safety. My heart was pounding and I began to cry. Tears of liberation. But I was still uneasy until the train stopped at the Gare du Nord.

The statement, together with my jewels, had gone into the pockets of my tormentors. I am sure they will go no farther up the line. If they reappear, it will be in the shop of a pawnbroker.

September 9, 1938. *S.S. Normandie:*

Safe aboard this gorgeous boat! It is almost too much for me to believe. Then, when I do become acutely aware of my good fortune, I feel almost guilty, remembering the unfortunate ones who wait, trembling, desperately hoping for their chance to get out. There *must* be a way to help.

The magnificent ship glides through the waters to the new land. I cannot get myself to join in the gay cheerfulness on board. There is an atmosphere of luxury and freedom from care, but I am not yet in a mood to breathe this air. I find I cannot yet stand fun and laughter.

UNDER FIRE ON GUADALCANAL

(FEBRUARY 1943)

Patrick Maitland

*The manuscript of this article was written by the correspon-
dent of the London News Chronicle, much of it under the
most difficult circumstances imaginable. It arrived here with
sundry passages scissored out by the Pacific Fleet censor. It will
help the reader to understand the significance of Mr.
Maitland's story if he remembers Hanson Baldwin's dispatch of
September 19th [1942] (five days after Mr. Maitland's story
begins), which said the American position at Henderson
Airfield was "as if the Marines held Jones Beach, and the rest
of Long Island were loosely dominated by the enemy." The
events Mr. Maitland describes were part of the crescendo of
Japanese attacks which culminated in the great land-sea-air
battles of October and November.*

—The Editors

GUADALCANAL—MONDAY, SEPTEMBER 14th:

I arrived on Guadalcanal yesterday—Sunday, September 13th. This
message is being prepared as I sit on a bank twenty yards from a field
kitchen and two or three yards from a rough table where we eat
beneath the palm trees, with jungle and tangled boughs and creepers

117

swaying slightly in a gentle breeze. This is just behind our front line.

From time to time a Japanese sniper's rifle cracks less than a hundred yards off, followed by the rattling bursts of our returning fire. Heaven knows when, or where, I shall finish this. We have alerts all the while—maybe it is an air raid on the field a mile north toward the coast, or some machine-gunning.

Good funkholes are rare around here and as a rule the few dugouts are packed tight by the time I get to them. So I have now taken up station beside a sandbagged dugout, formerly Japanese. I plan to bound in in three hops at the word go.

* * *

Those dots mean "alert." I planned wrong and am now boiling inside the dugout after a disagreeable experience. Sweat is pouring down; I mop my face at intervals with a handkerchief that was clean this morning and is now a messy yellow. There are ten Marines here, pretty cheerful on the whole, ever friendly to the war correspondent. ("Say, you tell those folks at home what this hell's really like: they've no idea. I thought it was all as easy as pie myself till I came out here. Now it's different. Still it's good to be in the Marines.") But they are always interrupting my knee-balancing-cum-typewriter turn. The machine got battered and the roller is not working too well, for just five minutes ago (it seems like an hour) three Japs, crying, "One, two, three, Banzai," came plunging downhill into camp shooting all around.

I dived first onto an ant heap, lay cowering beside a sandbag, ruefully reflecting that war correspondents should all go around armed, hearing the crackle of bracken as nimble feet scampered about, hardly daring to breathe for fear that this was a large party of visitors rushing the whole place, one of whom would bayonet me any moment.

It is faintly surprising how one buries one's nose in the earth, dives beneath any sort of cover, cares not a whit for torn trousers or anthills, and curses only for the interruption.

In fact there were only three Japs, one officer and two soldiers; two are dead now, for the price of one Marine. The third escaped.

When I arrived here yesterday I found Till Durdin of the *New York*

Times, with raincoat and British tin helmet and canteen from Malaya; Bill Kent of the Chicago *Times*, unshaven and looking like a central African explorer; Tom Yarborough of AP, who has a beard to match the Ancient Mariner; and the lofty figure of Dick Tregaskis, of I.N.S., cool and calm always. Durdin enjoys excitement. But the others were all dead tired from a sleepless night in the jungle. They had to bundle out of their tent when Jap warships, thought to be a cruiser and two destroyers plus a submarine, shelled the place for two hours last night.

"The Japs are only a few hundred yards away over there, sniping away at intervals. They're quiet just now but with nightfall they're certain to be at it again and you'll be spending the night with us in the jungle over the ridge. If that isn't enough excitement for you, then you'd better go aboard the *U.S.S. Dash* and get some more." That was Bill Kent's warning; but he declined to explain what he meant about the ship. Maybe I'll learn. We had plenty of excitement last night as it was.

As I write now (out in the open again, for "Condition Green" has just been signaled) a wounded Marine sits beside me puffing a cigarette to soothe the pain of a fresh shrapnel wound. Two hours ago four Marines slumped dead over their machine gun five or six yards away from me on the ridge. Five minutes later I was yelling for a stretcher to fetch in another, badly hit.

This is the continuation of last night's battle, the biggest Jap effort yet to get back the airfield. Some weeks ago they landed a thousand or so on the beach and I'm now satisfied, as I wasn't when I first read the story in New Zealand, that at least seven hundred *were* killed. Since then bodies have been washed up daily. And in parts the jungle stinks of dead.

Since then the Japs have made nightly landings east and west of here up the coast and down, and their men have thrust into the jungle till they met each other. They may have landed anything up to ten thousand men—perhaps more—but nobody knows. They've infiltrated past the airfield, inland past our positions. That means they surround us on the landward side—hidden in the jungle.

They brought plenty of stores and a good deal of artillery. A party of the Marine Raiders, in one of a string of thrusts up the coast which should be famous for their Commandolike daring, took several batteries of seventy-fives. The Japs seem to have plenty of food as well. And not all rice either. Last night I supped from a captured tin of goulash, highly salted but most nourishing. The enemy are fairly well supplied with candy in red and white sticks, captured boxes of which are now serving the Marines. They have mortars enough and plenty of ammunition, to say nothing of machine guns.

The attack last night began around 8:00 P.M. An officer bade us skip over the ridge quick before something happened. We took our bed rolls and made uphill. Figures furtively slipped around in the dark. One heard whispered voices, low words of command, last bits of encouragement, advice. "Now remember," I heard an officer mutter to his band, "you guys just gotta sit tight. If you hear a Jap, don't move, don't fire till you see him and are sure of a hit. He can't see you so long as you're still. Let him do the moving and give his position away. . . . Unless of course there's a breakthrough. Then give 'em all you've got. Just now they're trying to infiltrate on both flanks and several snipers have got through already. Keep calm and don't move." Silently the patrol slid away.

A few hundred yards off machine guns opened up and mortars sent their bombs flying over the treetops only a little above our heads—like great flaming oranges. It reminded me of a fireworks display. Between the boughs against the stars we saw one, two, half a dozen, three, five, two, of these fiery balls sail away into our lines behind us.

Soon snipers began showing their positions. There were vicious needle points of flame spurting out from trees thirty yards to our right and left, and nearer. This was the start of the attack. Its aim was to seize the ridge north of our tent (I was now cowering on the north side of this ridge), which commanded a road to the airfield.

Farther away on our flanks to east and west were lighter diversionary attacks, begun with light shelling by a cruiser and some destroyers. Away in the distance we heard the plump of shells, then every few minutes (later every few seconds, in bursts of two minutes each) the whang and whistle of the mortars tracing their fiery path, snapping a twig sometimes as they went.

Now and again a falling twig or piece of bark would drop close by. It could do no possible harm. But each time it reminded me of that King of France who took the court jester to the guillotine and then let a drop of water fall on his neck. It killed him—and in the state my nerves were in I felt each time that the first falling twig to catch me would do me in.

Our field artillery spurted back and still we lay in the dirt on the ridge side. I am usually hyper-careful about sores and abrasions in the tropics and doubly particular about soiling them with infected earth. But now such things mattered little. Around ten, I suppose (I hardly dared uncover the luminous face of my watch for fear a sniper twenty yards away should spot it and fire), we had word to press down into the bowl of the saucer of which the ridge made the rim.

The firing was hotter now, much hotter, and our gunners seemed to be getting their range. But so were the Japs. All the while figures crept through the undergrowth. There went a half-dozen men in line with American helmets, packs, and rifles or tommyguns—obviously Marines. They were silhouetted against the sky as I lay full length in the muck. My heart stopped a second. There was one among them slighter than the rest. He had no pack. His footsteps made less noise. He seemed to know the leaves by instinct.

I muttered to Bill, "That looks like a Jap." "Pipe down, you fool," he spat back. "It probably is and you'll only give us away by talking." I pressed myself into the undergrowth praying my khaki would blend with the dead palms.

Two more hours passed. Once I crept into the dugout for a cigarette. It was hot enough outside; within it steamed. I could stand it only a few minutes, stamped out the cigarette, slid back to my bedroll. . . . Just in time. The main attack came right away. Shells banged away and plunked overhead. A stray one hit a tree and sent shattered splinters showering about us with a splitting crack. The snipers were now working overtime. I could spot their jabs of fire in three or four places either side of us. The glow of flying missiles above the treetops was so frequent now that it looked like a stream. The noise rose. There was a racket in growing crescendo. It is queer, and I suppose traditional in war, that at the tensest moment somebody makes a wisecrack that just brings the rest back to earth and sanity. A Marine ran out of ammunition. "Say," he shouted, "gimme some more of that stuff. I want to join the band and make some noise too. You can't beat the drum and play the cornet and do everything else all by yourself."

Around two there was a positive turn for the worse. Glumly we sat or cringed or clung glued to the ground, our eyes caught by one sight, and one only, our thoughts fastened on a frantic new phenomenon. It made me feel so sick I can only describe the sight as filthy.

The Japs aloft to our right and left now dared more openly. They were strong enough now to disclose their position without fear. They fired tracers back behind to indicate where their comrades should bring up ammunition. Away to our right, say one hundred yards, was a machine gun spitting away from a treetop clump.

I understood what "infiltration" meant—that catchword from Malaya and the Philippines. They were on three sides of us already. There had been that very breakthrough of which I'd heard an officer warn his men hours (it seemed days) before. They were pushing forward. One could trace their movements farther on by each new spit of fire, a few yards ahead each time. Soon they'd be around us. We'd be cut off.

I cursed my dauntless refusal, back in the Hebrides, to take a gun. You feel so helpless. I had the same feeling of sickening nausea that I had had several times before: once in Albania when I escaped three would-be assassins by hiding in a Turkish harem; once in Poland when we had to mend a flat in the dark on a road the German Panzers were chasing; once when I trembled in a shelter during the crashing bombardment of Belgrade, April 6th last year; once the day I was taken prisoner by the Italians.

From time to time the enemy sent up star shells to signal to one another from different sectors. They came, like the snipers' shots, from behind us, to our right, to our left. I gloomily rethought all the horrors I'd read of Hongkong, Singapore, Manila, pictured a bayonet in my stomach, grimly wondered if I'd manage to stifle the pain, feign dead, and escape.

The hours passed terribly slowly. The night was now cool and I'd have been glad to sleep; but behind my knees, along my forearms, around my neck, streaming down my forehead, I could feel the damp warm beads of fear.

Then around five, as we consoled ourselves the twelve hours of tropical darkness would end about six-thirty or seven, there came a change. The Marines sent up a terrific barrage. Shells poured over in a stream that made the night's shelling till then seem a mere trickle. They poured pounds of iron and blazing hell into the enemy, sent it on and on. More came, still more. The Japs flung back the best they had. For half an hour the racket seemed unendurable for noise, for cracks, for rumbling, for the sputtering, stuttering bursts of small-arms and machine-gun fire. Much of it was over our heads, for an hour at least.

Then slowly the firing receded. It seemed our men were getting a new range. The Japs were growing irregular, ragged. I returned to the dugout, took another smoke, three cigarettes this time, stifling as it was. In there the noise was muffled. And maybe our senses were numbed a little too. I rested, crouched with three others on a creaking cot the Japs had fashioned by twining telephone wires between two poles on uprights, with another bunk above us—four on that. In a corner a man snored—he'd been on special work of a highly delicate sort till he had been relieved an hour earlier.

Someone burst in with news that the tide had turned. The Japs had pushed ahead from one ridge nearly to the top of another linked with ours. Then they had been held.

I must have dozed a while after that, for when I came to, about seven, it was light. The firing had died down to an irregular stutter. The situation was in hand. I came out to breathe some cool, fresh morning air. And on the flanks the Japs had been repelled decisively.

As I write now they're lying fairly low. Our pursuit planes are wheezing over the jungle two ridges away pouring explosive lead into the mess where a bunch of Japs are still rattling away with their .35's. A colonel told me we're going after them with tanks, indeed everything we've got. We're on the offensive ourselves now. For results, we'll see tonight when darkness falls and the jungle's still again.

"A few thousand shillings needed from Australia."

Thus ran a radio message from our troops at the captured Jap airfield a few weeks after the Marines had landed. For Japanese cost one shilling each—alive.

Native police, who went bush when the Japs invaded, are now equipped with captured enemy rifles and sent out by Captain Martin Clements, their chief, former British District Officer, who led them into the jungle. They go out to bag what they can. They slink through the undergrowth, hide behind trees, creep through the dead palm leaves, stalk the enemy. They hunt and track till the hated Jap runs out of food or ammunition, then bring him in alive and get their reward—one silver Australian shilling, about twenty cents.

The natives are loyal. Take the case of Sergeant Major Vouza. Fuzzy-headed and dark-skinned, he had been twenty-five years in the Solomon Islands Police and was the first native to welcome the Marines ashore. He did so saying he had a Marine airman who had crashed wounded in the jungle and whom he had cared for. A while later Vouza slunk off up the shore to scout for Jap outposts. He fell in with a Jap officer who recognized Vouza, took him prisoner, led him to a Japanese hideout where they questioned him about American positions.

Vouza refused to talk; so they tied him to a tree, slashed him about the chest and thighs with bayonets, threatened death. Still he remained silent. There went the crack of a Marine's rifle, and the Japs scattered. The last to flee turned back and stuck his bayonet through Vouza's neck to the tree. It just missed the jugular vein. Vouza bit through the rope, removed the bayonet, and crawled to safety and the attention of the Medical Corps. Such a tale could be duplicated twenty times. It is just part of the war for the Solomons.

Not that the Jap is always keen to fight. One prisoner, who had been working on the Guadalcanal airfield at Lunga, said he'd had more than enough of this war already. "We were cheated," he began. "They promised we'd be sent back home after a few weeks in a labor battalion. But that was two years ago. We were sent from one island to another, always working, ever assured the next job would be the last and then we'd go home."

But that goes only for the labor battalions. They are the slaves of the military, so despised that Japanese soldiers protested when we locked them up in the same prison camp. The labor corps lads are generally polite and smiling, if uncommunicative. All know two phrases: "Cigarettes" and "Thank you."

True to type elsewhere, all are ashamed to be caught alive, whether soldiers or slave labor. As soon as they are missing, said one, they are listed as dead by the Naval Code. "To return," said another, "would be to shame two brothers in the Army and two more in the Navy. If I'd had my gun you'd never have caught me alive."

All expect to be shot when captured and are amazed when the Marines treat them decently, bind up their wounds. And they are cleanly. I inspected the corpse of one dead officer who must have been fighting a week in the jungle. His hands and face were clean; and from his vest pocket protruded a snow-white toothbrush. The average ration seems to be a small bowl of rice, sometimes with the added delicacy of dried fish heads, a packet of chocolate, and a packet of cigarettes. In a pack each carries a square khaki bandage and two lint pads.

And, though the bulk of experience has been the opposite, it may be wrong to think every Jap is out to rape the first white woman he sees. There is a story of a soldier whose job was to accompany some horses south from Japan to the Philippines, and who commented on his friends' raping of white women: "I'll never so defile my service for the Emperor." This man also cursed his officers for their surly and overbearing behavior. Once he waited by the road, trying to thumb a ride into a town. A car of officers, with two seats empty, merely accelerated as he signaled.

And while there is no reason to underrate the Jap's crazy valor, that too can possibly be exaggerated. For instance, once the Japs had fled—in terror, I repeat, in sheer terror and nothing less—from Lunga airfield at the Marines' approach, the enemy had to parachute mimeographed pep pamphlets to them—brought probably from Rabaul. "Friendly troops are producing substantial results in this war," read one. "The enemy, one after another, are collapsing before your eyes. Relief by friendly troops, including a landing party, is near. We are confident of Divine Intervention and Heaven's Grace. Be circumspect. *On no account run away from your position precipitately.* [Italics mine.] Bestir yourselves with caution." Another gave a heavily exaggerated list of Allied naval losses, before we had been able to tot them up ourselves.

September [censored]

This afternoon I walked over last night's battlefield. Machine guns were still crackling their angry fire. Now and again a mortar—who could tell if it was ours or theirs?—whooped overhead. I stooped to inspect the gorgeous engraved Samurai sword of a dead Jap officer. A minute after I stepped aside, a sniper's bullet laid a Marine low on the same spot. Maybe it's just my luck. Everything was tense. The day was calm. There was no taint of breeze. You walked everywhere with an eye alert for snipers. You'd catch sight of a swaying tree, reckon it couldn't be the wind, for there wasn't any, dive for cover. If the wind wasn't swaying the trees it must be a straggling sniper from last night.

I counted a good hundred and fifty Jap corpses—wizened little men, sprouting beard over sallow skins, with swollen eyes, flies at their wounds, their teeth white as ever, grinning. Some clutched the jeweled handle of a long curved sword. Some in the loose hold of death gripped as they fell a little printed charm, a Shinto abracadabra, a colored picture of the Emperor flanked by Shinto deities.

They wore cleft sandshoes for tree-scaling. Many had photos of their families back home. Several had photos that were recognizably themselves—with this difference—that weeks or months of tropical campaigning had made tough, stalwart, stocky men look like crusty ancients. Among the Jap dead were a number (far fewer) of Marines.

One lad of eighteen was wandering round sadly, turning up the faces of dead Americans "looking for my buddy."

In twenty-four hours I have collected enough stories to keep my paper satisfied for days. The next job is to get to Pearl Harbor and see how the stuff's censored, then get back again to Guadalcanal. So this evening I went aboard the *U.S.S. Dash,* sailing south. She pulled out as dusk drew on. As we slid out into the channel between Guadalcanal and Tulagi the sinister crackle of Jap infiltrating snipers could still be heard from shore. Occasionally the clear sky was eerily lit by flying star shells—the enemy's jungle signal.

Then I learned the meaning of Bill Kent's allusion to more excitement. For ten days now this feebly armed merchant cruiser has been chugging in and out of Lunga, playing hide and seek with Jap cruisers as she tried to get in to unload a cargo of gasoline and explosives. She has had hair-raising escapes from bombing and shelling. Yet one touch with an armor-piercing bullet and everybody aboard would go sky-high. Talk of running the gauntlet . . . There is one boat and there are twenty rafts aboard for two hundred and fifty men. All have lifebelts save me.

Ten minutes after I came aboard we were ordered to "General Quarters." Fourteen Jap seaplanes zoomed above and bombed. I don't know whether they aimed at us. But none hit, or I should not be writing now. As we let go with every arm aboard we sent up a racket that made the steel walls of the wardroom konk in and out like a sardine can. It lasted ten minutes. Four Jap planes were downed in flames. We steamed into the open sea. I was glad to be under way.

Looking back on the past forty-eight hours, I see we've much to learn. The enemy are crazy fighters, use every wile that a nimble imagination can devise. Their snipers are sturdy men picked from the jungle veterans of night fighting in Malaya and the Philippines. Their cleft sandshoes are ideal for tree-climbing. Have our men got these? Are our Marines taught similar tactics?

The Japs tie themselves to the treetops and await their chance. They wear dungarees and cap and jerkin of a drab color unlike our blazing khaki—to tone with the trunks and foliage. One such sniper, speaking good American, lay quiet till he knew the Christian names of the men moving below. Then he called out, "Bill," and Bill turned to expose himself. Crack—and he fell wounded. Others have shouted to one another from the treetops in American.

The Japs are using weapons we have still to throw in. Today they used flame-throwers on our tanks, disabling three. They have a special contraption for hurling grenades with a leg-thrower. Have our men anything as good?

Earlier some Jap soldiers, trapped in a cave, sallied out against machine guns with rocks and stones. Elsewhere unarmed Japs who had escaped the fire from a tank crept up beneath the traverse of its guns, then beat the armored sides with their fists. The charred bodies of airwomen have been recovered from shattered Jap plane wrecks. They seem to have been radio operators. Japs have lain on the ground feigning dead and then, at the approach of a Marine, let go a grenade which killed both the American and themselves. One day a Jap bore a white flag to our lines. He came to say a hundred fellows were waiting in the jungle to surrender and he would lead an American party to the spot. A colonel took men to get them. They were ambushed. Two escaped. Sometimes in the bush they deliberately rattle chopsticks to draw our fire so that we give away our positions. Other times their snipers fire only when we fire, to hide their hideouts.

One batch was trapped without ammunition in a house at Tulagi. Marines surrounded the place and were closing in. A Jap burst out, made for the heftiest Marine, did a champion jujitsu throw which hurled his opponent several yards, then ran back inside while the other Marines split their sides with laughter. The Japs refused to surrender and our men had to tommygun their way into the house and kill the lot.

There is little evidence, it is true, but the Japanese seem to have learned the German technique of doping themselves for battle. That may of course be the effect of opium. For in a village formerly under Jap occupation we found quantities of opium pipes, a stock of opium, and the equipment for every sort of orgy. Supplies of rouge and other cosmetics indicated that geisha girls were expected, though they apparently had not yet been actually installed. There was red wine, Japanese beer, and sake in plenty. One captured officer was found to be wearing a fifty-pound steel bullet-proof vest. I talked to the man who caught him short of ammunition.

For our men this job is terribly depressing in this heat. They have no liquor (not even warm beer, to say nothing of Coca-Cola, whiskey, or cool milk shakes). Water is always warm and often from rusty cans. They have little enough candy and, now that captured Jap stocks are exhausted, few cigarettes. Matches are a luxury. They have no books, no magazines, few short-wave radios for news; they never see a white woman. As for magazines and books: American Red Cross, please note. Urgent.

But morale is high nevertheless. Ashore again and again one meets a sergeant or an officer. "Say, I'm bored," is a typical opening. "Let's get some grenades and go kill a few Japs." And off they go.

The British in the Solomons have a sage of their own. Captain Martin Clements is only one of many here. Out in Malaita Island lives Bishop Baddeley, head of the Diocese of Melanesia, who runs a dozen Episcopalian missions throughout the islands. He and his male staff chose to stay when the Japs came. And some of his women workers stayed as well. The same is true of the Roman Catholic missions. Throughout the islands the missionaries' slogan is "Business as Usual," both for themselves and for their flocks.

A priest at Marabovo, Guadalcanal Island, stayed till the Japs seized his place, took the garden vegetables; then he made off into the jungle with a teacher and two or three boys. From an eminence a few days later they watched Allied planes blast their life's work to smithereens. Never again shall I swallow the stupid tales of missionaries being the kind of men who made natives wear pants and shirts. This lot in the Solomons are brave as only men of great faith can be.

Another Britisher arrived in camp yesterday with several days' beard growth. He had made a fearful trek for a week. On the way he was signaled by an enemy patrol and replied by waving a walking stick—all he had for self-defense—then dived into a bush. Presently three officers approached and passed within a yard of where he lay, then sat down to smoke and gossip but a few feet farther on. They talked all afternoon, from two till sundown, then departed. The Britisher lay still the whole while and escaped when they had gone.

September 25th

The *U.S.S. Dash* has been ordered back to have another go at unloading her cargo. She couldn't get rid of it on Monday, for the situation ashore was too critical. Now we're in at Lunga. We've had our share of excitement as Bill promised. Last night we missed our escort and decided to sail on. On the way, we now learn, we passed within a hundred miles of a Jap task force, plunging in where angels fear to tread.

We were sighted early this morning by a friendly plane which must have known what was aboard, for it went into a victory roll of sheer delight. Flashing signals ashore, a combined Allied task force stood out in the roads as planes whirred above in endless cover. Tank and jeep lighters by the score sped out and back with goods, with men, with equipment, and stores. In twelve hours some thousands of tons of material must have been unloaded by us and by the other ships. They were unloaded with a minimum of fuss and confusion as the lighters dashed into the bay, set down their loads at deposit points marked by colored flags or signboards.

Instantly trucks rolled up in a cloud of gray sand and wheeled off to dumps beneath the palms. Some were brown-painted Chevrolets and Fords—remainders of the days of Pacific appeasement, for they were captured from the Japs who had made off in such haste when we first landed that they failed to disable more than half the eighty vehicles they had around.

As we sailed up the channel we saw a pall of smoke arise from the hills west of Lunga—where our warships this morning shelled an enemy-occupied village. Farther down the beach we saw through binoculars a dozen stranded Jap landing-barges, wrecked and useless, once capable of taking thirty to fifty men apiece—one more landing caught just in time. In the distance we heard desultory gunfire, sometimes caught the flash of an explosion.

It is easy to think of the front as simply the line we're holding round the airfield. But what of the men behind, the men who man supply bases and airfields to the rear? The war may not be as exciting to them; indeed it's a war first of all against boredom. But without their efforts Guadalcanal could be nothing.

Behind our tactical success in the Solomons is a grim tale of battle with jungle and disease and savagery to the rear, on little-known coral islets where the surgeon's knife and his drugs have wrought wonders, where savages roam beauty spots the tourist would pay thousands of dollars to see if he could.

Up here in Guadalcanal things have been pretty quiet since Monday when, we now reckon, we killed at least five hundred. "Pretty quiet" means this sort of thing: One night snipers caught a body of men sitting down to supper. Several nights the Japs have shelled from the sea for an hour or two. There have been small patrol clashes, and after one such skirmish a group of our men were cut off. We made one raid up the coast to catch some more infiltraters. A Jap cruiser sniffed her way into Tulagi yesterday and was damaged by an aerial torpedo.

Ashore this afternoon the biggest change I noticed was in our own men. Officers and men alike were fairly clean and all were shaved. There was grave-digging and I passed several neat, sad rows. The graves are tidy and each has a wooden cross.

But how long things will stay quiet is anybody's guess. General Vandergrift, the Marines' commanding general on Guadalcanal, driving around the airfield in his jeep this afternoon, was far from sanguine that the Japs have been irrevocably repelled. "They're a determined lot, these brown devils," he said, "and they'll try again. But unless you want to get shot around you can tell your paper that any further fighting here'll be pretty much the same as you saw on Sunday."

FRANCE FROM THE INSIDE

A REPORT BY THE "LAST MAN OUT"

(JUNE 1943)

C. J. Fernand-Laurent

LET ME GIVE you a glimpse of Paris in summer. Busses and taxis
have disappeared. Horse-drawn vehicles are rarely seen. All Parisians
ride bicycles—or walk. An elderly couple, very correct, pedal by on
an ancient tandem.

From the great lady to the midinette, every woman goes bare-headed and bare-legged. In the great dressmaking houses of the Place
Vendôme and the Avenue Matignon the simplest ensemble costs from
fifteen to twenty thousand francs; only the wives of the Germans, the
profiteers, and the collaborators patronize these places.

There is a great vogue for print dresses—made out of scarves dug
out of bottom drawers and ingeniously assembled. Thus it happens
that Parisiennes run around the town showing on their backs the most
unexpected designs: the coats of arms of our provinces, the map of
Europe, boats, airplanes, the coronation procession of King George
VI. Miraculously, they succeed in remaining attractive. There is no
more leather of course, and so they all wear wooden-soled sandals. For
a long time our ears will recall the double sound of footsteps in Paris
under the occupation—the dull thud of the Germans' boots and the
light, brisk patter of the Parisiennes' wooden sandals on the sidewalks.

And a glimpse of Paris in winter: Since the Nazis have put the country on Berlin time—which is two hours ahead of sun time—it is still dark at nine in the morning. Men and women slip rapidly, like shadows, through the dark and the cold. Many are wearing their old winter-sports costumes: they go to work in ski clothes. All hasten toward the warmth of the metro. In the corridors they pause, stricken-faced, before little white posters which they scan with a rapid glance. These posters, bearing the signature of von Stuelpnagel, announce to the population, by way of warning, lists of hostages shot the previous day.

The houses are glacial. The whole family lives in a single room, which there is no longer any means of heating. There has been no coal for a long time, and hardly any wood. During the winter of 1940–41 electric or gas heaters could still be used, but since then rationing has been so severe that it is practically impossible to run them. So as often as they can people seek the collective warmth of the movie houses.

In November, 1940, when a picture of Pétain shaking hands with Hitler at Montoire appeared on the screen there was an uproar of catcalls in most of the movie houses. After that the showing of newsreels usually set off demonstrations which to the Parisians became the most important part of the show. To prevent these demonstrations the Germans ordered the lights to be kept on in the theaters while the newsreels were being shown. With one accord the Parisians, as soon as the newsreels began, hid their faces behind opened newspapers. A new order prohibited the reading of newspapers in movie houses. Whereupon what appeared to be an extraordinary epidemic of grippe began to rage all over Paris. As soon as the newsreels appeared there began a great coughing and sneezing. In the end newsreels were forbidden except in the theaters reserved for German troops.

Right after the Armistice Paris swarmed with Germans. They were authorized to travel first class in the metro—whereupon all the Parisians, even the richest, took to traveling exclusively in second. The attitude of the population toward the Germans has remained one of complete and scornful indifference. They never speak to them, and literally rub elbows with them without appearing to see them.

There are infinitely fewer Germans in uniform to be seen in Paris now than in 1940. On the other hand, there are many German civilians, refugees from bombed cities and men sent to relieve the military of all possible administrative duties in France. And while the first soldiers sent in after the Armistice were smart, freshly shaven young men with punctilious manners and excellent morale, those who remain would obviously no longer be of any use on a fighting front. Like the German civilians, they are a pathetic lot; if they were not Germans one would feel sorry for them. After a German has been in France for a while, especially if he is one of a small group stationed in some out-of-the-way place, he is likely to become lonely and begin to make overtures to the sympathy of the French, perhaps pulling out a photograph of his wife and children; and when they tease him by suggesting that he will never see Germany again it becomes evident that he believes his side has lost the war.

I have often been asked about the black market in France. There is no black market in basic necessities, first because there are almost literally none, and second because even the vilest thief would be ashamed to deal in such things under present circumstances and would dread the terrible consequences if he were caught. But in goods of the luxury class there are two black markets. On both of them furs, leather, and jewels are dealt in as well as rare foods and wines. When I left France the price of a turkey on the black market was about 5,000 francs; of a ham, 7,000 or 8,000; of a goose, 3,000 or 4,000. One of these black markets is run by the Germans, the other in competition with it. If the French know that a German official is getting luxuries on the black market, they will often try to outbid him. For instance, in one town it was common knowledge that a huge *pâté de foie gras* was being held for a local German *gauleiter* who was going to give a Christmas party; whereupon a group of Frenchmen pooled their resources to outbid the German, and on Christmas day the dealer simply said to the German, "Something happened. It didn't come after all." The German knew perfectly well what had happened, but what could he do?

I am also asked often about travel in France. Transportation has become very difficult because the Germans have taken at least two-thirds of our rolling stock. Trains are extremely infrequent and are

135

incredibly crowded—corridors so jammed with people that they cannot move and sometimes it is impossible to open the doors when a station is reached. One must buy one's tickets several days ahead of time and make known one's identity and reason for traveling in order to get an *Ausweiss,* or permit. As for Jews, they are simply not allowed to travel.

Many Americans ask me about the present status of the French universities. The answer is that the Germans have not carried out against the French intellectuals the kind of campaign of complete suffocation they have been guilty of in some other countries; though some members of the university faculties have been imprisoned—usually not so much because of what they have done as because of what they have refused to do—the Germans have not had the teaching personnel to replace the French ones, and so the universities have remained comparatively untouched. They are valuable strongholds of the spirit of freedom.

The passive resistance of the French people takes unexpected and picturesque forms. Numerous stories of the jokes they have played on the Germans have reached America, but you may not have heard of the gala concert of the Berlin Philharmonic Orchestra at Lyon in the winter of 1941-42. All the principal German and Vichy authorities were to be present at this concert, and apparently it was an assured success, for there was a great rush to buy tickets. But when the great night came, though all the officials in uniform were in the boxes the theater was three-quarters empty; patriots and students had bought all the tickets and stayed away.

That same year all the teachers in the primary and secondary schools received an order from M. Abel Bonnard, the Nazi academician, who has become Minister of Education in the new regime, to address their pupils for twenty minutes, a certain Thursday morning, on the subject of the Marshal. In the town where I happened to be at the time, the teacher announced: "My children, I have been ordered to speak to you about the Marshal. I am going to obey the order." He began: "The Marshal was a great soldier. . . . The Marshal was as intelligent as he was courageous. . . . The Marshal was a great Christian. . . . The Marshal was as modest in victory as valiant in battle. . ." and so on for twenty minutes. The twenty minutes over, the teacher concluded, "Children, I thank you for your attention. I have just told you about Marshal Foch."

In the summer of 1942 a battalion of Chasseurs Alpins was crossing the public square of a little town in Auvergne. When the commanding officer came to the monument to the dead he ordered his men to form a square, present arms, and sound the bugle; and in the midst of a breathless, expectant crowd he raised his voice: "Chasseurs, we bow before our dead. All our dead—those of the Great War, those of 1939-40, and those who tomorrow will fall in their country's fight for freedom." In the afternoon the mayor of the town, who of course was a man of Vichy, asked for a public concert. The Chasseurs gave him one. Standing in front of the bandstand in the civic park, the commanding officer announced, "You are going to hear one of our traditional refrains"—and the troops struck up an old popular song, *"Non, vous n'aurez pas l'Alsace et la Lorraine."*

If in 1942 resistance—founded on disillusionment—was organized, in 1943 the storm of revolt is breaking. It is breaking because Laval has recently committed the most odious of sacrileges. Promising the exchange of one prisoner of war for every two volunteer workmen, he has called this arrangement *"la relève."* This word is sacred to the soldiers of Verdun, for *"la relève"* was the arrival on the firing line of fresh troops coming to relieve their exhausted comrades who for days and nights had held fast in the mud of the trenches under merciless fire and were now able to go back to a hot meal and sleep. The shamelessness of Laval's daring to use this word shocked the French people beyond measure.

The great mass of the French had expected that the first result of the Armistice in 1940 would be the liberation of the prisoners. But in actual fact an infinitesimal number were returned to us; the Germans never sent back any, even under the "relief," except those whom they would have had to send back in any case on account of their health. For instance, in a little town in the southwest it was announced that two prisoners, freed by the relief, would return home. The wife of the first arrived in Lyon just as her husband was dying; the second died two weeks after he got home.

More than thirteen hundred thousand French soldiers are still prisoners in Germany—in addition to the civilians who have been taken there by force in the course of the past few months.

Why were there so many prisoners in the beginning? The explanation is simple. The order to cease firing was given on the night of June 16, 1940, when the negotiations for an armistice had not even begun; the Armistice was signed the evening of the 21st and was not actually put in force until the 23rd. For seven days, therefore, the Germans were able to take their time surrounding and capturing hundreds of thousands of men who, against their will but in obedience to orders, had laid down their arms.

The relief did not bring back these prisoners, but it did mark the beginning of a sinister manhunt.

In the beginning—officially, at least—enlistment for work in Germany had been purely voluntary, and volunteers had been so rare that the government had to hire people to act the part of volunteers. In Nice, Darnand rounded up a gang of unemployed whom he paid to do nothing but this special kind of work. Every time a trainload of "volunteers" left Nice—after a great deal of advance publicity in the press—these wretches were collected in the station, put in special cars on which were scrawled in chalk, "Vive Laval! Vive la collaboration!" and sent as far as a way station just beyond Toulon, where they got out of the train and went back to Nice to play the scene over again when the next train left.

But since October, and more especially since the occupation of the whole country by the enemy, the manhunt has become serious—and tragic. There is no longer any thought of getting volunteers. All men under thirty are systematically trapped by the administration and the police and, through the use of threats, blackmail, and often physical force, made to leave for Germany. It is a real slave hunt.

Many prefer to run every conceivable risk rather than go. They abandon their families and their homes and take to the woods, where they find officers and non-coms who are hiding from the Gestapo—

remnants of that Army of the Armistice, limited to forty-five thousand men, which was demobilized at Hitler's order toward the end of 1942. At that time all the officers of one cavalry regiment, from the colonel to the last second lieutenant, crossed the frontier and took refuge in Spain. Other members of that army are in hiding within France itself; they form a part of the underground army who await with anguished impatience an Allied landing so that they can enter the struggle again and give the signal for a general uprising.

If these insurgents are able to stay hidden month after month without dying of hunger it is because of the magnificent solidarity of the peasants. In the course of this account I have often spoken of the workmen in the cities, but the attitude of the men of the countryside is no less admirable. It is true that farm workers are in theory exempt from the relief and that Vichy has done everything possible to gain their support. The return to the land and the exaltation of the peasantry have been two of Pétain's favorite themes. Nevertheless he has not been able to win them over. When—on a day that is not far off—we see the uprising of revolt, the terrible, desperate army of the oppressed and the hungry will find in the French peasantry its firmest supporters.

To the superficial observer the France of 1943 might seem out of the war. But not only are the French fighting overseas with the magnificent armies of General Köning, General Leclerc, and General Giraud; there is also the immense, pitiable, and magnificent army of suffering and rebellious France herself.

Toward the end of the First World War, I arrived in the Somme with the British troops, in a village that had been bombarded and pillaged, only a few days after its evacuation by the Germans. And I saw an old peasant standing at the door of what had been his house. The poor old man, his head bent low, was brooding on his sorrow. But as he saw us coming he straightened himself proudly, looked us in the eye, and said, *"Allons!* The walls are still good. I can rebuild it."

In the house of France—devastated, pillaged, enslaved though it is—the walls are still good. We will rebuild it.

FROM HOUSEWIFE TO SHIPFITTER

(SEPTEMBER 1943)

Virginia Snow Wilkinson

WHEN I WAS given my first real shipfitting job, I was taught to put chocks on the double bottom. Chocks act as supports when the unit is turned over and put into the waiting hull. For weeks the craftsmen of our skids had worked on a huge section of double bottom, labeled XAK, which was at last passed as finished. It was prepared by the riggers to be lifted by the cranes—and then the whistle blew and we all went home. In the morning we learned that while the cranes were lifting the sixty tons—on the graveyard shift, mind you—the great weight suddenly broke loose and dropped, breaking a crane, smashing the roadway and concrete walk, and quite ruining the unit itself.

If the work in the basin on Hull 6 was not to be held up we had to rush a new XAK to replace the other. All hands were thrown upon it—even my hands. I was told to locate the chocks on the blueprint, to measure for them, to find the chocks, to get a welder to put them on, and to check to see that they were square.

It was nice to be a part of the co-operative spirit that was humming over this great smoking honeycomb. Men crawled in and out as furiously busy as wasps. I went my way blithely, saying "Ah-h-h" to myself. When it came to getting a welder, why, I knew welders. They were clothed in brown leather and wore black helmets. Dozens of them were about. I approached one of them.

"Would you please weld these chocks on, over here? They are in a hurry for the unit."

The welder looked at the project and drew back coldly.

"That's a job for a tacker," he said.

"It's welding, isn't it?"

"Tacking is a temporary weld. You'll have to get a tacker."

I went up to the next brown-leathered man.

"I haven't my hose over on this side. It would be too much trouble to haul it over for just those few chocks."

I approached another welder, who tried to crush me with a look.

"I'm a welder, not a tacker."

I selected next a tall masterly-looking man of much dignity.

"There are a few chocks which must be tacked in unit XAK. Can you do it? The unit is supposed to go right away."

Heavens, what had I done now? This man looked at me, just looked at me, while he blew out the cigarette smoke from his mouth. Slowly, quietly he spoke these few concentrated words:

"I am a tacker leaderman."

I wondered if I was supposed to back away bowing.

This was getting me nowhere. And this was my job. I looked about the skids until I recognized a welding foreman. I took my case to him. More experienced now, I did not ask him to weld but only to obtain a welder-tacker for me. He produced a very young boy whom I led to my chocks. I made them square and on my lines before he welded. When he finished they were neither square nor on my lines. They had to be broken off and rewelded. They were not his responsibility. But I felt sorry for him—not so many years older than my children, and earning ninety-five cents an hour before he had lived long enough to know what that meant or the importance of the education he was not getting. When he had welded three or four chocks he stood up with his eyes wandering all over the skids and murmured something about not being able to do any more because he ought to be with another crew and besides, he didn't think his hose would reach much farther.

Then I looked about the assembly myself. I found a tall young woman standing with her tools and hose with that baffled look of the newly idle. I approached her.

"I don't know whether you're a tacker or a welder or a helper or a trainee or a journeyman, but there are a few chocks which must be welded to unit XAK before it is picked up by the riggers. Do you think you can do it?"

"You bet I can. I'd love to," she said and was on her way at once. "I haven't done a thing all day." I was surprised how quickly and efficiently she gathered her paraphernalia and stooped over the job. When she raised her helmet the chocks were on the lines and square. She was interested to know where they should go and she took the responsibility for their being there when she had finished. "You shouldn't hold them or look at them," she told me. "You might burn your arm or get a flash. I'll hold them to the mark." After she had finished she told me that this was her second day out of welding school. "My husband was called into the Army and I went into welding school. If there's anything I can do to help build ships I'm going to do it."

I could well believe what was said so frequently in the Yard: that women make fine welders.

A few mornings later, as soon as we stepped upon the skids, we perceived that something new was astir. The shipfitting women—there were three of us—were called together.

"We're going to give you your own unit to work on together," the leaderman said. "XAK is your baby now. Study your print, square your frame lines down the vertical keel, and get the crane to bring you your steel."

Alice, our naïve nineteen-year-old, glowed. "Golly," she said. "Really?" The colored girl was more sophisticated but we were all pleased.

"Let's be so accurate and careful that they won't be able to find a thing wrong. Let's check and recheck everything. . . ." "We'll work it out together. If one of us makes a mistake we'll tell her and correct it and no bad feelings. . . ." "We'll all stand and fall together on it." That was the way we talked.

I never saw such a change in three workmen as in these three girls. We became integrated persons working together on a project which focused all our interests. I noticed how quickly we ran our own errands, how conscientious we were in checking, how we abhorred sloppy measurements. For once we had been given responsibility, for once we had been put on our own, for once we had enough to do.

"When we finish we'll hold open house and invite you in to tea," we told our leaderman.

Our enjoyment was such that we did not notice that something was amiss until late in the afternoon. Then we became gradually aware of the hostility of the men. Our woman burner reported that they were "seething with resentment" that women should be given a unit to construct. The women checkers said, "You should just hear what we hear outside our checking shed, my dears." This was the first time I had come up against the hostility of one sex toward another and I could not believe it. The men had always been so decent, so respectful, so kindly. But this was the first time that we had been seen in the light of competitors. We had been amusing little creatures only too happy to take what crumbs of jobs were dropped to us.

Our leaderman said, "I know, but pay no attention. They'll have to get used to women shipfitters. Half these men may be in the Army this January. They might as well accept the fact that women will have to take their places."

Our woman checker said, "In September I was one of the first women ever to be admitted out here in the yards. You could have cut the resentment with a knife and spread it thick. But it's gradually being worn away."

The next day, with no explanation, our XAK, "our baby," was taken from us and given to the men. We had to stand aside and see the men working on what we felt was our project. Cora, whose boy friend was one of the group, said the men were afraid the assemblies would become like the plate shop—overrun by women. She took herself over to the unit where her friend was working, to lean against the steel.

Alice took out her lipstick: "Oh, what the heck do I care so long as I get my dollar five an hour. But it *was* fun."

I tried to reflect that there must be another side to this thing. Maybe the men who were heads of families, straining to take care of several dependents, and who had known the bitter struggle for a living—maybe these men resented the fact that any eighteen-year-old could come out without a day's training, without a grain of tool sense or mechanical sense, and draw the same pay as they and rise at the same rate—even these girls who would go at once into debt for fur coats and "perfectly adorable" evening gowns. The pay was too high for the beginner, I knew—for the boy who had quit high school as well as for the girl. The experienced workman might easily feel resentment. But this I knew too: that the responsibility placed upon these girls had made them almost in one day into serious workmen.

One night I had an adventure. It concerned my getting home. Tired of having my hammer stolen so many times, I had brought a cheap little hammer from home and kept it in a little leather holder on my belt (a Christmas gift from my son). Now as I was going out the gate, a little late, I was held up by a guard.

"Sorry, lady, you can't go out with that hammer. Step back. "

"This?" I asked and brought the hammer forth. "But it is my own from home."

"Sorry, but you'll have to go to the police station."

"Where is the police station?"

He gave me the direction with his thumb.

"But I'll miss my last bus."

"There'll be others later on."

"Not for fifty or sixty minutes later on, and then perhaps not in my direction."

At the police station: "You can't go home with that."

"It's my own."

"But you can't go out the gate with it."

"I have for two weeks."

"You can't any more."

"Will you check it for me then and let me catch my bus?"

"No. You'll have to go all the way back to the plate shop and let them release it."

"That is blocks and blocks back. The plate shop has nothing to do with this—they've never seen it. Can't I leave it with you and go out the gate?"

"No."

"But you'll have the hammer."

"We don't want the hammer."

"Do you mean to say you are going to keep me here for a twenty-five-cent hammer, without a warrant?" I looked at the three uniformed policemen, at the heavy galvanized fencing, at the guarded gate, and shook myself. This was like some movie I had seen of Nazi Germany.

"I insist on seeing the American Consul." But they didn't smile. "May I use the phone then?"

"No."

By this time I had a splitting headache; I was furious; I was longing to reach my husband and have him come in true movie fashion to the rescue. Outside the station I put my little hammer in an ashcan near by and approached the gate. The guard stood stiffly and stoutly before me.

"Where's your release?"

"I haven't one but I haven't a hammer either—see?" and I showed him.

"You'll stay here all night then."

I turned and began my furious walk to the plate shop. Often in the yard I had seen people pushed round and marveled with a little disgust that Americans would take it. I had often seen utter disregard for individual liberty and great injustice done to employees, and had noticed that it was taken with pained resignation by some, and by others with apathy, with whining complaint, or with "My God, someone is going to hear of this!" But for the Resigned, the Apathetic, the Plaintive, the Angry the situation remained unchanged. Now I understood.

The plate shop seemed puzzled by my request; it was evident they had not often had to meet such a demand. The tool checkers looked at my puny hammer; they looked at me; they shook their heads, for I was a suspect character. Finally a checker brought a man in charge who produced, after a time, a form which stated that the tool chest which this workman was carrying out of the yard contained no plate-shop tools. The employee at his elbow said, "For a two-bit hammer, my God!" I walked the blocks back to the gate, noting when I arrived that all busses had disappeared.

I presented my piece of paper to the guard, who stepped aside and allowed me to pass. I clicked my heels and saluted. "Heil,'" I said. But he did not smile or speak, for he was a serious man and I had tried him greatly. I now realized I worked for something Big. I was deeply impressed all the way home.

I had promised myself two months in which to find myself here in the shipyards but my probation was not to last so long. It seemed that we, the women, were being assimilated gradually, if slowly. For a while we had floated on top, undissolved, but the broth was big enough with a little stirring and stewing to absorb us all—or almost all. The great need was for experienced workmen, men or women; and time on the job, doing this and a little of that, adds up finally to experience. I was given more and more to do. (When I told my leaderman that I liked having more to do he answered, "Well, neither you nor I nor the shipyards are as new and green as we were; we're all getting under way.") Six weeks from the date of my arrival at the yard I was given a unit to handle by myself. I guess it was not so much but it was my own.

I measured for and located the steel material which was to go on this unit. I labeled it with chalk and engaged the riggers to lift it. I asked a flanger and a tacker to be on hand to put the steel in place and to tack (weld) it up. And then I stood while the crane—one of those beautiful gray cranes which trail steel through the air with a motion as graceful as the soaring of a hawk on an upcurrent of air—picked up the material and sped it to our unit. It wasn't so much, no more than anyone could have done, but I felt the keen exhilaration of getting under way. It was good, I thought, this working together on a ship.

Standing so elated, I felt a ripple of interest run from workman to workman. We all looked up and out to sea where a gray troopship was being towed past us silently. Our ship. My first day in the yard I had helped make a scupper for it and these other men and women standing grinning had made the double bottom.

"There she goes!" we said and watched it as it slipped away. Then I turned back to my work, for at last I had a job.

NOTES ON AN ENGLISH VISIT

(JANUARY 1944)

Frederick Lewis Allen

I. *Blackout*

I reached London early last October at seven o'clock of a cloudy evening, just as the nightly blackout took effect. Stepping from the bright interior of the train onto a station platform whose gloom was only faintly alleviated by an occasional hooded lamp of low candle-power, and wondering how anybody could recognize anybody else in this crowded dimness, I was nevertheless recognized and hailed and led away to a car which whirled me out into the vast dark of London. We drove at what seemed to my unpracticed eyes a wildly confident speed—down half-empty avenues, round almost invisible corners, past traffic islands marked only by a small $\overset{x}{\text{X}}$ of light; past an occasional taxi tearing along with the same sublime confidence, its headlamps playing dimly downward on the roadway ahead of it; past vaguely illuminated double-decker busses thundering through the night.

We stopped before a hotel—not a glimmer showing from it—while my companions went inside to inquire about reservations; and for a few minutes I stood waiting beside the car in a silence broken only by the rush and rumble of infrequent taxis and busses, by the clicking footsteps of shadowy people striding by on the sidewalk (as briskly, it seemed, as if they had cats' eyes), and by the fragments of their conversation as they passed. Now and then a flashlight would blink as some pedestrian checked up on the location of the curb he was approaching. Across the street a tier of office buildings and apartment houses loomed lightless and immense. There is always, to me, something majestic about London; in this portentous obscurity its majesty was intensified.

I left the city a little over five weeks later, likewise by blackout. And so my last impression of it complemented my first. It was of standing on another equally dim railway platform in the midst of a clamorous and shadowy confusion: soldiers, sailors, and civilians tramping along to their trains, the soldiers and sailors laden with heavy kits, and some of them accompanied by wives or parents as they searched one dark crowded railway carriage after another for a vacant space; baggage trucks, heaped high with blanket-rolls and military equipment, being dragged clattering through the throng; smoke pouring from panting locomotives into the high black vault of the train shed, through the glassless skylights of which I could catch glimpses of a full moon weaving in and out of bright-edged clouds. About me I could half-see the farewell embraces as families were separated; and it seemed to me that the sense of overwhelming urgency that hung in the smoky air, the sense of imminent departures for unknown and perilous destinations, the sense that individuals were being implacably lost in impersonal groups beckoned by fate, was strangely accentuated by the blackout gloom which turned men into mere moving shapes.

And as I look back now upon those English weeks, it is the blackout which stands out in my mind as the most striking, and also the most wearing, single circumstance in British life today. Millions of words have been written about it, yet to the visitor who experiences it for the first time it comes nevertheless with a shock of surprise. For as he sees how the blackout circumscribes his movements from day to day he realizes how profoundly it must circumscribe the lives of millions of English men and women as they enter *the fifth winter of darkness.*

The English seem today a worn and tired people. For over four years they have undergone deprivations and manifold inconveniences similar to those which the war has imposed on the people of the United States but much more intense. On the average they have become more deeply immersed in the war than we, and their lives are more distorted by it than ours are. Their food is more drastically rationed than ours and is short of so many things—meats, butter, citrus fruits, and so on—that although there is enough to sustain health there is seldom enough to make eating a pleasure. Their gasoline is much more dramatically rationed than ours: there is no basic ration at all; nobody can get a gallon unless he can prove absolute necessity—as for a family in the country to go marketing once a week, or for a government official to go on war errands. Their clothing is so sharply rationed that the purchase of a new suit will eat up half a man's clothes points for the year. All manner of goods which we regard as necessities are lacking; matches, for instance, are almost unobtainable (and good cigarette lighters are expensive and hard to come by). Every form of transportation is infrequent and overcrowded, and the sight of men and women standing quietly in long queues at the bus stops is ubiquitous. People mostly look a little shabby, down-at-the-heel; the women's cotton and wrinkled rayon stockings, for instance, and the fact that half the young girls are bare-legged even in October, reflect a situation in which supplies are often lacking even if one has the ration points to buy. (One morning in Cardiff I saw a long double queue of women stretching along the sidewalk, and asked one of them what they were in line for. "Stockings," she said. Some shop had got hold of a supply.) As for living under government regulations, the British are far more circumscribed in their day-to-day freedom than we: consider the single circumstance that no one may change his job without government consent. For four years they have been working long hours under the spur of wartime necessity. All these conditions of life are wearing—yet none of them seems to me to bear down upon and hamper the individual quite as does the blackout.

In summer its impact is comparatively slight, for the evening twilight lasts long. But in winter things are different. When I was in Glasgow, toward the middle of November, the blackout began at about 5:20 P.M. and lasted till well after eight in the morning. Think what it must be to work a shift from 8:00 A.M. to 8:00 P.M., and in one's free waking hours, all week long, never to be able to move outdoors save in blackness.

151

Make no mistake about it, this blackout is strictly enforced. When I reached my hotel room on my first evening in London I found the windows already shrouded by heavy overlapping black-lined curtains. Under the glass top of the dressing-table was a warning notice:

BLACK-OUT

PLEASE DRAW CURTAINS

BEFORE

SWITCHING ON LIGHT

Another sign amplified the warning:

IMPORTANT

By the door was a third:

AIR RAID PRECAUTION

ALL LIGHTS MUST BE TURNED

OUT BEFORE THE ROOM IS LEFT,

IN CASE WINDOW DAMAGE OCCURS.

I switched off the light, groped my way to the windows, parted the curtains, and looked out—across a hotel court—at what one might have imagined to be a quite untenanted building, with not a sliver of light showing. Actually it was another wing of the hotel, with every room occupied. Later I moved to another room looking out over a wide stretch of London—rooftops, chimney pots, apartment houses, hotels, office buildings; a view at least a mile deep. Invariably there would be no ray of artificial light visible anywhere after nightfall except at one point among the rooftops where a single not-quite-sufficiently curtained window, invisible from the street, showed a tiny line of brightness. Every evening as dusk approached a chambermaid made the rounds of the hotel rooms, both occupied and vacant, darkening every window: the inevitable routine which someone must go through every evening *in every house in England*. One afternoon I was talking with a publisher and a novelist when the novelist glanced at his watch and leaped to his feet. "My wife is busy this afternoon," he said, "and I've got to get home to my suburb in time to black out thirty-eight windows."

To the newcomer to England, particularly if he has a map to consult beforehand and a bump of direction, the game of trying to find his way about London in the evening is rather good fun. When the moon is near the full, even if the sky is quite overcast, it is easy. Most curbstones are marked at the street intersections with white paint, as are projecting cellar doors and other obstructions; and as there is almost no traffic by night you can stride along rather confidently (with a wary eye out for unmarked garage entrances and other changes in the sidewalk level in the middle of a block) provided you can keep track of how far you have gone without ever being able to see a street sign. But in the dark of the moon . . .

You go out through the revolving door of your hotel (this door has been made lightproof by stretching a black strip of cloth over each of its glass panels) and find yourself in blue-black gloom. Ahead of you you can see a dull blue light set into the curving brick blast-wall which protects the hotel entrance against any bomb explosion outside—but you can see no steps at all. You feel your way with your feet, step down on the sidewalk, steer out past the end of the blast-wall (which is vaguely visible to you now because it is painted with black and white stripes) and stand bewildered in what seems total blackness. You can hear people walking by but you can't see them. Better grope your way to the hotel wall—unless you have a flashlight (you are permitted to carry one if you have one)—and stand there a minute till your eyes adjust themselves. Then you can set out.

Whenever a car comes by, your way ahead becomes half-discernible, for its dim downward-shining headlights reveal a bit of the street and diffuse enough light even outside their direct path to indicate the line of the curb. As you approach a street-corner there will be a tiny hooded overhead street light to guide you, and perhaps a small traffic light. If the pavement is wet these lights will make thin paths of reflected light below, which will help to orient you; but if the night is overcast and the pavements dry you may stop helpless in the middle of a block, unable to tell which way to move until a car approaches. Your concentration upon the effort to find your way, the brief glimmer of flashlights glowing here and there, the almost invisible people groping their way along, the snatches of their overheard talk, the computations going on in your mind—"There—here's the corner—now two blocks in this direction and then a block to the left"—take on a strangely dreamlike quality: this episode in your evening is as sharply set apart from what preceded and what will follow it as if you were sleepwalking. You reach what you think must be the approximate location of the building you are seeking; you ask a passing shadow if you are right and he tells you to go a little farther on; you make out a faint bluish glow, find yourself moving in behind another blast-wall and climbing steps and laying your hands on another revolving door; it revolves— and then suddenly you are in a blaze of light: a hotel lobby full of activity. The dream is over and wakeful life resumes again.

With all this inconvenience goes a special beauty: the beauty of the ghostly streets by moonlight, with every Renaissance pediment and column, every bit of white stonework in the brick houses, shining under the moon; the beauty of starlight, with a powder of stars overhead so clear that I have plainly seen the faintest of the seven stars of the Dipper (the one where the handle joins the Dipper itself) from the sidewalk of as traveled a street as Park Lane; the sudden unexpected effects (as when once I noticed that a supposedly full moon seemed to have had a piece bitten out of it, and saw as I walked on that the bite altered its shape, and realized that I was witnessing a partial eclipse of the moon by a barrage balloon hanging above the city); and the somber beauty of the scene from a high window on a foggy night, the dark shapes of the clustered buildings looming like castled mountains through the mist till one imagines one is not in an inhabited city at all but in some silent land of ghostly slumbering peaks and turrets.

But even the beauty palls on people who have endured the blackout winter after winter—never able, waking at night, to turn on a light without first closing the curtains, never able to let night fall without blacking out every window, never able to set out of an evening without calculating how to get to their destination and home again. Of all the things English people dream of doing when the Luftwaffe is reduced to helplessness, perhaps the first on the list is to see the lights turned on again.

It has gone on so long! An English friend of mine heard a little girl, pointing to an electric-light pole in the street, say to her mother, "What's that thing for?" The child couldn't remember ever having seen a lighted street.

I heard another anecdote which involves both the blackout and the obstinate pattern of habit which helped to carry the English people through the horrors of the bombings of 1940–41: An English county official told me that one night when the Luftwaffe was ranging over England and bombs were falling he was himself in a plane flying above his county at about three thousand feet, inspecting the adequacy of the blackout arrangements. As he looked down into the darkness, he began to see little subdued flashes and gleams here, there, and everywhere. "What's that?" he asked the pilot. "Oh, that," said the pilot. "It's ten o'clock. They're putting the cat out."

II. *The Scars of 1940–41*

My first morning in London, as I walked out in the streets, my first reaction was similar to that of many other newcomers these days: "I don't see much bomb damage." It was a fine sunny morning, the busses rolled mightily by, the sidewalks were busy with people (perhaps a third of them in uniform, and over half of this third in American uniform); everything looked very active and normal—though the traffic was far lighter than in New York. Presently I'd come to a gap where a couple of houses had been removed and the neighboring buildings showed patched walls, but there didn't seem at first to be many such gaps.

Soon, however, I'd come to a bigger gap where several houses were missing. Next to this gap there would be perhaps a half-wrecked house whose front wall and floors had been sliced off, disclosing some such sight as a second-storey drawing-room, its fine wainscoting still in place, its green wallpaper torn and fluttering in the wind, its ornamental fireplace a mere niche in the side wall, its ceiling and floor quite gone. (London offers an endless variety of such odd stage sets; where the side wall of a ruined apartment house has been left standing, for instance, one can see running from the top of this wall to the bottom identical patterns of bathroom tiling, with identical arrangements of holes for the plumbing fixtures.) Then I began to notice that around each such area of total destruction there was a fringe of still apparently intact but untenanted houses, most of them with FOR SALE or TO LET signs before them—buildings so gutted or shaken that they would be unfit for use until labor and materials, and presumably government money, became available for their repair. And I noticed another thing: I could walk for two or three blocks along a street that seemed to have suffered no damage whatever—but just out of sight around the corner on a side street would recur the familiar picture of the yawning gap and the houses all about it damaged and empty, their glassless window-openings covered with building-paper. About these scars of the blitz the life of London flowed on unregarding, for now that the wreckage has been mostly cleaned up Londoners have become as used to the marks of destruction as New Yorkers in the nineteen-twenties were used to seeing in every other block along Fifth Avenue a building being demolished or a lot standing vacant to await a new skyscraper.

Of the desolation wrought at the end of 1940 in the region east and north of St. Paul's Cathedral much has been written; but the descriptions have mostly, it seems to me, failed to suggest its vast extent. Translating it roughly into American terms, it is somewhat as if in New York a zone a mile or more wide from east to west, and stretching from near the Woolworth Building on the south to say Washington Square on the north, were broken into a chain of what might be called lakes of desolation, involving in all perhaps half of the zone. St. Paul's, with its great Wren dome, stands virtually intact; about it on the north and east stand a few unsmashed buildings and a few gaunt blackened skeletons of brick and stone; then come the open spaces in which almost every wall has been demolished down to the street level, and you walk along almost trafficless streets past endless rows of deep cellar holes in which moss and rank grass grow greenly. At intervals stand oddly surviving remnants of the City's former pride—a carved stone Renaissance doorway or a pair of stone statues that once flanked an imposing office building. Here and there, in front of a yawning cellar hole, a signboard informs you that John

Bates & Son are continuing business at such-and-such a new address. In one island, as it were, of surviving buildings I came upon the Church of St. Giles-Cripplegate, its tower partly intact, its walls mostly intact, some fragments of stained glass still in place in its windows, but its whole roof gone and its interior burned out; beside the entrance doorway there still stood an announcement-board listing the weekly schedule of Morning Prayers and Holy Communions and Vespers. Close by, where some cellarless buildings must once have stood, a row of vegetable gardens flourished among the wreckage.

I saw similar bomb damage in other English cities and towns (for on such a trip as mine one becomes something of a connoisseur of modern ruins): in Canterbury, where whole blocks along its busiest streets have been wiped out; in Swansea, where the shopping district was smashed; in Coventry, where the central part of the town was eliminated; and especially in Dover and Plymouth. One detects among the residents of these places a certain rivalry for the prestige of living in the worst-bombed town, but on one score Dover's pre-eminence is secure. It certainly is the most frequently hit town.

The Dover air raid headquarters reminded me a little of some I had seen in New York—the same sort of maps, and charts of available equipment, and girls sitting knitting by the telephones—but with this difference: the number of alerts in Dover since the war began is numbered *in the thousands.* And in addition to occasional night bombings Dover now has to submit to frequent shellings from across the Straits. at any hour of the day or night a shell which has taken just one minute to travel from the Nazi-held French coast may approach in complete silence and land on a house and blow it to bits. No wonder that in some parts of Dover half the houses have been hit; no wonder that the population of the town, which was 45,000 before the war, has now dwindled to 18,000 or 19,000 people, of whom about half spend every night on iron cots ranged along labyrinthine tunnels carved into the celebrated white cliffs.

Dover was having a quiet day when I was there—not a shell dropped—and as we stood on the cliff top and looked across the

Straits, where a stiff southwest wind was kicking up a rough gray sea and had blown the air quite clear of mist, the wrinkled cliffs of Cap Gris-Nez looked singularly peaceful; and to the left of them a few faint vertical marks on the horizon, which powerful field-glasses revealed as high chimneys and a crane and a graceful tower in the town of Calais, looked hardly less innocent. But the Doverites, going on about their business within eyeshot and artillery-shot of Hitler's Fortress Europe, have to be ready every instant for trouble, and they still get a nasty amount of it.

Yet no place that I saw has had to face such wholesale ruin, in proportion to its size, as Plymouth. There a city official with a gift for the graphic phrase told me how the ruin began on a March evening in 1941. "We heard a sound," he said, "as if an immense hive had been overturned." The Plymouth searchlights played, but the city of 220,000 people was almost helpless as the German planes came over by the hundreds; within a couple of hours one whole section of the city was mostly in flames. The next night the Germans came again, turned their attention to the adjoining section of the city—the main business and shopping district, containing most of the public buildings—and made a similar shambles of it. The third night bad weather came to Plymouth's rescue. "If the Germans had come again that night," the City Clerk told me, "I don't know what we'd have done. We were almost helpless from exhaustion; I know I hadn't had my clothes off for sixty hours."

The Germans didn't come to Plymouth again in force, as a matter of fact, for about a month. Then they resumed their campaign and smashed a third adjoining area and a fourth. (I have seen a series of maps on which are marked the places where each bomb hit, night by night, and it is clear from the patterns that the German intent in this series of raids was not to go for military objectives so much as to plaster the city area by area and render it unfit to live and work in.) By the time the Plymouth blitz was over, two hundred acres of buildings had been ruined, some fifteen hundred lives had been lost, and the city was such a wreck that now as one drives through it one exclaims with surprise if one discovers a whole block of houses standing complete.

I find my Plymouth notes crammed with items of the sort that will undoubtedly live on as legendary tales of the great ordeal, handed on from generation to generation in Devonshire. The item, for instance, about Dingle's big store, which was demolished in the March raid: the proprietors of the Dingle business leaped into action and promptly rented twenty-four other small properties in which to resume business, department by department—only to have fourteen of the twenty-four smashed before the end of April. . . .The item about the keys: the ARP officials after the first raids forehandedly listed one hundred houses which would be available for emergency occupation, and stored away the one hundred keys ready for instant use—only to have the ARP Headquarters burned, and the list of houses burned with it, and all the key-tags burned off the keys! "You learn by experience," said the man who told me this; "the fact that key-tags are inflammable just hadn't occurred to us." . . .The item about the old woman who had been vainly pestering the city fathers for bricks to build a shelter, and who, when she was dug out of the ruin of her house a few nights later, stood up, blackened but uninjured, and looked about her and yelled, "*Now* they can't say there are no bricks for me!" . . . The item about the city's supply of firewood, which was buried under the rubble for safety, but was set into a huge blaze when incendiary bombs pierced the rubble—and now is stored under water in an estuary. . . . And the item about the completeness of destruction wrought at the center of a high-explosive bomb blast: the bomb, I was told, reduces everything within many feet to a fine blue-gray dust, when a big bomb made a direct hit on a piano shop the salvagers found nothing at the spot but a ten-foot length of piano-wire—and a layer, over everything, of that blue-gray dust. . . .

Those horrendous days are receding into history, and the people who endured them, in Plymouth and elsewhere, wonder now how they got through the exhaustion and sleeplessness and menacing suspense that dogged them week after week and month after month; and they feel too, one sometimes notes, a little yearning of regret for the exaltation that took hold of them then: the exaltation of discovering that all of them, rich and poor, were knit together by the sharing of labor and peril. Little by little in the intervening years that close bond has been loosened. Of course this had to happen: the human spirit cannot long live on such a plane. But the bond has not been quite undone. No one can travel by train in England (to select one test which the visitor can apply himself against his pre-war experience) without noticing that the Englishman who withdraws into the traditional frigid reserve has become a rarity. There is as much, or almost as much, give-and-take of conversation as there would be among Americans in a similar setting. And though the fiery resolve to remake post-war England which accompanied the exaltation of 1940–41 has likewise weakened as the peril has receded and men have begun mentally to wrap themselves about their property, privileges, and settled habits, and to say, "At any rate you shan't change *this,*" the psychological momentum has not all been spent. Though you will hear people say sadly, "There's been a great letdown since then," you will also hear them add, "But we learned something that we won't ever quite forget."

THE AMERICAN WAY IN WAR
A BRITISH ESTIMATE
(MAY 1944)

D. W. Brogan

A COUNTRY HAS the kind of army its total ethos, its institutions, resources, habits of peaceful life, make possible to it. The American army is the army of a country which is law-respecting without being law-abiding. It is the army of a country which, having lavish natural wealth provided for it and lavish artificial wealth created by its own efforts, is extravagant and wasteful. It is the army of a country in which melodramatic pessimism is often on the surface but below it is the permanent optimism of a people that has licked a more formidable enemy than Germany or Japan, primitive North America. It is the army of a country whose national motto was "Root, hog, or die." When convinced that death *is* the alternative, the hog roots. It is the army of an untidy country which has neither the time, the temperament, nor the need for economy. It is the army of a country in which great economic power is often piled up for sudden use; a final decisive military blow is merely a special variety of corner. It is the army of a country of gamblers who are more or less phlegmatic in taking and calculating their losses, but who feel with all their instincts that they can never go wrong over a reasonable period of time in refusing to sell America short.

161

So the American way of war is bound to be like the American way of life. It is bound to be mechanized like the American farm and kitchen (the farms and kitchens of a lazy people who want washing machines and bulldozers to do the job for them). It is the army of a nation of colossal business enterprises, often wastefully run in detail, but winning by their mere scale and by their ability to wait until that scale tells. It is the army of a country where less attention is paid to formal dignity, of persons or occupations, than in any other society, where results count, where being a good loser is not thought nearly as important as being a winner, good or bad. It is the country where you try anything once, *especially* if it has not been tried before. It is a country which naturally infuriates the Germans with their pedantry and their pathological conception of "honor." It is a country that irritates the English with their passion for surface fidelity to tradition and good form. It is the country of such gadget-minded originals as Jefferson and Ford. It is a country whose navy, fighting its first great battles a century and a half after it could boast of Paul Jones, recovered from a great initial disaster and taught the heirs of Togo with what speed the heirs of Decatur and Farragut could back out of their corners, fighting. The Coral Sea, Midway, these are dates for the world to remember along with the new Thermopylae of the Marines at Wake Island of the new Bloody Angle of Tarawa. It is a country— and so an army—used to long periods of incubation of great railroads and great victories. It is the army of a people that took a long time to get from the Atlantic to the Pacific and found the French and the Spaniards and the Russians before them. But they got there and stayed. The two hundred and fifty years from Virginia to California, like the four years from Washington to Richmond, must be remembered by us—and the Germans. The memory of General Washington, after six years of barely holding his own, combining with the French fleet to capture a British army as easily as taking a rabbit in a snare— that is to be remembered too; for it was not a matter of fighting but of careful timing, of logistics.

That typical Western soldier and adventurer Sam Houston, waiting patiently until the Mexicans had rushed on to deliver themselves into his hands at San Jacinto—he is to be remembered. It is not Custer, foolhardy and dramatic with his long hair and his beard, who is the typical Indian fighter, but great soldiers like Sherman and Sheridan planning from St. Louis or Chicago the supplying of frontier posts, the concentration of adequate force. The Indian chiefs Joseph and Rain-in-the-Face were often artists in war at least on a level with Rommel, but war to the American is a business, not an art. The American is not interested in moral victories but in victory; no great corporation ever successfully excused itself on moral grounds to its stockholders for being in the red. The United States is a great, a very great corporation whose stockholders expect (with all their history to justify the expectation) that it will be in the black.

Other countries, less fortunate in position and resources, more burdened with feudal and gentlemanly traditions, richer in national reverence and discipline, can and must wage war in a very different spirit. But look again at the cast-iron soldier of the Civil War memorial. A few years before, he was a civilian in an overwhelmingly civil society; a few years later, he was a civilian again in a society as civilian as ever. Such a nation cannot "get there fustest with the mostest." It must wait and plan till it can get there with the mostest. This recipe has never yet failed; and Berlin and Tokyo realize, belatedly, that it is not going to fail this time.

MacArthur and the Censorship

(MAY 1944)

The Editors

WE RECENTLY ACCEPTED an article on General MacArthur by an experienced correspondent of high repute who for over a year and a half had been accredited to the General's headquarters. Following the arrangement in force for all accredited correspondents, we sent the manuscript to the Army for review. Publication was "objected to on grounds of military security." We therefore may not print the article.

This act of censorship was not based on the inclusion of military information of value to the enemy; for if the article contained any at all this could readily have been deleted. It was based on the fact that the article contained, along with some praise, considerable criticism of the General; and on the contention that "as written" it "undermines the confidence of this country, Australia, and particularly the troops in that theatre, in their commander and his strategic and tactical plans," and that "such a result would be of great value to the Axis and damaging to General MacArthur's very difficult campaign in the Southwest Pacific."

We have always approved the censoring of information which

might be of military value to the enemy and have voluntarily submitted for review, as a matter of course, every article which we felt might contain such information. (The Office of Censorship has been consistently unexceptionable in its treatment of our material, and the armed forces usually, though not invariably, have been so.) But there is a perpetual danger that censorship may be extended to the concealment of military losses, mistakes, and shortcomings, and we believe it is better in the long run that the publicity given to, let us say, a Patton incident should cause acute discomfort in high military quarters than that mistakes should be hidden. We acknowledge, however, that in specific cases—which those on the outside may not be in a position to estimate—censorship of criticism may sometimes be justifiable if military matters alone are at stake.

But the present case wears another and graver aspect. As we go to press, General MacArthur has not denied receptiveness to a nomination for the Presidency of the United States. No candidate for the Presidency, tacit or otherwise, should stand hidden behind a veil of censorship.

One may write what one pleases about the other candidates; about General MacArthur no opinions based on recent direct observation may apparently be given publicity unless they are flattering.

This situation is intolerable in a free country. It may be that General MacArthur's apparent grievances against the Administration are justified. It may be that the many unfavorable criticisms of him which we have heard—even those which we sought to publish—have been misjudged. But that a man who stands protected by censorship should permit his name to be considered for the Presidency mocks a central principle of democracy—the right of the people to see their political candidates in the light of free discussion.

Before this page reaches print the General may have unequivocally withdrawn his name. Or the censorship may have been relaxed. Otherwise let the public stand warned. The accounts of this candidate which have been appearing are incomplete, biased by censorship, and therefore politically unreliable.

24 Hours of a Bomber Pilot

(AUGUST 1944)

By One of Them

A BOMBING MISSION doesn't start with the take-off or even with the briefing. It starts the evening before, when the word goes round that they are loading bombs.

There is a world of difference in the targets. Some are very lightly defended; in attacking some we have friendly fighter cover all or part way; in attacking others we know we will have to fight our way all the way in, flying through heavy barrages of flak over the target then slugging our way all the way out. So when the bombs are being loaded, there is a lot of speculation as to just what the target for tomorrow is. You do have some indication from the type of bombs being loaded.

After supper you have nothing to do except to wonder, write letters (which is hard to do with your mind filled with other things), and try to get some sleep. You can hear the R.A.F. going out and wish them all the luck in the world and hope they manage to keep Jerry awake most of the night, so he will be as sleepy as you are going to be the next day. You know that sometime after midnight the CQ will be in to get you up, and you wonder if it is worth while going to bed, because you know you'll feel twice as bad for just a half-hour's or an hour's sleep. But you convince yourself it is best to get undressed, hoping that it may be an afternoon mission.

So you go to bed and listen to the other fellows working very hard at the job of relaxing or going to sleep. And then when you finally have your bed nice and warm and it seems as if you have just closed your eyes, the lights go on and the CQ repeats several times (so that it sinks in), "Breakfast at — o'clock, briefing at— ."

You are so tired that the very idea of getting up is a physical pain, but you do, and stagger through the blackout to the mess hall. The sky is crisscrossed with a magnificent display of searchlights in patterns to signal the R.A.F. the way home.

Even your wife or mother would find it hard to recognize you as you sleepily eat breakfast with the questions of the night before still unanswered. When you see an old friend you make an effort to think up a joke of some sort, but this effort is becoming less and less necessary. You see the new replacements looking not too well and you try to help out a bit but really can't feel sympathetic for them, because they don't yet know enough of what the score is to be scared.

The target for the day determines how tough it's going to be, and anyone who draws "Purple Heart Row" knows it is going to be tougher. When you file into the briefing room, the map showing the route to the target in pretty colored yarn, with bright-colored pins showing enemy fighter staffels and red areas for flak, is covered up, as is the blackboard showing the position assignments. The Colonel starts off by asking the group leader for the day to make the opening remarks. He gets up and says "Gulp" and sits down. Then they open the blackboard and you see your squadron has drawn THE position (depending on the group's position in the wing) and you have THE spot in the squadron. Then they unveil the target map and it looks as if they had had to go out and buy some more yarn to cover the distance to the target.

There is definitely a hush as the Colonel outlines the operations of the day. All this time you have held your breath until he gets to the group's position in the wing formation. Then the worst has come to be a reality—you have drawn the "Purple Heart Corner" in "Purple Heart Row." You smile cheerfully as the others look around at you, obviously with sympathy, and you wonder if your cheerful smile looks as sick as those others do.

You hear, too, that you will have enemy fighters to contend with all the way in and out, made up of two to four hundred FW190's and ME109's. Looking at the map, you see the size of the red spot around the target which means flak concentration. You know you can avoid the other red spots on the map but not the target. About now you are convinced that even Lloyd's of London wouldn't bet on your chances of getting back.

It is cold when you go out to get the ship ready and still quite dark. Your gunners are probably already there, and they uncertainly ask you what you think of the position assigned to the ship. Then is the one time your smile cannot be sick, for you must somehow convince them that you have a good fighting chance. Confidence is absolutely essential for a fighting crew, because in an even fight with ten or fifteen fighters the decision will probably go to the side with the most confidence, and that must be you.

Carefully you check everything to see that it is all in working order and that nobody has forgotten anything. You know you already have two strikes against you and you don't want to have the third one a called strike due to carelessness or an oversight.

Your stomach feels queer, and it is a relief when "stations time" arrives, for then there is a chain of events that keeps you moving and puts an end to the awful waiting. The crew goes into a final huddle to check signals and exchange ideas of what to expect and how best to handle it. We get into the plane a little too early and again check our positions, because it is a strange plane. The ship we brought back yesterday was too full of holes to fly again today.

In the cockpit you check your watch again and take another look at the map of your route. You don't want to start the engines too soon because that would waste the precious petrol, but you must have everything warmed up and checked before take-off.

Again you look at your watch and wonder if you hadn't better start 'em. If something is wrong maybe you will have time to get it fixed. But you decide from previous experience that those extra gallons are too valuable.

You happen to look at the co-pilot and find him looking at you also, and you exchange grins, sort of; and you go over emergency procedure. It will be hard to talk during the raid itself and things will happen so fast that you must have a teamwork system all set in case anything should happen. As you glance at your watch again you see it is finally time to get going, and with a sigh of relief you go into action. The engines start, everything checks O.K., and you take your place in the line of taxiing ships.

Then the lead plane starts down the runway and you settle yourself in your seat. At any time up to now, from the first rumor of bomb-loading to the take-off, it would have been quite possible to have the mission scrubbed for any one of a number of reasons and you would have had your work and worry for nothing. This might happen several times for every mission you actually undertake. Or worse yet, when you were all set the schedule might have been delayed an hour or so and you would have had some more of that waiting. After take-off this is still likely but not so likely.

Then it is your turn and you get into take-off position. At last, for the first time since bomb-loading, you feel like mustering a grin. A check with the co-pilot to make sure you are all set, and you give her the gun. The lady is a little heavy this morning; those bombs with the chalked greetings on them slow her down; but well before she reaches the end of the runway she is on her tiptoes and you are air-borne.

Assembling the smaller formations into larger ones keeps your mind and hands busy. Gradually the beginning of the day's operation unfolds before you in your grandstand seat, right on schedule. Reluctantly you watch the coast of England slip beneath your wings. A last look and you settle down to the business at hand. Actually you feel pretty good and wonder why.

Soon the climb to altitude starts. That is the critical period. If you can nurse those engines to take this heavy load up there, without straining them unduly, they probably won't let you down. This climb period is where the weaknesses show up and also where most of the fuel goes. So it behooves a man who wants a future to use all the controls available to get the mostest for the leastest from the engines without punishing them. Plenty of time to strain their guts later in a pinch.

The last couple of thousand feet of climb, with the enemy coast in view, you do with your fingers crossed; but the lady pulls herself up to the assigned altitude and levels off to catch her breath for the battle to come. Almost immediately your searching eyes pick up a swarm of sinister dots coming up to meet you. So soon today? At that distance it is almost impossible to see such small objects, but you do. Experience is a hard teacher. There is no mistaking. Nothing else looks quite like a bunch of enemy fighters coming up to blast you out of the sky. They come up from behind, some of them, and pass you at your altitude as if you were standing still. Climbing, they go on ahead, after making several feints to see where the inexperienced gunners are who will fire when they are out of range.

There is a short period of looking each other over as you each choose a likely opponent. You know at the same time they are getting in position behind and possibly above you—and you sincerely hope your gunners see them.

The different enemy fighter groups have different tactics, and you watch the preliminary feints to see how the first attack develops, to see if it is the first team you are up against today. Then in they come right at you, four or five of them. At the same time you can feel your rear guns opening up and know there is an attack coming from the rear that you can't see. But you set your ears to waiting for some signal that your gunners want the ship moved this way or that to uncover a gun. You can get some indications of the tail attacks too by watching the rear guns of the ships in front of you as they try to cover you.

It is funny what you think of in a split second before the fighters in front of you, very rapidly coming closer, open fire. There is that argument you have been having with your navigator about the color of the flashes from the business end of a 20-millimeter. Now you can settle it. You watch the incoming fighters to see which have chosen you as their target—because when they open fire you want to have just left the spot they were aiming at. Some of these boys are pretty good shots.

The leading edges of the wings of the first three suddenly erupt in a series of flashes. (There, by golly, they *do* look greenish. Wait till we get down; I told Benny so.) They are going after that ship to the right. You notice they start a half-roll, keeping their fire on the selected target. It takes a darned good pilot to do this. It *is* the first team you are up against today.

Watch it! That pair are coming at you. Yes sir, it is you that they are after. It is a comforting sight to see your nose guns' tracers going out to meet them and even more comforting to see the supporting fire from the other ships in your formation. One attacker doesn't like it and peels off, but the other keeps boring in. Before you expect it he opens fire and you see the burst of his 20-millimeter in a row of little white puffs in front of your nose. He was too anxious and opened fire out of range. Your guns were pushing him too hard. He breaks off and goes out of sight to the rear, surrounded by a stream of tracers. A beautiful sight.

You feel your tail guns go again and hear your tail gunner yell, "I got one of the so-and-sos," and a pleasant glow goes through you. They come up again and hover out of range in front, but not so many of them. In they come again but not so enthusiastically, as a wall of fire goes out to meet them. Our formation is tight and the fire support is terrific.

After a few more spasmodic attacks they just stay out there and watch. They have failed to break the formations up and there were no stragglers for them to butcher. All right, they will wait and get us on the way back after the flak has shaken us up a little. With a final pass at us they peel off and go down to refuel. There weren't enough of them, but they will see to that on our way out.

You turn the controls over to the co-pilot and take a look around to see if you were hit. You check the crew and they are fine. The enemy never touched us. You check with the navigator to see when you are due over the target and then relax a bit. Without realizing it you were working pretty hard there for a while; but there was plenty of incentive to work.

You check your ammunition with the gunners and look at the gas gauges. Oh, oh, 3 and 4 are getting pretty low—and you are still going into Germany. Well, there is no help for it. The trouble you were having with No. 1 engine on the climb seems to have ironed itself out. Thank goodness the formation ahead is turning in to the target. It was a long way in but you know it will be twice as long out.

The formations ahead are approaching the target. There can be no mistaking its position—and by now every Jerry knows what the target for the day is. Just ahead of the leading elements appear little black puffs of smoke. Flak! Over the target is one place you can't dodge it. You are working a hundred per cent for the government and zero per cent for yourself. You just sit there and take it.

Those harmless-looking little black puffs now seem to sprinkle the first group of planes and you wait for one to go down, but they all go through it apparently unscratched. It takes a lot to knock a Fortress down.

Formation after formation goes over the target and the little black puffs have spread out into an ever-darkening black cloud. Jerry knows that you have to go through that one place in the sky and he is putting up everything he has got. When your turn comes the cloud is actually too thick to see through. You have heard stories of flak so thick you could get out and walk on it, and you see again the basis for those stories.

Then you are in range and the little black puffs are sprinkling your own formation. It somehow seems different when it happens to you. A puff, a second, and then a third appear just off your wing, each one getting closer so that you see the fourth one will be square on you. You really sweat out that fourth one for a second or two that seems an eternity, but it never comes. You rarely see the one that hits you.

Now you are really being peppered with them. Bursts appear between you and the next ship with loud whoompfs. Several puffs appear dead ahead and there is a strong desire to pull up or go down to avoid them. But that can't be done on the bomb run. You can hear the spent particles rattle off the tough hide of your ship. At least you hope they are spent.

As you enter the black cloud over the target the air becomes quite bumpy and you have your hands full keeping her steady and in place, so you don't see all the close ones. Maybe just as well, but your poor co-pilot has to see them.

All this time you are waiting for the bombs to drop from the ship ahead. It seems like a very long time to have to fly straight and level and serve as such a darned good target and not be able to do anything about it. Suddenly beautiful sticks of bombs begin to appear in neat stacks from out of the ships ahead, and then comes that feeling you have been waiting for so long—one you'll never forget. The ship gives a startled little jump and seems to shake herself free of the load she has been carrying all this way for Uncle Sam, and the bombardier sings out, "Bombs away."

Brother, from that moment on, you and your ship are working a hundred per cent for yourself. Your job for the government has been done and all you have to do now is to get home.

In the midst of your feeling of elation there is another feeling. The ship takes a sharp lurch. Flak! You're hit. A hurried glance assures you that all the props are there and the engines are not burning. Then a light smoke and a smell of hot oil permeates the cockpit. Something is burning. A search of the engine instruments again reveals everything in order. It was evidently only the fuselage that was hit. Something down in the nose is burning. As your co-pilot looks down there, you check the instrument panel again for trouble. Out of the corner of your eye you catch something wrong. The hydraulic pressure is down to zero.

The bombardier's head appears from down below and signals everything O.K. Then as your formation shakes itself free of the flak you put the evidence together and decide the hydraulic line below was hit and sprayed hot oil around a bit and maybe the flak smoldered a bit in the blankets you had down there for first-aid purposes. Nothing serious yet.

Free of the flak, you take careful inventory. Yes, the fuel in 3 and 4 *is* running low. Really too low. But there is nothing much that you can do about it for the present.

You look out at the formation, and the effects of the flak—the harmless black puffs—are beginning to be apparent. Here and there a ship is straggling in the formation. Flak doesn't knock a ship down very often, but it can easily get an engine or a supercharger or an oil line, and the resulting loss of power makes it impossible for the ship to stay in formation. These stragglers are cold meat for enemy fighters.

Soon you should be getting fighter escort again—the unfriendly kind. You check everything carefully again. The lady is behaving fine but that gas is getting awfully low. Someone is calling you on the interphone and you realize the interphone system has been fuzzy for some time. It takes careful repeating to get over to you that the right waist gunner is having trouble with his oxygen. A check assures you that the pressure for the cockpit is still up, and not knowing just what is wrong, you tell him to do what he can. There is quite a bit of talking going on back there but you don't get much of what is said. That gasoline is worrying you. . . .

Suddenly all that is forgotten or pushed to the rear of your mind. There are those darting specks again. Enemy fighters! Wearily the formation tightens up a little—at least the planes that can.

You can see the fighters picking off the stragglers in the formation ahead. A Fortress suddenly picks up a wing and heads for the ground. Perhaps it is hit or perhaps it is just heading for the cloud cover below. Little white dots appear. Parachutes. It must have been hit. You count seven dots and hope that you missed a couple.

Then a flash of fire catches your eye. A Fortress blazing from nose to tail slowly peels off. There are no parachutes. When it happens way out in front it is kind of like a show. Too bad. Again you check your group and notice one of your squadron has begun to straggle, and a careful look shows an engine gone. Flak, probably, and the trouble just now showing up. You catch the ship's number and realize that the pilot is a buddy of yours. You have flown, eaten, and drunk with him for several months. An old friend in this business, and now he is slowly dropping out of formation. Your heart bleeds with the desire to drop back and cover him, but it would be two ships down instead of one. Besides, there are nine other lives on your ship you are responsible for and so you can't do it. If you were alone, then it would be just your own life—but you are not alone.

All these thoughts go through your mind as you see him slowly dropping back. In your heart you already know the answer. With few exceptions there is but one answer to dropping out of formation so deep in Germany with enemy fighters in sight.

He dives a little and with extra speed is able to get into a lower formation. But soon he is slowly dropping back again. Really there are few more pitiful sights than to watch a good friend of yours in such a condition. His crew is probably fine and the ship well able to fly home but not able to stay in formation; so finis.

Then you see eight German fighters going in on him; your group opens up with protective fire but you see the tracers dropping short, out of range. He is on his own.

As the fighters close in they open fire. White puffs of 20-millimeter surround his ship and then they are on him. All up and down the fuselage and wings are bright flashes of exploding shells. His No. 2 engine belches smoke and the ship gives a lurch. The fighters pass by him and the ship rights itself momentarily and the smoke dies down. For an instant it looks as if he has weathered the first storm; then slowly his ship peels off and heads down. The fighters are on him again. Twelve butchers on one crippled Fortress. As the Fort disappears into the cloud below, the top turret is still firing. Stout fellow. . . .

Then they come in at *you*, again and yet again, and you feel it will never end but are afraid it will. As each comes in from the front, or when the signals from the gunners tell you they are after you from the tail, you do what you can to make yourself a difficult target. It is physically hard work but the stimulus of seeing fighters and bullets coming at you does away with any feeling of tiredness for the moment.

A red light on the dash catches your eye. One gas tank is at warning level and you are still over Germany. You don't see how you can make it. Then a tremendous explosion rocks your ship and as you look around, first one engine, then another, and then the wing of the ship above burst into flames, and it quietly slips out of formation and is lost from view. You hope there were parachutes but can't see.

Another red light winks on as a gasoline warning and you decide you'll have to call the engineer from his gun to transfer and even up what is left in the tanks. You squint ahead for a welcome glimpse of the coast and can't see it, so you have the sneaking hunch you are still over Germany.

The navigator announces that our own fighter escort is due—the friendly ones—and you feel better. Sure enough you see them coming and call your gunners not to fire at the 47's. You want them to come in nice and close. For a moment you relax, almost forgetting that the enemy fighters are still coming at you.

Then it happens. Although physically it is not possible, you see at the same time 20-millimeter and tracers exploding along both wings and skimming the glass overhead. In a split second you take this all in and wonder vaguely why you aren't hit. But already you go into action, as you know something is very wrong, for there was no warning from your gunners. And then you realize what else was wrong; not a gun on your ship was firing. Since the ship is already on her nose and the tracers are still coming, you stand her on her tail and tuck yourself back tight into the supporting fire of the formation, loving each of those gunners covering you. Then suddenly the attack is over and you are still there, though those Jerries should have got credit for a "probable." They had you dead to rights.

It surprises you to find all your engines are still operating when you survey the holes and gaping tears in the wings. Cautiously you check pressures for a hit in the oil or fuel lines, but there is nothing wrong except the amount of gas left and the distance yet to go.

Then you find you have been trying to get some answer from the rear of the ship but there is only a dead silence to greet your anxious calls. One by one you call the men, but there is still no answer and you fear the worst. You try to figure out something to do but see nothing except to keep going.

A faint voice comes to you and you glue the earphones to your ears. "Tail gunner to pilot . . ." Eagerly you call back, and then with a lot of clicks and breaks comes "Tail gunner to pilot . . ." There is nothing more and your calls go unanswered, but although the indications are bad, you feel great. Mike is still alive.

The front part of the ship is isolated from the rear half. The bombardier calls to ask if he should go back and find out what is what and you agree that the loss of his gun is worth it to find out just what the answer is. Besides, the friendly Spits and 47's seem to have the situation well in hand—there are only occasional single enemy attacks now—and there in the distance is the welcome, oh so welcome coastline of Fortress Europe.

In a moment the bombardier is back, collecting all the emergency oxygen bottles in sight. You can feel his urgency and appreciate that he can't take time to plug in and let you know what he found. There must be someone still alive or there would be no need for the oxygen.

As you cross the coastline and head out over the water, more red warning lights wink on—the oxygen system is at warning pressure too, and the gas gauge is about worn out from testing tank after tank again and again. With the English coast in view (how you love it at a time like this!) you decide to drop back out of the formation to save gas enough to make the coast.

In a long slow glide, doling out the precious gas by spoonfuls to the faithful engines, you sweat out your chances of any enemy fighter having followed the formation out for stragglers. You can now see several other Fortresses doing as you are, under the watchful protection of your escort. Finally you reach the altitude where you think you can exist without oxygen and, turning the ship over to the co-pilot and navigator to find the nearest field, you start back to find what's wrong.

Moving slowly to conserve oxygen in spite of your eagerness to know the answer, you work yourself way back. And you discover that the oxygen system in the rear half of the ship has been knocked out. The whole picture fits together in your mind now—you remember the waist gunner calling in about oxygen, and all that senseless chatter before the silence.

After over half an hour at twenty-six thousand feet without oxygen, the gunners had finally succumbed to anoxia. They had tried to load and fire in their weakened state and then they had collapsed. Wise old Jerry had been watching, and had noticed your flexible guns waving in the breeze and the turrets no longer tracking (you had called the engineer out at that critical moment); and three or four enemy fighters had come in close and let go with everything they had.

Nobody had been hit but Mike, and he apparently got only a flesh wound in the leg. The bombardier is taking care of him now. Duke, the radio man, is still on his feet, staggering around trying to help but having no idea what he is doing. His flesh is quite black and icicles have formed on his eyelashes and hair. The others look the same way. You practically have to clip Duke to make him sit down and conserve what little oxygen there is left in his system.

All this time the ship is going down to more oxygen and warmth, so they will be O.K.—but what a shambles! You marvel that nobody else was hit. Somebody must be looking out for you and your crew.

You want to get home, where medical attention is surely waiting for Mike and the crew. You check with the navigator in the nose to see what distance remains. You are over England now. He is carefully pinpointing your route and keeping the co-pilot on the shortest course home. He knows that he can't afford to make a mistake.

When you get back to the cockpit, the co-pilot is looking longingly at each field you pass, and he even points out a few of the more likely ones; but you want to make home if you can, for the ambulance will be waiting and it may be a little messy, landing without brakes.

A check of the gas gauges shows that the engineer has kept them level; each is below thirty gallons; they can no longer be trusted. Of course all the red lights are on across the instrument panel, like a Christmas tree. But you are still flying.

Then when you have used up all but a minimum of your altitude and are about ready to grab the nearest field, the navigator calls in, "There's the field." Sure enough.

The bombardier wants to move Mike up to the waist in case of a messy landing, but you are afraid of moving him with a chance of a broken bone. Besides, there is no reason for your luck to stop now.

Making a circle to the long runway you discover that your radio is shot out. Firing all the signal flares you have (your engineer seems to like to shoot them) you come in on the final approach. The wheels look O.K. and then you are on. As soon as you have her under control you turn off into the grass to slow down, trying to judge your stop to end up near the ambulance.

Then she stops and you wave the ambulance to the tail and sigh— your job is done. Whew!!

Quickly, though, you jump out to check the doc's opinion of the crew's condition, especially Mike. Everything is functioning smoothly and efficiently without you, so you just watch. Mike looks up and smiles— "Nice landing, Bud"—and a lump comes to your throat.

As the ambulance drives away you turn back to gather up your equipment. There is a big crowd of curious ground crew and officers marveling that the ship came back with all those holes. A Fortress is tough. Suddenly you are terribly and desperately tired, but the job isn't done yet. There is yet the interrogation.

So you gather the crew's stuff together, and what is left of the crew, and climb on the truck to go to the interrogation. There you must go through it all over again, remembering everything in detail, remembering in each case time, place, and altitude.

The coffee and sandwiches help, but you miss familiar faces. Your squadron S2 officers come up and say so-and-so isn't back yet—did you see? Yes, he won't be back, is your answer. And his name is crossed off the list of doubtfuls.

Too tired to eat a meal, you head for the barracks. You shiver as you enter and see the beds of the crew that didn't come back. Clearly you can see each of their faces and remember things they said and did. It is funny, but you can remember a fellow much better when you believe him gone. You had so enjoyed living with those fellows. But you are awfully tired, too tired to figure it out.

Before your nerves have a chance to relax, men come in to collect the clothes of the crew that didn't come back. It makes you sick.

In a couple of days there will be another crew to get to know and like, new names on the board and new faces in the mess, and a little later more new faces. How long will it go on?

With these crews gone from the squadron it will be harder to get passes. There will be more practice missions you have to fly with new crews. Just as you doze off into a troubled sleep you hear, "We are alerted for tomorrow," and hope it isn't an early mission, you are so tired.

WHAT THE GERMANS TOLD
THE PRISONERS

(NOVEMBER 1944)

William L. Shirer

ON MAY 9, 1943, an innocent-looking little weekly newspaper of four pages, printed in English, was distributed for the first time by the German government to American prisoners of war in the Reich. It had a temporary name on the masthead—*The (What?)*. The prisoners were asked to suggest names, and a prize of 120 cigarettes was offered for the best suggestion. May 30th, when the fourth issue appeared, the paper had a name. It was *O.K.* The subtitle read *The Oversea Kid*. A captured doughboy by the name of A. R. Mawr received the 120 cigarettes.

Through *O.K.*, tens of thousands of American prisoners of war have received a weekly dose of Nazi propaganda, some of it so subtle and so expertly done that it would almost certainly influence all but the most worldly-wise young American prisoners.

The front-page editorial in the first issue was a minor masterpiece of deception. In a tone of great modesty and sincerity, the Nazi editor assured his readers that it would be the paper's purpose "to serve you the news, good or bad, in a simple and straightforward manner."

Actually, *O.K.* (which, one must remember, furnished American prisoners the only means—with the exception of German broadcasts which few could understand—of learning what was supposed to be going on in the world) served up as "news" little but Nazi propaganda in all its varied forms.

There was the typical Nazi appeal to prejudice against Jews and Negroes. There was the usual Nazi bias against Russia and Britain, the material prepared in such a way as to appeal to the latent feelings of some Americans about the British and about "Bolshevism." There was of course a steady barrage of propaganda purporting to show that Hitler was not the evil figure "the Jews" had depicted him as being, but a humble fellow whose only concern was the common man of Germany and indeed of Europe, and who moreover had nothing but the most friendly sentiments toward the American people.

But above all else there was a constant effort to convince the American prisoners that they had been swindled by their own government in being thrown into a war which was none of America's business; that the home front was not backing up the American troops; and that when they went home they would find a country which did not appreciate their sacrifices and had hardly been worth fighting (and being captured) for. Maury Maverick, for instance, was falsely quoted in the June 6th number of *O.K.* as stating that "the ten million American soldiers will be out of work when they return home."

Now the German government was perfectly within its rights in distributing propaganda to tens of thousands of captured American boys. Though our own Army authorities for a long time did not know that such rights existed and hence refrained from doing any "educational" work among Nazi prisoners of war in this country, there is nothing in the Geneva convention which forbids subjecting prisoners of war to propaganda. But the way in which the German government exercised this right was highly interesting. For it transparently revealed the Nazis' purpose.

The short-term objective of discouraging the prisoners as to the progress of the war by false military news and depressing items from the home front was, it seems to me, of slight importance—since these particular Americans could never fight again. But the long-range objective was of considerable importance. For even though they lost the war and were forced underground, the Nazis aimed, I believe, to send back to America thousands of American youths whom they had primed with poison about Jews, Negroes, striking unions, profiteering employers, and a corrupt democratic government. Thus, in their calculations, the seeds of Nazism might be made to sprout overseas and eventually aid them in their comeback in Germany and Europe.

In the first number, the editor gave his address as Saarlandstrasse 60, Berlin. It just happens that I used to know that address well. It housed, among other things, a Nazi bureau, made up mostly of officials from the Propaganda Ministry and the Foreign Office, which specialized in propaganda for America and Americans. One German official of my acquaintance there had been a student at Dartmouth; two others had taught at American universities. They knew America, its racy language, its likes, dislikes, and prejudices. And they knew our youth and put their knowledge to good purpose in the columns of *O.K.*

I have before me a complete set of copies of the newspaper from the date of its inception on May 9, 1943, through the Christmas number of December 26, 1943.

O.K. was tabloid in size, with four columns to the page. The front page usually carried four standard heads: "Editorial," "World and War News," "Military," and "Home Front."

The military news was merely a digest of the official communiqués of the German High Command for the week. In the very first number the sinking of the American aircraft carrier *Ranger* by a German U-boat was announced. For this false news, however, the High Command and not the editor must be blamed.

Under "World and War News" in the May 9th issue there were twenty-six items averaging five or six lines each. Every one of these was either a propaganda falsehood or had a propaganda slant. An example of the first: "The Jewish Press in Palestine is complaining of the introduction of the numerous clausus [*sic*] of all medical faculties in the United States, introduced with the object of safeguarding America from immigrant Jewish doctors." An example of the second: "Reports from Teheran received from Ankara speak of conflicts between Soviet and Polish troops."

The entire second page of the first number was devoted to an illustrated article on the Nazi "People's Car" to show the Americans what Hitler did for the "Poor Man." Said the author of this article: "I could, of course, make great capital out of the 'People's Car' for propaganda purposes. I shall avoid doing this however and remain strictly objective and technical." He also avoided telling his readers that not a single "People's Car" ever reached the hundreds of thousands of people who had been forced by Dr. Ley, head of the Labor Front, to make down payments.

Half of page four was given over to what appeared to be an admirable purpose. It consisted of a weekly German lesson by Otto Koischwitz. And who was he? Some readers will recall the name. He was none other than the one-time instructor at Hunter College who, after becoming a naturalized American citizen, betrayed the country of his adoption and returned to Berlin to become one of Dr. Goebbels' star propagandists against the United States. His very first "German lesson" for our boys contained a silly crack about a Jewish name.

The second number of *O.K.*, which was distributed on May 16th, differed little from the first. A front-page editorial attempted to convince the prisoners that while the "Anglo-Americans" had won a "tactical" victory in North Africa, it was the Axis which had won a "decisive strategic victory." And it went on to "prove" that the "Anglo-Americans" could never invade the continent of Europe. Among the misleading items under the heading "World and War News" were these: "The Australian government is negotiating in Washington for the transport of U.S.A. workers to Australia." And: "Donald Nelson announced that in the first quarter of 1943 only 18% of the production figure envisaged for the whole year has been reached."

Beginning with the May 23rd number, more space was given to

"Home Front" news. After all, a prisoner of war is more interested in news from home than in any other kind. But the kind of "news" from home which the Nazis fed our prisoners of war may be judged from these items in the "Home Front" column on May 23rd. One began: "A report from Washington deals with the ever increasing number of deserters in the U.S. Army." Another said: "A report published in the 'Philadelphia Record' states that the inmates of U.S. prisons and federal penitentiaries are being accepted by the United States Army for military service. . . . Convicts whom the board finds fit for service will be sent immediately to a training camp." And, wedged in between an item about increased taxes and one which said that Willkie's book proved that the Soviets "had wiped out the whole upper and middle classes," there was one beginning: "Of all countries in the world, the United States have experienced the greatest increase in Jews," which went on to give phony statistics.

Already these lonely American youths must have been beginning to get a discouraging picture of conditions back home.

For the next number they dug up a passage from an article by Ernest Hemingway which had appeared in *Esquire* in 1935. Entitled "Notes on the Next War," it was very strong stuff. The passage read: "They wrote in the old days that it is sweet and fitting to die for one's country. But in modern war there is nothing sweet nor fitting in your dying. You will die like a dog for no good reason. . . . A hell broth is brewing in Europe and we shall be brought in if propaganda and greed can swing us in. Europe has always fought. The intervals of peace are only armistices. We were fools to be sucked in once on a European war and we should never be sucked in again."

If you were sitting behind the barbed wire in Nazi land far from home, wouldn't Mr. Hemingway's words make you think? And wouldn't the utterances of other writers? The Nazi editor of *O.K.* knew his literature. He roped in several well-known authors to rub his message into the prisoners.

In the same issue that presented Mr. Hemingway, James Joyce was also brought in under the title "Another Prophet?" Thus: "James Joyce, whom experts consider the greatest English-language writer of our century, made one of his characters in his novel *Ulysses* (page 635) predict: 'A day of reckoning is in store for mighty England despite her power of pelf on account of her crimes. There will be a fall and the greatest fall in history. The Germans and the Japs are going to have their little lookin . . .' "

But the Nazi propagandists really went to town with Mr. Louis Bromfield, who unwittingly gave them a chance to score a hit with current material. *O.K.* for October 31, 1943, ran on its front page a two-column photograph of an American butcher shop which from the looks of the window and from the signs in it was obviously empty, closed, and for rent. Underneath the photograph the Nazi editor had written the following caption: "There are two things you must have in order to run a meat store—meat and butchers. Neither being available, this U.S. shop is now for rent. (See Article on Page Two.)"

The article on page two turned out to be the complete text, with suitable illustrations, of the famous piece which the famous author and gentleman farmer wrote for the *Reader's Digest* of August, 1943. In *O.K.*, as in the *Digest*, it was entitled: "We Aren't Going to Have Enough to Eat."

It is not difficult to imagine the feelings of an American prisoner in Germany whose own stomach was kept satisfied only by extra food sent him by the United States Army and the American Red Cross when he learned that his folks back home weren't going to have enough to eat and that specifically "by then [February] most of our people will be living on a diet well below the nutrition level. Before we have finished, this tragic food situation will go down as one of the most senseless scandals in American history."

After all, the German people were eating well enough. Even a prisoner of war could see that. America must be in a bad way if it was letting its people starve so early in the war. Or was the Nazi-edited *O.K.* putting something over on them? Propaganda? Misquoting the *Digest* and Mr. Bromfield? Some American prisoners of war must have entertained such misgivings and must actually have written in to the editor about the Bromfield article, for on November 28th *O.K.* came back with a vengeance. The middle two columns of the first page on November 28th carried an editorial with the heading: "Propaganda?" The editor frankly admitted that "inquiries from several Prisoner of War Camps" concerning the Bromfield article had reached him. Was it propaganda? Well, he would give his American readers in the camps "some systematic information."

"This article," he wrote gleefully, "was taken word for word—even the same title was used—from the *Reader's Digest,* August, 1943. The pictures were taken from the *Saturday Evening Post,* August 14, 1943." Whereupon to clinch the argument he reproduced, directly under his editorial, a photostatic copy of the first page of Mr. Bromfield's article as it appeared originally in the *Digest.* There could be no doubt of its authenticity.

"It was and still is our policy," the editor wrote, "to publish a Newspaper for you which is purely an informative and entertaining journal." As for propaganda, he would enlighten the poor doughboy prisoners a little. "In order to influence people propagandistically," he continued, "one must know: why—and in what direction. Are you Germans to whom we want to bring our way of thinking? No! . . . Aren't you after all 'involuntary guests,' Oversea Kids, whom we are trying to bring a cross-cut of world-wide happenings in an informative manner?

"Do you call that propaganda?"

All in all it was as effective a job as I have ever seen a Nazi propagandist perform. The falsehoods in *O.K.,* of course, continued in almost every line in the paper, but I cannot help but feel that after the Bromfield incident the American prisoners of war swallowed the distorted reports on home-front degeneration more fully than ever before.

Some of the American writers served up to our boys by *O.K.* are not familiar to me. There is one Curtis Thorn Ley, for example, described as "an American," who contributes an article on France which actually turns out to be primarily about the United States. I give a sample quotation: "Truly this is another tragic era. The United States of America, who might have maintained peace for their own people and have secured peace for the world, chose instead—in the hope of establishing a super-imperialism—to associate themselves with England in the support of atheist Russia for the spread of terror and total war throughout the world. . . . 'My dear friend Stalin'—as Roosevelt addresses a murderer without parallel in history—is being supported by the United States and Great Britain with money, arms, and munitions. Thus the real issue of the war today becomes: European civilization and culture versus godless Bolshevism. . . . In 1941 President Roosevelt solemnly promised American mothers that they need never fear the loss of a single American son in wars on foreign soil. Already, however, thousands of American sons have lost their lives in attempts to deliver American supplies to the Bolshevists and today thousands more are being sacrificed in the invasion of North Africa and the nightly bombing of the civilian population on French soil."

As we have seen from the Hemingway and Bromfield affairs, a favorite technique of the Nazi propagandists is to make use of American publications to influence the American war prisoners. On June 13th, part of the front page of *O.K.* was given over to a photostatic copy of an editorial from the Chicago *Herald and Examiner* of January 5, 1937, in which one of Mr. Hearst's editorial writers let go on the subject of "Soviet Russia: Foe of Peace." The Nazi editor gave it his own title: "Lest We Forget."

This, in part, is what our prisoners read in Mr. Hearst's own peculiar type: "The basis of all the trouble in Europe is Soviet Russia and its militant communism. The armed forces of Germany and Italy are not formed to fight England and France. BUT TO REPEL SOVIET RUSSIA. Democracy is not iron-handed enough to deal with communistic sabotage. . . . After Fascism was chosen in preference to communism in states that put order above anarchy, Russia persisted in its impudent interfering. . . . No state is safe, no civilization, no culture is safe AS LONG AS RUSSIA SURVIVES." (Capital letters Mr. Hearst's.)

That, after all, was exactly what Hitler had been blabbering for years, but it undoubtedly was more effective with American prisoners of war to have it come from a Chicago newspaper of large circulation.

Another Chicago paper of even larger circulation—or at least its publisher, Col. Robert R. McCormick—also came in handy for Nazi propaganda to our prisoners. *O.K.* for November 14, 1943, published in its "Home Front" news this little item: "McCormick of the Chicago *Tribune* complains bitterly of the way censorship is handled in America. McCormick points out that originally censorship was introduced for strictly military purposes. Now, however, he declares, censorship is used to keep the political failures of the U.S. government a secret from the American public, and to influence its general attitude, while the simple truth is withheld."

In all fairness it must be said that the Nazi propagandists in *O.K.* did not confine their newspaper quotations to those from the Hearst or McCormick press. They took anything they could use from any American source—newspapers, magazines, and radio broadcasts—to drive home to our prisoners their propaganda line that the home front had let the soldiers down. Thus the August 22nd number of *O.K.* published on the front page and editorial from the Philadelphia *Inquirer* under the heading "American Home Front Seems a Tragic Picture." The editorial was quoted, in part, as saying: ". . . food grows scarce; labor troubles increase, the coal strike cannot be settled by any sensible formula. This picture would not be satisfactory in peace; it is tragic in war." Again, on December 5th, quotations from the *New Republic* attacked the State Department and reported disputes among two factions of "the Jewish community." And on July 18th, a CBS broadcast was quoted as saying that the battle of production was going poorly.

This theme was dinned into the hapless prisoners week after week until some of them must have raged with anger at the home front and others must have been profoundly discouraged with their native land. *O.K.* for August 1st carried a half-column story from the Philadelphia *Independent* under the heading: "War Dept. Asked to Keep Negro Troops out of Miss." In the "dispatch," Governor Johnson is reported to have asked Senator Bilbo to advise "Secretary of War Henry Stimson to promise that no more northern Negro troops be sent to this area."

Hatred for Jews was fanned more by the constant publication of little items, true or false, week after week, than by any direct attacks. The Nazis were rather good at this form of propaganda. A typical example was in the issue of September 12th. It was just a little false item under "Home Front" news: "Shakespeare's 'The Merchant of Venice' has been banned in the United States. The reason given is that the celebrated play might wound the feelings of the Jews."

Devious and persistent attempts to stir up hatred for America's allies, Britain and Russia, were made in almost every number of *O.K.* In the number for July 18th, whose first page was given over largely to stories of American strikes, the entire second page was devoted to a hair-raising account of "The Mass Murder of Winniza" which the Russian GPU [secret police] was alleged to have committed. Even to a propaganda story of this kind, the Nazis knew how to give an American slant. Thus the author turned his thoughts from the mass murder of Winniza to: "I have been thinking . . . of the dead of Dieppe taken away from the blood-stained beach in big hay-wagons last summer. They died in battle so that the killers of Katyn should triumph. And the boys are dying again on the shores of Sicily this summer, so that the slayers of Winniza may live."

Feeling against the British was worked up by both the direct and the indirect approach. Thus a captured American prisoner in North Africa was quoted: "There was always trouble and friction with the British, who happen to be our Allies. Our losses in men and equipment were large and our morale sank still lower, especially when we got to thinking about Algiers and the States. We asked ourselves: 'Why all this nonsense?'"

In the July 4th issue, there was a head: "The Fourth of July"—with a blank space below it. "This space," explained the Nazi editor, "had been set aside for a short meditation on today's Fourth of July. Just as we were going to Press, the editor decided to take this article out, as under prevailing circumstances it might be misunderstood or misinterpreted by our readers as a joke on America's independence of Britain."

The "friendliness" of Hitler for the American people was stressed. *O.K.* for September 9th carried a whole-page article entitled "Hitler and the Western Hemisphere" with a note that it was published "by the request of the American war prisoners." There is a nice gentle picture of Der Führer. Most of the article consists of an interview which Hitler gave on June 14, 1940, the day that Paris fell, to "an American newspaperman" (I recall it was Karl von Wiegand of the Hearst press) to the effect that he had no quarrel with the United States.

Do not think that this weekly paper published by the Nazis for our prisoners in Germany was all propaganda. The Nazis knew how to make propaganda palatable by mixing it with other things. They obviously made a special effort to give the prisoners sport news from home. The July 18th issue had three columns of sport news complete with major league baseball standings as of a month before and with batting averages. Sometimes the editor apologized for the lack of sport news. No American papers were received that week, he explained.

In the very first number of the publication the editor made an appeal for contributions from the prisoners themselves. He knew that if he could get the men to read what their fellow prisoners were writing they would read his propaganda as well. His object was to get the captives to feel that it was "their" paper. "The editor aims," he wrote, "at making this weekly something of value, a friend of your Sundays and an integral part of your communal life. But he cannot possibly achieve these aims without your collaboration. He would be glad, therefore, if you would co-operate by sending contributions."

At first the contributions were slow to come in but later there were so many that a two-page "literary supplement" was occasionally published. Even so, an unaccountably large proportion of the contributions are by a single person—one Frank Stebbing. The supplement for July 25th, for instance, has an "editorial," a short story, and a poem—all by Stebbing. But some of the poems and prose pieces that came in from the P.O.W.'s tear your heart out, for they are the expressions of profound loneliness and hunger for the love of women. There were, to be sure, verses and essays and especially cartoons which attempted to portray with true American humor the plight of the war prisoner. But even in these you can sense the overpowering longing to be home which is expressed in the opening lines of one of Stebbing's poems:

"Home sometimes sounds so far away. So lost in ancient yesterday,
Now and again it seems, That I was never there at all. . . ."

It was with such homesick contributions from fellow prisoners, plus baseball scores, cartoons from *Collier's* and the *New Yorker*, cheesecake pictures of the glamour girls of Babelsberg (the German Hollywood), crossword puzzles, cute pictures of babies (and sentimental poems about them), reproductions of pre-war advertisements for La Salle convertibles, and all the other entertaining or nostalgic items which might appeal to prisoners of war—it was with all these that *O.K.* surrounded its phony blend of real news and distorted propaganda. The overall purpose of the paper seems to have been to amuse and interest the prisoners while deftly planting in their minds the seeds of doubt, mistrust, and fear for the future which might set them against their fellow Americans and their country's allies after the war—thus contributing in post-war America to the kind of dissension and internal weakness upon which the enemies of the United States have always—unavailingly—relied.

REPORT FROM A CONSCIENTIOUS OBJECTOR

(JANUARY 1945)

William Fifield

WE'RE LOCATED IN an old Civilian Conservation Corps camp near Elmira, New York. There are 165 CO's in this camp, which is the Eastern reception center for Quaker-administered Civilian Public Service—the alternative service provided for men classified 4E (conscientious objector) in the draft.

The men here in camp now are quite young, as most of them are new draftees and thus likely to be eighteen-year-olds. They fall into three divisions: the men who object to war on the basis of the religious precepts of their church or of their personal interpretation of the Bible, all holding that they owe their allegiance to a higher law than that of the state; the humanitarians who object on the basis of Jesus' philosophy of the brotherhood of man and the sacredness of human personality; and the so-called "political" objectors, the socialists, independent liberal thinkers, and so on, who subscribe to the ethic of cooperation as against coercion, but certainly don't consider themselves religious in the conventional sense. This last group is small; the first group is the largest of the three.

This camp, though a Quaker camp, is only about one-third Quaker in membership. There are even fewer Quakers in the other Quaker-administered camps, though in the Mennonite and Brethren camps the ratio of men holding the faith of the administering church is much higher. In this camp the eleven Methodists are second numerically to the Quakers, and there are five Baptists, seven Congregationalists, eight Presbyterians, one Catholic, an Orthodox Jew, four Jehovah's Witnesses, a follower of Father Divine, eight Christadelphians (the Christadelphian church is one hundred per cent pacifist; in fact a man is expelled from the church if he takes any other position)—and there's a perfectly normal young fellow from New Jersey who sleeps on the cot beside me and who's studying to become a Ramakrishna Hindu monk. About half the men are married, and a fifth are fathers.

The camp is the labor source for the U.S. Soil Conservation Service nursery, and we put in fifty-one hours a week of labor for them. Most of my work since I've been here has been in the big trees—climbing seventy- and eighty-foot pines and picking the cones for seed to be used in reforestation. I've also put in some long days on my hands and knees weeding seedling tree beds, a day latrine-digging, two days spreading manure in the rye fields, and have done other assorted jobs. Most of the men are engaged in this kind of work, only a small number being held in camp to make up the kitchen, maintenance, and clean-up crews.

During our work day—from 7:25 A.M. till 5:00 P.M.—we are under the supervision of government men, civilians. The rest of the time we are under camp government, with rules worked out by ourselves in keeping with the general camp plan laid down by the Quakers and Selective Service. We are allowed two overnight leaves per month, which enable a man to leave camp after work Saturday evening and stay away till Sunday midnight; and we earn thirty days' furlough a year at the rate of two and a half days a month.

Conscientious objectors are not paid and receive no dependency allotment. This has worked a severe hardship on men with families. We wear no uniforms and provide our own clothes. When able to pay it, we are responsible for our maintenance of approximately thirty dollars a month. We have no accident or death compensation; this has caused quite an issue, as a large number of men have been injured, some seriously, and several killed. Some of the men in Civilian Public Service do very hazardous work—notably those in the smoke-jumper unit in the West who parachute into forest fire areas, and the human guinea pigs who submit themselves to various diseases and disabilities. One of the most dangerous—and significant—of the experiments in which these men have taken part has begun this winter in Minneapolis, where a group of volunteers is being systematically starved for six months until their condition parallels that of the most severe war sufferers abroad; they will then be restored through the use of various rehabilitation diets. The data obtained will indicate the most effective ways of feeding debilitated peoples after the war.

There is a very considerable disagreement about pacifism here in camp, though there are no men who could reasonably be suspected of being draft dodgers. The careful FBI investigations—of well over ten thousand cases to date—have seen to that. The disagreement is largely between the humanitarians, who feel called upon to make their pacifism work in the practical world, and the fundamentalists, who are content to let God's word stand at face value without the need of human modification. The humanitarians believe that only through the spreading of the gospel of love as against the doctrine of force can permanent peace be obtained and a better world achieved. The fundamentalists—many of whom believe in the Biblical War of Armageddon which according to their interpretation of the Scriptures will bring the end of the world—feel that they must adhere to the injunctions of God as they understand them, even if by this they accomplish no positive good on this earth.

The men vary as widely in type as they do in belief. Here we have fewer farmers than in other camps because of the area from which we are drawn, but the majority of the nation's CO's are farmers. This is because two of the historic peace churches—the Mennonites and Brethren—are so generally rural. The farmers are inclined to be fundamentalists, or at least conventionally religious—but along with them we have the philosophical and "political" objectors. These fellows are from the cities, and are inclined to be highly educated. Exclusive of farmers, there are more teachers in Civilian Public Service than men of any other profession. One-sixth of all the men in this camp are teachers—enough to staff a good-sized college. We have a number of men with doctor's degrees, seven scientists, eight history professors, a Broadway actor, the author of a standard textbook on atrocity propaganda, Massine's understudy from the Ballet Theatre, a casket salesman, a relief worker caught by the Germans in France and released from internment in Baden-Baden only last March, three fashion designers, four radio announcers, and to round things off a weight-guesser from a carnival.

HOW WE PLANNED THE
INVASION OF EUROPE

(MARCH 1945)

C. Lester Walker

ON JULY 1st, over two and a half years ago, a dull and cloudy Wednesday morning, at about a quarter to ten, certain British and American officers began to arrive at the sandbagged entrance of London's 20 Grosvenor Square. Each man was detained at the door—for papers and personal recognition. Then each made his way inside, entered an old-fashioned, slow-moving elevator, and ascended to a room on the fourth floor. Here, shortly after ten o'clock, twenty-five to thirty colonels and generals took their appointed seats at a conference table and began the detailed planning for the invasion, through France, of Nazi Germany.

What happened between that date and the morning of June 6, 1944, when the great expedition struck the shores of Normandy, was beyond doubt the most gigantic as well as the most extraordinarily complex single operation two nations have ever undertaken. From the outset it depended on combined planning between the military leaders of the United States and Great Britain, with particular parts and missions assigned to the forces of the country best able to carry them out quickly and efficiently. What follows is chiefly the story of the American side of the operation as it was conducted both in this country and in Britain, the great base from which the invasion was launched.

It can be revealed now that the planners, at that date, had not one but at least five overall plans. Each had its own code name, and as the meeting progressed the conferees kept referring to *Falcon, Matador, Afghan, Épée, Tamarack.* *

Falcon was the original British plan for return to the Continent, and had been worked up soon after Dunkirk. Long before this meeting it had selected all possible invasion landing areas. *Matador* was the air offensive—the long-range strategic bombing plan.

Afghan was a plan for an emergency which might, conceivably, occur. It represented an American force being built up in northern Ireland with all speed. The force would be ready to jump off in September if, by chance, Russian resistance at that time seemed to be faltering.

Épée was the Normandy operation. And *Tamarack* was the plan for the United Kingdom—the buildup of men and materials in preparation for *Épée*.

Taken as one these plans called for the biggest organization job in human history. The American Army had to put over a million men into the United Kingdom by D-day. Its own and the British Army Service Forces had to supply them with more than a million different items. In over 1,100 British towns the Engineers must build a hundred thousand buildings, all this in addition to the vast amount of supplies and services rendered to the American forces by the British under Reverse Lend-Lease. The air plan ordered landing strips equaling in total length a highway from Moscow to America. At least 18,000,000 ship tons of cargo would be unloaded at United Kingdom ports, and tens of millions of individual crates and packages piled mile after mile on thousands of country lanes all over England—and piled

---

Except in the case of Torch, *which appears later in this article, fictitious code names have been substituted for the correct ones. Such substitution was requested by the War Department for the purpose of continuing security.—The Editors.*

so that someone would know what was in each pile on each lane when invasion time came. For the Channel crossing 660 different kinds of landing and escort craft would be designed and built; and for the great day itself the British and American navies would have to co-ordinate the movements of many thousand vessels, each one scheduled to perform a particular task with a particular load of men and equipment at a certain place at a certain time.

Preparation for the July London planning conference had been made in this country in April with the appointment of one man. One day General Somervell, head of our Army Service Forces, called into his office in the Pentagon Building fifty-seven-year-old Lieutenant General John Clifford Hodges Lee of the Engineers. "We're making you Commander in Chief of the Services of Supply in the European Theater of Operations," Somervell said—and the American end of the logistics for *Tamarack* and *Épée* was under way.

Lee's colleagues are fond of saying, "Today the way General Lee set about getting started on that colossal job seems a little quaint."

Lee took an obscure office in the down-at-the-heels Munitions Building and came in with no staff, just one officer aide. He talked with Generals Pershing and Harbord—on how supply had been organized in the last war. He read the books on the subject, which were few. Then one day he suddenly picked some men. The heads of the technical services—the chiefs of Engineers, Ordnance, Transportation, and the rest—were called in on a ten-minute schedule and asked, "Who's your ablest assistant?" Lee, as General Somervell's deputy, then picked that man for his staff in the United Kingdom.

On May 23, 1942, less than a month after appointment, he was in England, shaping up things for the July conference. That meeting laid the framework for execution of the different plans and underscored Lee's primary problem: airfields for prosecution of Army Air Forces' *Matador.* Hundreds of them. With all speed.

So important did Combined Chiefs of Staff consider *Matador* that they gave it priority over all other plans—a rating which continued practically up to D-day.

This enabled Lee's Engineers to rush construction on a network of airdromes which to some of our British cousins must have seemed utterly fantastic. The *Matador* planners intended that by January 1, 1944, it should be physically, geographically, and operationally impossible to put another airfield in Scotland or England. It was. On that date any plane three thousand feet up anywhere over England could make a dead-stick landing on a concrete runway.

While this vast construction went on, the Air Forces people were working out *Matador*'s strategical plan. In simplest terms, they conceived of this as stopping the heart of the German Wehrmacht by smashing such industries as combat aircraft, ball and roller bearings, rubber, and oil.

So in Air Force offices here and in England hundreds of specialists began working out the infinite details of the target plan. Facts had to be assembled by the thousand. Every German factory which produced one of the vital target items must be uncovered. Its exact location, its production, and the ratio of that production to the total production of Germany must be known. It was not enough, for instance, to know that Huls produced great amounts of synthetic rubber. It had to be determined (as it was) that it made 29 per cent of all Nazi buna. Schweinfurt, it was ascertained, produced 40 per cent of the ball and roller bearings. But it was also necessary to know on just what streets in just which three factories.

A legion of Air Force researchers, names unknown as far as history is concerned, worked thousands of hours over dull statistical records, charts, and tables. Other Air Force officers called on agencies like the Board of Economic Warfare and the Office of Strategic Services and on thousands of key men in industry. As the data piled up, a committee of military and industrial experts, some of the best brains of England and America, analyzed every factor relevant to the *Matador* bombing plan. They would discuss for hours, say, a certain steel plant to determine just how crucial to the enemy's front-line fighting effort would be the loss of a million tons of prime-quality steel for plane engines and gun barrels. Finally the *Matador* planners knew what they wanted to know:

just how many towns the German Wehrmacht depended on, and how many of these were truly important and should be bombed out.

The highest headquarters in Great Britain then had to plan a system of objectives and an order of bombing; next the whole operation must be broken into phases, and for each phase a time limit set. An operation must be completed within the specified period, or the cumulative effect of the bombings would not be achieved.

On individual targets some of the planning got down to such fine details that the planners could (and did) write a prescription for destruction of, say, a particular wing of a particular precision tool plant, which would grade the target's vulnerability, specify the type of bomb to use, the type of fuse for the bomb, the minimum number of bombs it would be necessary to drop, the area of effective radius of each bomb blast on that particular target, and the exact number of hits which would be required to demolish it. There were even error charts—showing that at 25,000 feet it would take fifteen planes to knock out the building, but at 10,000 feet only five planes, and at 5,000 feet only three.

The plans had to specify the right planes for the right jobs. Certain types of bombers for certain types of targets. Certain fighter protection for certain missions. Unless this was carefully studied and watched, costly upsets occurred.

Frequently there were interruptions in the *Matador* plan. Any one of a hundred contingencies could monkey-wrench parts of the time schedule and make replanning necessary. An example (one of the most spectacular) was the submarine campaign. It came close, we know now, to ruining *Matador*.

While General Lee was building up airfields in the winter of '42–'43, the subs, working in packs, were sinking shiploads of Air Force supplies and planes faster than in the planners' worst nightmares. The Combined Chiefs of Staff decided that the subs would have to be stopped or the invasion plan as scheduled just couldn't go on.

The British urged that planes be taken off *Matador* and put on

Atlantic patrol. The Americans demurred. Icing, they thought, over the north Atlantic in wintertime would make maneuver of the big bombers impossible. But the British argued that the R.A.F. Coastal Command had been operating its Halifaxes and other bombers on Atlantic patrol for months. In addition they cited their previous winter's flying from Montreal to Prestwick, Scotland. They had had only three days' interruption and only four planes lost. Winter or no winter, they insisted, American Liberators could help. In due course some American anti-submarine Liberators were based in Britain and, co-operating with other long-range aircraft of Coastal Command, covered the convoy lanes (the British navy working the waters below) in a great oval stretching from England to the American coasts. They photographed and bombed—and Nazi orders at that time were for submarines to surface and fight it out with the planes.

Despite these tactics the pilots went down to two hundred feet and photographed. The shots were delivered to the central anti-submarine control room, located underground, and from these records it was soon possible to tell the cruising range of the operating enemy submarine.

"Those were days," one Air Forces planning officer has remarked, "when the men of the A.A.F. and R.A.F. really put in time. Crews would work on their planes twenty hours at a stretch. I saw them— with a wrench in one hand and a sandwich in the other—fall asleep by the plane, nap for an hour, and then get up and work again. They loaded the planes so full of gasoline that when they took off, the ground crews would involuntarily squat, and then rise up with an 'Oof' as if to help lift the plane off the ground."

As a result of this intensified effort, submarine sinkings in the first three months increased notably. Still, to the planners it seemed a long, long road ahead to *Matador's* completion. Despite the quantities of planes operating against the submarines, winter would pass, spring, and summer, and it would be well into autumn before the A.A.F. would get enough aircraft in England to equal the minimum number which the planners estimated would be necessary to complete *Matador's* task.

However, the Engineers *were* building the airdromes fast. "So fast," one of them reporting on those hectic months has said, "that last year's Brussels sprouts, I remember, were still being gathered up between the runways even when we began to use them."

During these months Lee had moved his headquarters from London to a country town and was there developing as fast as possible the basic organization for *Tamarack*.

Port accommodations were his earliest worry. There seemed to be not enough ship berths in the United Kingdom to handle all the American shipping planned. Remember that the ports were already over-taxed supplying Britain's own far-flung forces and were seriously under-manned owing to the labor shortage. In addition the Luftwaffe was then doing its blitz; so every ship's cargo had to be cleared out of every port within twenty-four hours. Now the Americans proposed to schedule six tons of shipping for every one of the more than a million soldiers, and nearly an additional ton per man per month afterward.

Army Transportation Corps men then performed a gigantic jigsaw puzzle job. They analyzed every kind of cargo and matched it against facilities at every kind of port, so that each port could be used to maximum efficiency. Clyde ports, which were poor on handling heavy lifts, got ships loaded mainly with subsistence. Vessels heavy with tanks were scheduled to Newport. Ships with Air Corps bombs went to the Humber, and tugboats were dumped off at Liverpool.

The same Transportation Corps worked out the intricate details of getting all these shipments of goods to their thousands of storage depots in England. Since railroads and highways were already war-strained to the breakdown point, Transportation imported railroad equipment and operating personnel from America. Rolling stock requirements for *Tamarack* were 57,000 cars (from ordinary box cars to refrigerators and cabooses) and nearly 3,000 locomotives. Freight cars came knocked down and were assembled at a place on the Thames in the biggest car shop in the world. A month before D-day these shops had to close because there was not a single empty siding in England.

To save shipping space, trucks for *Tamarack* arrived in "twin-unit packs"—another product of some planner's fertile brain. "You took two trucks," a Highways Branch man of Transportation Corps has described it, "and took their wheels and some other stuff off and then slapped them in that coffin tight as two figs." So much shipping space was saved that huge twin-unit-pack assembly plants were set up. The packaged trucks were swung off the ships, assembled by Chrysler, Ford, and General Motors mechanics, given a one-mile trial, loaded up, and rushed off to a crossroads hamlet where was the biggest supply dump in the world.

Locomotives and freight cars which we supplied the French in World War I were, the *Tamarack* planners knew, now being used by the Germans. Locomotives for *Tamarack* were, therefore, built so as to last only four years. Freight cars were made to last three years—of plywood!

On the south coast our assault training center was being laid out on beaches where the surf had been "tested" and found most like Normandy's. Behind the training was a planning board which had sat in London and meticulously worked out "the doctrine." All the amphibious assault knowledge available had been sifted and weighed. Still it was necessary to make thousands of practice trials to be sure just what was the optimum way tactically to divide up thirty men— the number in each assault boat—into teams. How many in the rifle team, the wire cutters, the flame throwers, the rocket gunners, the automatic rifle team, the demolitionists? How many in each and in what order would they go in?

Day after day, beginning in September of '43, the theory was tried out with live ammunition and tens of thousands of American G.I.'s. Changes would be made and the new wrinkles tested next day under the guidance of the training school's "faculty" of six thousand officers and men. The whole problem involved a most delicate adjustment, for one man too few on any one team might spell the difference in invasion attack between success and fiasco.

Despite all the forethought, the invasion operation was so big that some breakdowns inevitably occurred. This meant replanning—someone, or a hundred someones, doing parts of the job over again. Some of the planners and personnel engaged on the already complex *Tamarack* organization were switched to work on another invasion plan. This was *Torch*. It was for the landings in North Africa and in itself a step toward the Normandy project. At first it was to be mounted entirely from the United Kingdom. Then the high-ups changed their minds—from both the United Kingdom *and* the United States.

Early in September it was discovered, to the general chagrin, that it was necessary to duplicate North African invasion supplies to the United Kingdom. Too much stuff already in England (and which by Normandy D-day *must* be stored so that someone knew what every package was and where) was too hard to find. Just before *Torch* shoved off for North Africa General Eisenhower had to be provided with nineteen rush shiploads of ammunition and equipment because he couldn't locate what he needed in time in British depots and warehouses.

Originally the British had stored our goods for us, as best they could under blitz conditions; and our own Service Forces had not arrived in Britain until after mid-July. Even so, replanning of *Tamarack*'s shipping, storage, and identification methods was obviously in order. Lee put some of his smartest colonels on the job, and this was the situation they found:

To order supplies, the commanding officer of, say, the Signal Corps had to know what he had on hand, what was en route from America, what items were in his requisitions now in the works, and his future needs over and beyond the above. And could he obtain all this information? Hardly ever.

When a ship arrived, he often found it impossible to know whether it contained his supplies. More than half our ships were arriving without manifests. Manifests which did arrive were unspecific. "Signal Corps Supplies: 24 Tons," they would say. But *what* Signal Corps supplies? For whom? Nothing on that. Markings on the individual packages were equally enigmatic. The package had to be examined in order to be sent to the right general's depots.

If a shipment of walkie-talkie radios arrived, the general couldn't tell what requisition they were based on. So he couldn't know the status of *any* of his requisitions! He was continually discovering that what he had ordered *rush* from the States had been on hand in the United Kingdom all the time. But he hadn't known where. One sad result, the officers working on the problem found, was that we were shipping thousands of tons of invasion equipment unnecessarily!

What was needed was a system which would tie in specific shipments with all their specific requisition and shipping papers, so that each one would cross-identify the other. A system so simple that the lowliest supply sergeant could operate it with two-thirds of his mind on his best girl.

In December the officers on the job presented Lee with their plan. It was called I.S.S.—Identification of Separate Shipments—and although perhaps an unromantic piece of work, it proved to be one of the masterpieces of planning of the invasion.

The whole system was based on a set of code letters and numbers. All covering documents showed these same markings. Port of embarkation in the States would send two copies of the documents in advance by air mail. When the ship was all loaded, the port would send a cargo-loading cable—a mere string of numbers and letters. Overseas, the Ordnance officers would compare the cable with previously received papers and know exactly what was on the boat. If the plane with advance papers was lost, or even if the ship went down, duplicate documents, or a duplicate shipload, could be made up immediately from the symbols of the cargo-loading cable.

"Now the commanding generals in England," one A.S.F. officer has stated, "could order five cotter pins and get them, and know where they were every minute. They knew what was in every box and where it was to go to. The plan worked so well it was even applied to dumps on the beach on D-day. We could say: 'At Dump 6, Aisle 2, Row 4, Tier 3, you will find your box of 300 spark plugs.'"

Don't imagine, however, that the planners' work was done once they devised the plan. Getting it accepted was something else. The British saw its merits right away and were enthusiastic, but our people were hesitant. Naturally—since adoption meant junking 100 per cent the existing Army systems, reorganization of every depot and every embarkation port in America—the change involved a colossal job.

The story goes that a certain colonel who had had a big finger in getting up I.S.S. became restive at its delay in adoption and suggested that he return to Washington, attend a certain High Command meeting in the Pentagon Building, and put the idea over. General Lee was willing; but the theater either wouldn't or couldn't furnish transportation. Remembering about several dozen detainees of German and Italian consular staffs from North Africa in British camps, the Colonel casually queried the American Embassy, "Shouldn't those people be sent to America?"

"Yes. But there's nobody to send them with."

The Colonel would take them. The Embassy was delighted and telephoned Washington and made arrangements.

A few days later, his presence in Washington unknown, the Colonel one morning at ten o'clock walked unannounced into the meeting—and into seventeen generals.

"What the devil are you here for?"

"To attend this meeting."

"By whose say-so?"

"I was sent."

"And then," the Colonel reports, "we closed the doors and for four hours went round and round."

The zealot returned to England some days later, official O.K. for adoption of I.S.S. in his pocket. In August General Somervell cabled him to return and present the new system to six thousand key officers. Just one man's work in one invasion replanning job!

Impatient armchair critics, of course, predicted frequently that the invasion would never come off. In those days *Tamarack* planners here in America matter-of-factly arranged to pile thousands of miles of four-inch petrol pipe in England, ordered the rotproofing of 500,000,000 burlap sandbags, the delivery of two and a half million miles of telephone wire, and scheduled the laying of special cable under the Channel.

Two years before D-day the Engineers were computing the bridging necessary for *Épée*. They figured thirty feet for every mile of French railroad and ordered it and stored it for *Tamarack* in England. On D-day American forces could produce replacements for every bridge in France.

The Engineers made 125,000,000 maps which went in with the attack troops. Their tide maps were so accurate that our tactical planners could predict the exact spot where a boat of given draft would touch down on any beach at any minute, and how many yards and what kind of footing a soldier would have to run over without cover. (Not like Tarawa, where the men waded a mile.) General Montgomery found difficulty in believing the claims, so one day he sent a plane to check on when the water would reach a certain row of obstacles. It was there, on the dot.

Even underwater obstacles were plotted on the maps by the Engineers. "There wasn't a pile driven," one Engineer planning officer has said, "scarcely a barnacle *on* a pile, that we didn't know about." Maps also showed the formation *under* the beach—whether shingle, peat, or limestone—and what loads it would bear. There was a map ready months ahead for pasting on the ramp of every landing craft — showing exits to the beaches and the walls nearby to be breached. Surveys showed when the surf would be likely to be three feet or higher, so as to break the silhouettes of men coming ashore.

Royal Navy Engineers practiced demolition of duplicates of underwater obstacles for months, until they knew how many seconds each kind would take. After them Engineer Special Beach Brigades checked the time it took to clear up the metal and debris.

To plan its casualty handling program accurately, the Medical Corps had to know both the country and the exact beaches of the landings as early as the autumn of '43. Its planners then estimated our wounded, using, among other data, reliable German figures for the ninety-day drive on Moscow. Every piece of medical equipment had to be packed so it was watertight and would float—from electric coagulation machines for stopping bleeding in brain surgery to hypo needles. Every individual soldier had to be provided with a sterile dressing and two 71/2-grain sulfanilamide tablets. The medical plan for invasion called for 800,000 units of blood plasma, 10,000 pounds of sulfa drugs, 600,000 doses of penicillin, 650,000 syrettes of morphine; and in planning the doctors had to allow for critical shortages of materials—such as alcohol, which goes into the making of aspirin, and the lack of which would reduce aspirin's availability.

Medicos in the Surgeon General's office set up a plan for evacuating the wounded which worked so smoothly that all casualties at the debarkation ports in England could be sorted out by categories (fracture cases, neuro-surgical, maxilo-facial, etc.) and each kind shipped on separate trains to proper similar-injury hospitals. Planning provided that every midnight the Surgeon General of the American forces would know the number of patients to be evacuated next day from the Continent and from England, and the exact number of vacant beds at that moment in every Army hospital in the United Kingdom. It was arranged so that if every telephone in England failed, the reports could still get in—by radio.

"Give aid as soon as possible," was the watchword of all the medical planning. So portable hospitals were devised which would land on the beach on D-day and perform major operations two hours later. Hospital planes were scheduled ahead by the hundreds. To save precious seconds there were special slings to transfer litters eight at a time from small landing craft to the big LST's. The latter were ready with specially anchored operating tables, and steadying straps for the surgeons, so work could go on no matter how choppy the Channel. "So expertly were the time-saving factors worked out," Surgeon General Kirk has declared, "that on D-day 80 to 90 per cent of the wounded received medical care within ten minutes after injury." And for the unexpected—just in case—doctors specially trained in gas poison treatment were held in readiness in England.

What the Intelligence men call "cover" forever added to the *Tamarack* planners' difficulties. This was the need to keep the enemy guessing about every phase of the huge project. Cover for the floating harbors which civilian contractors and Royal Engineers were building for use off the D-day beaches proved an especially difficult Intelligence task. There they were, building up all over Britain—like huge floating apartment houses. Concrete caissons over fifty yards long—as obvious as aircraft carriers. And around them the Royal Navy practiced buoying up their vertical barriers of floating sheet steel. Finally, for concealment, the harbors were sunk, to be pumped out, towed, and sunk again off the beaches.

In the middle of all these million-sided activities, General Eisenhower was made supreme invasion commander and came to London. He found 600 officers on the *Falcon-Tamarack-Épée* plans and shook his head.

"No. This invasion has got to be planned *big,*" he said, and increased the planning staff to 6,000.

Last March it was a common quip in England that if invasion didn't start pretty soon, and if materials and equipment kept on piling up, the island would sink beneath the waves. "Just cut the barrage balloons," American troops were fond of saying, "and she'll go down six inches."

Then, early in April, the windup began. It was like the coiling of a spring. Invasion phase plans which had lain quiet but ready for months began to tick now.

The last stages of *Matador*'s strategic bombing plan went into action on April 1st. Every major operation of the next sixty-five days had been scheduled ahead in minutest detail. At Air Force Command Headquarters elaborate charts showed that over 58,000 tons of bombs must be dropped in April, over 70,000 in May. First, on 99 railroad targets. Second, beginning May 7th, on the Seine bridges. Third, May 16th, on almost 50 airdromes within a radius of less than 150 miles of Caen.

Transportation Corps, which had begun planning for these days a year ago June, now began to move men and supplies toward the *Épée* embarkation ports. Every unit and every shipment had to be kept track of, its whereabouts always known. For this Transportation had ready ingenious charts on which was shown the progress of all units from camp to concentration area, to marshaling area, to embarkation zone, to the beaches and the boats, at any hour of day or night.

The months spent on loading plans and practice began to pay dividends now. Supplies flowed smoothly into the right trucks and goods wagons, in the order the Army tactical commanders wanted them in. So they could be reloaded in the opposite order of need on the cross-Channel craft. Converted Liberty ships—loaded on paper five months back, and double-checked with the Navy for safety—now gorged themselves with jeeps and trucks and rode steady on even keel.

Equipment not feasible to load was prepared for towing by tug—as planned. There were nearly 1,400 pieces of such floating equipment. Huge bundles of telephone poles were lashed together by cables so they would ride the roughest seas, and were so fastened that they would dismantle in a jiffy on the far shore under the hands of an Engineer construction man.

Midway in all this loading and dispatching a crisis arose. In May the Americans exceeded their monthly quota of ship arrivals. Thirty-eight extra vessels from the States were on hand—and no facilities. The ships dropped anchor and waited—prey to any Nazi bomber—until the dilemma should be solved. It was arranged with General Lee to move the cargo ashore. "But a lot of it," Lee said, "will have to be merely dumped behind the port areas. There's no protection for 40 per cent of it from ruin by exposure. We'll save 60 per cent of it, however." The Transportation Corps Port Battalions then unloaded 100 per cent and got 100 per cent to sheltered depots!

Finishing touches were now put on arrangements for handling prisoners of war—an example of co-ordinated planning between the Military Police of Provost Marshal General's Office and Transportation's Passenger Branch. From south England ports prisoners would be sent to a camp elsewhere. Someone had had to remember to specify non-corridor railway cars (so prisoners would be always under surveillance) and barbed wire strung on the ships which would take them thence to America (to prevent jumping overboard), and that the Germans and Italians must be segregated.

These regulating points were beautifully co-ordinated with Service

Forces units operating on all the roads. M.P.'s checked the flow of traffic and patrolled every mile. Ordnance teams were everywhere with spare parts for repairs. If a motor burned out, a new one was put in on the spot. For accidents and injuries, Medical Corps doctors were stationed every few miles. In case storm or sabotage disrupted communications, Signal Corps messengers were standing by. Details of specially assigned men popped up wherever a truck convoy halted en route, to keep the G.I.'s from talking with the populace.

How well the highway traffic plan performed is indicated by the remark of one colonel of the Engineers. "I flew over it," he said to me, "and in all those southern counties I saw not one traffic jam."

As the last remaining days rushed up, the air plans laid down so long before were working out their final fulfillment. Beginning a few days before D-day, 1,350 sorties would be flown to lay mines at predetermined areas in the Channel. On the night before invasion the ten German coastal batteries (thirty inches of solid concrete) guarding the three beaches would be hit with 7,500 tons of bombs. At dark on the eve of D-day twenty Pathfinder planes would leave the coast of England and head for points over Normandy where airborne troops would land. In addition to British airborne troops, two divisions of U.S. troops (1,000 transport planes and fighter escort) would follow thirty minutes later, by the clock.

It was estimated that to control the beaches and the waters off them on the first day, 12,000 sorties would have to be flown. Every one of these flights had to be integrated with other parts of the operation. Infantry commanders had to know where the bombs would hit and how many and when. In previous planning conferences, bending over the maps, they had carefully specified, "I shall want 95 tons at *these points.*" Five squadrons of planes would cover the convoy continuously, half of them sixty miles off England, the rest eighty miles. At exactly H-hour minus thirty minutes, 1,350 heavy bombers would plaster the beaches, and lay their eggs just so: 530 tons to every brigade front of 2,300 yards!

Controlling the vast air armada—that is, knowing where every plane was and how it was doing at any given moment—would be a staggering task alone. All directives (for both British and American planes) were to issue from one executive control center hidden in England. Through here every aircraft which flew on invasion day would have to be cleared. This center was in touch by radio with forward control points which did the actual plane directing. Then on each Army division's headquarters ship on the water was an Air Force officer in a little operations room, with a map on which he could see all planes working with that division. Bobbing on the water, further ahead, would lie fighter tenders: one in mid Channel to control fighters over the ships, and two just off the beach for fighters over the land. Meanwhile, back in England, the central executive control must continue its routine checking with R A.F. Coastal Command aircraft out on anti-sub sweeps on both sides of the Channel, and must maintain the usual schedule of defensive fighters day and night over United Kingdom harbors and headquarters.

So perfect was the advance planning, and so diligent the work of the unsung ground crews, that when the day came every plane took the air—except one. And that was because at the last minute its whole side was blown out when some of the airborne infantry inadvertently set off a box of hand grenades.

Since planning is supposed to think of everything, all the planners abhorred eleventh-hour emergencies. Every care was taken to prevent them. In April General Lee and all his chiefs of A.S.F. Technical Services (Engineers, Quartermaster, Chemical Warfare, etc.) were called to Washington from the *Tamarack* theater to confer with the War Department on shortages. Item by item the generals reported on the current status of *Tamarack* supply. A Critical Item List was made, giving the quantity and the deadline date of every article lack of which might endanger success of the invasion. Thereafter a report on each critical shortage was published weekly and dispatched by air courier to the United Kingdom. Here in America the status of every item was checked daily.

The constant variations in the list give a graphic picture of the complexities of invasion planning in these intense weeks of the windup period. On April 15th the list showed 115 items. Because of information from the United Kingdom, 86 were added in the next seven weeks. They were on and off—133 were dropped! The total kept jumping up and down as crazily as the temperature of a patient with successive fever and chills.

On May 7th, a Sunday, supply officers in England called A.S.F. headquarters in Washington on the telephone:

"We have to have 100 per cent re-equipment for some airborne divisions. They're going to land, be pulled out in four days, return to England, re-equip, and drop somewhere else. We'll send you a list of shortages Wednesday. Deadline? Here—June lst."

Wednesday, the 10th, the list arrived, by radio: 327,272 articles. Paracrates, tractors, inflatable boats, ointment, telephones, weather balloons, demolition sets, air compressors, litters, flame throwers, gas masks, fuse setters, four stop watches! Port of embarkation was immediately advised that May 14th was set as deadline sailing date, and all A.S.F. branches were flashed their sections of the list.

A lot of dinners never got eaten that night. The list had arrived late in the afternoon, but by dark stuff was moving from all over the Union. Whether it came by rail, truck, or plane, it was kept track of at every point by officers on the telephone. Special priority markings on every shipment gave it open switches or motor escort through all bottlenecks right up to the port ship-convoy loading platform. Cross-country one shipment was lost somewhere. A duplicate was sent by air. One item only—helmet liners—failed to arrive at ship side on time. Those were put on a fast troop ship. They too arrived in England before the deadline.

This equipment was for the first airborne troops who landed in Normandy. Their fate there illustrates how the mischances of war can make all plans go awry. The planners estimated re-equipment for the losses of four days in combat. But the tactical situation was so hot that it kept these troops fighting in Normandy as infantry until D-day plus thirty-five. Then they returned to England and were re-equipped for the September landings in Holland.

Morning of D-day minus nine found the planners' Nemesis—the list—standing at 77 items of vital equipment still undelivered in the United Kingdom. Of these, 20 were already afloat or in ports of embarkation. For 51 others, substitutes were found in time. As for the rest: unrecorded by history, in obscure offices in the War Department, A.S.F. colonels and majors lived at the telephone day after day, determined to get the remaining items on time—just six out of more than a million.

"We've got to have that tape for that division," they pleaded. "General Lutes himself ordered it from England just a few days ago. He said it was an *absolute must.*"

It got there, by plane, six hours before the shove-off.

Then, finally, at different times, from scores of different invasion embarkation ports, the thousands of vessels got under way. And now it could be seen how well the Navy had planned.

"A stack of papers as big as a desk," is how one admiral describes the size of the Navy Operating Plan. "More complicated than the Army's," one general admits. For this plan had to co-ordinate the Navy's *and* the Army's timing—with no margin for error allowable, because there was always *the tide.*

Down on the beaches and the hards, where the troops got aboard, occurred probably the trickiest timing of all. The Navy must get the right boats to the right beach and section, each on the dot. The Army, which had broken up battalions and companies, in the marshaling areas back of the ports, into craft loads of thirty men to a boat, must march up the right thirty men for the right boat. And no lagging and no waiting around; for loading time for the thirty men, from long practice with the stop watch, was fixed and scheduled. Then the small boats must put each thirty men aboard the right LCIL or LCT anchored offshore.

The Navy had worked out D-day loading plans for these larger vessels in cooperation with the Army months before. For every vessel a detailed list had been made: so many jeeps for Service Company No. 74; so many weapons carriers; so many men; at a certain part of the ship so many Engineers for blasting obstacles on the beach; at another place on board, so many Navy demolitionists for underwater blasting in case the ship couldn't land; special places for four tank dozers; one tank integrated with demolition, three with infantry. "All written down," as one general said to me, "for each ship—all on mimeographed sheets—a pile three inches high."

Suppose the invasion didn't come off? There was a plan to take care of that, too. It read that if D-day were delayed X number of hours after the men were on the water, all men in the smallest craft, since these had no toilet facilities, should be taken ashore. If, after everything was ready, there were a four-day delay, all men in all vessels should go ashore. If there were a month's delay, all personnel would be returned to the marshaling areas.

Every American soldier, once in the boats, received a sealed letter from General Eisenhower, telling him that this was it—not another practice, but D-day. And ready for every coxswain of every landing craft was a little panorama map of his particular section of *his* particular landing shore on "Utah" or "Omaha" beach.

From the ports the Navy minesweepers had swept specific lanes out into mid-Channel, marked them with buoys visible in moonlight, then swept the Channel itself—like a roadstead for the battleships and cruisers to perform in. Beyond this another sweeping cleared a space for the transports, the area where deployment into the battle area would occur. This last was marked by control boats, which at assault time would call up each wave of landing craft to go in.

Although some boats had to put to sea for the rendezvous several hours before others even moved, each craft had to enter its lane at an appointed time (wind and tide regardless), be in the roadstead, and take its predesignated place in the battle area on the tick of the clock. LCM's, under their own power, had to be alongside particular transports, to get the right men waiting at the rail at just that minute to clamber overside. And all in darkness. And total radio silence. No communication ship to ship of any kind.

What could be done, and was, in the way of co-ordination is graphically illustrated by the manner in which one particular general made the cross-Channel trip. He was to leave England in Landing Craft H. This would proceed to the transport area and at X minutes after Y o'clock would come up on the port bow of Transport T, from which an LCVP (Landing Craft Vehicle Personnel) would be delivered, containing one jeep for the General's own purposes. The meeting, the timing, the transfer were all accomplished in the dark without a hitch. "And every detail of it," the General points out, "had to be written down, in the orders, in advance."

He might have added that it was because so many things *were* written in the orders in advance—so many millions of details thought of, and painstakingly worked into the thousands of plans by the thousands of planners—that the greatest feat of organization in history was rolling so smoothly on its way. More right men with more right equipment had been gotten more precisely to the right places at the right time than ever before—thanks to the months and months of tireless planning behind them.

219

WAR AND THE POETS: A SYMPOSIUM

(APRIL 1945)

Edited by Oscar Williams

I have just finished editing an anthology called The War Poets. Manuscripts came to me from all theaters of war, from poet-generals and poet-privates, from commanders and yeomen, from men and women outside the armed services. When I asked the poets to send me manuscripts, I also asked them to send along prose comments giving their ideas on the relationship between poetry and war. The comments I received are of such interest that I have selected, for quotation in full or in part, a few of them that speak representatively for all.

Some of the poets are civilians, some are in uniform, but they are all war poets, in a general sense, and they are all essentially in agreement that there is no such thing as a poet made by war. The collection of commentaries they have written is a kind of Gallup poll of the soul, and we receive a hint of its accuracy from the fact that the poets have come to similar conclusions.

—Oscar Williams

GEOFFREY GRIGSON

You ask about war: one must be self-deluded if one simplifies something so muddled as a twentieth-century complete war into causes,
either good or bad. The only clear thing that I can see is that humanity has walked into a mess: the only clear duty is to endeavor to regard
the mess as clearly as possible, and to endeavor to be as honest and as
unmessy as one's powers allow. Nothing new has happened in this war.
Men have been tortured, women have been murdered, explosives have
exploded; and I am in debt to a letter of Rilke's in which he said that
the whole possibility of human suffering has already been, and is
always being, experienced. It is the quantity, not the quality or depth
of suffering, which has been increased by this war. That helps one, not
to be indifferent, which is impossible, but not to be taken in by surprise and by the lewd rhetoric of a war, and to keep at least that degree
of sanity one had before Chamberlain's voice announced over the air
that England was fighting with Germany.

Should one's poems before have been about roses, and now about
blood? Or shouldn't the blood and roses, the mortality and life, have
been mixed, as they always have been, at the times when a writer was
most deeply possessed by life?

In this country, the Black Militia of the Pen ask where the war poets
are; and they only mean, where are the thumps on the tub, the morale
poems. They don't mean, where is Goya saying, "I saw this," or
Whitman recording a fight under the eternity of the moon, or Wilfred
Owen saying, "Red lips are not so red." If one moves among the dying
and bewildered as Goya did, or Owen, or Whitman, one may write
about those direct experiences or draw them. If a war pushes one into a
civilian job (as it has pushed me), one is still in the midst of life. A war
may numb you, as Rilke was numbed, or it may complete your sense
of life. You must believe in the value of men, and war means that you
must not weaken in that belief. If there is such a thing as a War Poet, it
must mean someone whose vestigial heart swells only when a vast
quantity of suffering mills all around him, a poet normally indifferent
to the intensity and quality of individual suffering. So only Peacetime

Poets matter at all. Pity, or *saeva indignatio,* is not only to be caused by an air raid or a concentration camp.

E. E. CUMMINGS

Is something wrong with America's so-called creative artists? Why don't our poets and painters and composers and so forth glorify the war effort? Are they Good Americans or are they not?"

First: are they Good Americans . . .

When I was a boy, Good Americans were—believe it or don't—adoring the Japanese and loathing the Russians; now, Good Americans are adoring the Russians and loathing the Japanese. Furthermore (in case you were born yesterday), yesterday Good Americans were adoring the Finns; today Good Americans are either loathing the Finns or completely forgetting that Finland exists. Not even the fact that twice during my lifetime Good Americans have succeeded in disliking the Germans can convince me that any human being (such as an artist) is a Good American.

Second: why don't they glorify . . .

When you confuse art with propaganda, you confuse an act of God with something which can be turned on and off like the hot water faucet. If "God" means nothing to you (or less than nothing) I'll cheerfully substitute one of your own favorite words, "freedom." You confuse freedom—the only freedom—with absolute tyranny. Let me, incidentally, opine that absolute tyranny is what most of you are really after; that your so-called ideal isn't America at all and never was America at all: that you'll never be satisfied until what Father Abraham called "a new nation, conceived in liberty" becomes just another subhuman superstate (like the "great freedom-loving democracy" of Comrade Stalin) where an artist—or any other human being—either does as he's told or turns into fertilizer.

Third: is something wrong . . .

All over a so-called world, hundreds of millions of servile and insolent inhuman unbeings are busily rolling and unrolling in the enlightenment of propaganda. So what? There are still a few erect human beings in the so-called world. Proudly and humbly, I say to these human beings:

"O my fellow citizens, many an honest man believes a lie. Though you are as honest as the day, fear and hate the liar. Fear and hate him when he should be feared and hated: now. Fear and hate him where he should be feared and hated: in yourselves.

"Do not hate and fear the artist in yourselves, my fellow citizens. Honor him and love him. Love him truly—do not try to possess him. Trust him as nobly as you trust tomorrow.

"Only the artist in yourselves is more truthful than the night."

HENRY TREECE

I volunteered for the Royal Air Force in order to fulfill a social duty: so that I should not be ashamed of myself as the years went on. As a poet, I was naturally cynical of such behavior. Nevertheless, the impetus of my pre-war craftsman energy carried me through the first two years of war, my work retaining much of its pre-war character. Gradually this impetus wore off and I was unable to produce more than a very thin trickle of verse, this being due not only to the limitations imposed on me by Service duties, but also to the fact that the *purpose* of my poetry, its warning nature, was now no longer required. The catastrophe had happened. Then, as a reaction to the complexity of the difficult early war years, my poetry became simple and often nostalgic. I wanted only to end the war and become a quiet, private person again. Now, after five years of war, there is so little to write about. War, as I see it here and now, is not the material of poetry. Lasting poetry must go down deeper than the superficial appearances of war machines: it must seek out the spirit of man in pain and glory, and must express that spirit and that pain and that glory in simple terms, in those fundamental statements to which the mechanisms of contemporary warfare are irrelevant.

This war, the last war—and possibly the next war—are all the same war, whether fought with flame throwers or stone axes: and it is the poet's function to seek out the germ of all war, isolate and parade

224

it as a warning against future disease of this sort and as a cure for the present disorder.

I feel that it is the poet's duty as a man to fight, physically; but I maintain that it is his duty as a poet to heal the results of that fighting now, and to attempt to prevent such horror for the future.

JOHN BERRYMAN

I should be sorry if the relation between one of man's most destructive and witless activities and one of his most purely and intelligently creative activities should seem to be very close or satisfactory. I do not think it has been so; it is less and less so as war loses its human countenance and living is hard enough. But poetry is not civilized. It takes its themes where it finds them, and some permanently interesting to it are thrown up by war: fear, departure, courage, loss, ambition, loyalty, intrigue, madness, faith, and death. Whether its themes will engage the poetry of a particular man is another matter. There are not many poets and there are no rules. War is an experience, worse than most, like illness or a journey or belief or marriage; those who "have" it will be affected in different degrees, in different ways; some trained to speech will talk about it, others trained equally and affected strongly will have nothing to say; those affected most—the dead—will be most silent.

Iwo Jima Before H-Hour

(MAY 1945)

John P. Marquand

LIFE ON A battleship is largely conducted against a background of disregarded words. For example, upon leaving Saipan, the radio loudspeaker on the open bridge produced a continuous program somewhat along the following lines:

"This is Peter Rabbit calling Audacity One—Peter Rabbit calling Audacity One—over . . . Audacity One calling Peter Rabbit . . . Come in, Peter Rabbit—over . . . Peter Rabbit to Audacity One—Shackle. Charley. Abel. Oboe. Noel Coward. Unshackle—over . . . Audacity One to Peter Rabbit—Continue as directed. Over . . . Peter Rabbit to Audacity One—Roger. Over . . ."

Sometimes these guarded code conversations, all conducted with flawless diction in clear unemotional tones, would reach a degree of subtlety that bordered on the obvious.

"Tiger Two is now in a position to give the stepchildren a drink. Will Audacity One please notify the stepchildren? . . . Bulldog calling Turtle. A pilot is in the water, southeast of Hot Rock. Pick him up. I repeat: In the water, southeast of Hot Rock. Pick him up. . . ."

There was never any way of telling whether or not the stepchildren received the drinks which Tiger was kind enough to offer, or whether or not the pilot was rescued from the slightly chilly waters off that unpleasant island of Iwo. Moreover, no one seemed particularly to care. The Admiral and the Captain sat upon the bridge in comfortable high-chairs, not unlike those used by patrons in a billiard parlor. Their staff officers stood near them, and behind the staff officers stood the men with earphones and mouthpieces tethered by long insulated cords, and next came the Marine orderlies with their .45 automatics. Occasionally a Filipino mess boy would appear from the small kitchenette below—doubtless called a galley—with sandwiches and coffee for the Admiral and the Captain. He would carry these on a tray, sparkling with bright silver, china, and napery, up two dark companion ladders to the open bridge. Once when the main battery of 14-inch guns was firing, some freak of concussion lifted him a good six inches off the deck. But guns or not, no one appeared to listen to the voices on that radio.

However, as hours merged into days during those vigils on the bridge, that constant flow of words could not help but appeal to the imagination of anyone whose experience on battleships and with naval affairs had been previously limited almost exclusively to an acquaintance with Pinafore and Madame Butterfly. Charley and Abel and Peter Rabbit, who kept shackling and unshackling themselves, gradually became old friends. You began to wonder what was happening now to Audacity and Oboe. It would not have been tactful to ask, since each was a special ship, a unit of the task force, but once one of those characters revealed its identity. This was when Little Abner had words with Audacity off the beach of Iwo Jima on D-day minus two.

"Little Abner calling Audacity," Little Abner said. "We've got three holes and so we're going back to the line."

"What line do you mean?" Audacity asked.

"What the hell line do you think?" Little Abner answered. "The firing line."

Little Abner was an LCI—Landing Craft Infantry, in case you do not understand naval initials. She was one of the LCI's equipped with rockets, assigned to strafe the beach, and the Jap batteries had taken her under fire at eight hundred yards.

In addition to the radio on the bridge, there was also entertainment down below. When the great ship withdrew from the area, and when General Quarters had changed to Condition Two, some unknown hands would place recordings of radio programs from home upon a loudspeaker that reached the crew's mess, the warrant officers' mess, and the wardroom. Thus, above the shufflings on the deck, the clatter of mess tins and dishes, would come blasts of music, roars of laughter, and blatant comedy. There was no way of escaping it if you wanted to eat. Though you were seven hundred-odd miles from Tokyo, you were back home again.

"And now Dr. Fisher's tablets for intestinal sluggishness present Willie Jones, and all the little Jones boys, and the Jones boys' orchestra." (Whistles, laughter, and applause from an unknown audience.) "But first a brief, friendly word from our sponsor. Folks, do you feel headachy and pepless in the morning? Just take one with a glass of warm water. But here he is, Willie Jones himself." (Whistles, applause, and cheers from that unknown audience.) "How are you tonight, Willie?"—"Well, frankly, Frank, I'm feeling kind of dumb."—"You mean you're just your old self, then?" (Shrieks, whistles, and applause from the unknown audience.)

There was no way of turning the thing off, but no one seemed to mind. Perhaps after having been at sea almost continuously for thirty months, as had many members of that crew, these sounds gave a sort of reassurance that a past to which everyone was clinging still waited back at home. At the ship's service, days before the ship was cleared for action, you could buy all sorts of reminders of that past. The shaving creams and toothpastes were like old acquaintances. There was even Williams' Aqua Velva, though this line was finally discontinued when it was found that certain members of the crew were taking it internally. There was a selection of homely literature, such as *The Corpse in the Coppice* and *Murder Walks at Midnight* and *The Book of Riddles,* and there were fragile volumes of comics and nationally known brands of gum and candy. When men went to battle stations nearly all of them took a few of these things along. When the ship was closed into hermetically sealed compartments and the ventilating system was cut off you could see them reading by the ammunition hoist.

You could see the damage control groups, with their gas masks, their tools and telephones, reclining on the decks slowly devouring those pages and chewing gum. They may not have enjoyed this literature for itself but it must have given them about the only illusion of privacy that there was in a life at sea where privacy does not exist.

"If you write this thing just the way you see it," an officer said, "maybe it might mean something to people back home. They might see what we're going through. They might understand—they never understand back home."

That was what nearly everyone aboard said. They all had a pathetic desire for people at home to know. Of course, if they had thought about it, they would have realized that this was impossible. There was too great a gap between civilian and naval life. There were too few common values. The life aboard a ship in enemy waters was even more complex and difficult of explanation than the life of troops ashore. There was a combination of small personal comforts and of impending danger verging on calamity that was ugly and incongruous. The living quarters of the crew were overcrowded, but they had hot water and soap, hot showers, and all sorts of things you would never get ashore. There were clean clothes, and all the coffee you wanted day and night, and red meat and other hot food, and butter and ice cream. Yet, at the same time, the sense of danger was more intense. You could not run away from it as you could on land. It might come at any minute of the day and night from torpedoes, from the air, from a surface engagement. Almost any sort of blow meant casualties and damage. Even a light shell on the superstructure might cause complications incomparable to the results of a similar blow on land.

There had been some hope that the task force of battleships, cruisers, and destroyers that was scheduled to bombard Iwo Jima for three days before the transports and the amphibious craft appeared, might arrive there undetected, but the force was spotted by an enemy plane on the evening of February 15th. No one aboard saw that speck in the dark sky.

In the junior officers' wardroom there was a complete collection of all the intelligence which had been gathered regarding the island of Iwo. Nothing was a secret any longer. It was possible to scan the latest airplane photographs, which had been taken early in the month. There were maps showing the target areas assigned every unit, with batteries, pillboxes, and anti-aircraft installations marked in red. There were reports on the soil of the island. The beach would be coal-black lava sand, and the land rose up from it quite sharply in terraces. Each terrace had been a former beach, since in the past few years the island had been rising from the sea. As one moved in from the water's edge the soil was a soft sand of volcanic ash, almost barren of vegetation and exceedingly difficult for any sort of vehicle to negotiate. Higher on the island were the cliffs of brown volcanic stone, suitable for construction of underground galleries. There were patches of coarse grass full of the mites that cause scrub typhus. There were hot springs, and there was the sulphur mine from which Iwo draws its name (Sulphur Island), and a small sugar plantation to the north near a single town called Motoyama. There were believed to be fifteen hundred troops on the island. The defensive installations were all underground or carefully camouflaged. There was only one practical beach on which to land and there was no chance for tactical subtlety.

The most interesting unit of this informational material was a large relief map made out of soft, pliable rubber, that gave a bird's-eye view of the island we were approaching. Every contour of it was there in scale—the cliffs to the northward, the vegetation, the roads, the air strips (two finished and one nearing completion), and Mount Suribachi, the low, brown volcanic cone on the southern tip.

There have already been a good many ingenious descriptions of the shape of Iwo Jima, including comparisons to a mutton chop and a gourd. The whole thing was about five miles long. Mount Suribachi, to the south, was a walled-in crater. Its northern slope was known to be studded with pillboxes and with artillery. Bushes and boulders on this slope ran down to the lowest and narrowest stretch on the island, which had beaches on the east and west. (The west beach, however, would not permit landing operations on account of the prevailing winds.) From here the land gradually rose upward, and the island broadened until it finally reached a width of two and one-half miles. The air strips were on its central spine. The northern shores came down to the sea in cliffs. There were only eight square miles of this bleak, unpromising, and porous dry land.

Anyone could tell that the plans for the seizure of Iwo Jima must have been the main occupation of a large group of specialists for a long, long time. Heaps of secret orders showed the disposition at any given moment of every one of the hundreds of craft that would take part in the invasion. The thousands of pages made a scenario for an operation which might take place in an hour or a minute. Veterans of other invasions were not impressed by the infinite detail. They spoke of the plans for Normandy and the south of France, or they discussed the arrangements for Guam and Saipan.

"If you've seen one of them," they said, "you've seen them all."

No one spoke much on the bridge. It was chilly and rain was falling before daylight. We were a silent, blacked-out ship, moving slowly, and as far as one could tell, alone—except for voices on the bridge radio.

"Battleaxe One," the radio was saying, "Area Zebra. Shackle. Charley. Oswald. Henry. Abel. Unshackle."

"We'll start firing at about ten thousand yards," someone said.

Then the first daylight began to stir across the water and we were among the shadows of other heavy ships, moving very slowly.

"Look," someone said, "there's the mountain."

There was a faint, pinkish glow on the rain clouds above the horizon and the first faint rays of an abortive sunrise struggling against the rain fell on a rocky mass some five miles dead ahead. It was the cone of Suribachi emerging from a misty haze of cloud, and cloud vapor covered the dark mass of the rest of Iwo Jima. After one glance at its first vague outlines, it would have been hard to have mistaken it for anything but a Japanese island, for it had the faint delicate colors of a painting on a scroll of silk.

Our spotting plane was warming up on the catapult aft and you could hear the roar of the motor clearly over the silent ship. Then there was a flat explosion as the plane shot over the water. When it circled for altitude and headed for the island, there was already light enough to see the faces on the bridge.

The Captain dropped his binoculars and lighted a cigarette. The clouds were gradually lifting above the island. It was unexpectedly tedious waiting and wondering when we would begin to fire. The island lay there mute and watchful. A bell was ringing. "Stand by," someone said, and seconds later one of our 14-inch projectiles was on its way to Iwo Jima. The noise was not as bad as the concussion, for your chest seemed to be pushed by invisible hands when the big guns went off. There was a cloud of yellow smoke, not unlike the color of Mount Suribachi. Then everyone crowded forward to gaze at the island. It seemed a very long while before a cloud of smoke and gray sand rose up almost like water from land. Then another ship fired. The bombardment of Iwo Jima had begun and the island lay there in the dingy, choppy sea, taking its punishment stoically without a sound.

Even at a distance of five miles, which somehow does not seem as far at sea as it does on land, one had the inescapable impression that Iwo Jima was ready for it and accustomed to taking a beating. This was not strange, as we had bombed it from the air for successive dozens of days, and fleet units had already shelled it twice. Nevertheless, this lack of reaction was something that you did not expect, even though common sense told you that there would not possibly be any land fire until we closed the range.

Another aspect of that three-day bombardment before D-day was even more unexpected, especially when one retained memories of the heavy and continuous fire by land batteries upon prepared positions in the last World War. The bombardment turned out to be a slow, careful probing for almost invisible targets, with long dull intervals between the firing. Occasionally one could see a cloud of drab smoke arise from another ship, and a long while afterward the sound of the explosion would come almost languidly across the water, and then there would be another plume of dust and rubble on another target area of Iwo Jima. Sometimes, when the breeze was light, the smoke from the big guns of another ship would rise in the air in a huge perfect ring. Of course common sense again gave the reason for this deliberate firing. The fleet had come too long a distance to waste its limited ammunition, and consequently the effect of every shot had to undergo careful professional analysis.

In the lulls between the firing there was always an atmosphere of unremitting watchfulness. While the crews of the anti-aircraft batteries below us sat by their guns, smoking and talking, hundreds of eyes were examining the sky and land. There was air cover far above us. In the distance were underwater listeners on the destroyers and DE's that were screening us. Our own air watch, besides, was covering every sector of the sky—and you also knew that the enemy looked back at us from his hidden observation posts. That consciousness of eyestrain and listening never entirely vanished in those days at Iwo Jima, and, because of it, not a moment on the bridge was restful.

The slow approach on Iwo Jima was somewhat like the weaving and feinting of a fighter watching for an opening early in the first round. To put it another way, our task force was like a group of big-game hunters surrounding a slightly wounded but dangerous animal. They were approaching him slowly and respectfully, endeavoring to gauge his strength and at the same time trying to tempt him into action. We moved all through the day, nearer and nearer to Iwo Jima. Planes from the carrier force came from beyond the horizon, peeling off through the clouds and diving toward the air strip; but except for an occasional burst of automatic fire and a few black dots of flak, the enemy was very listless. Our minesweeps, small, chunky vessels, began operating very close to the island. There were a few splashes near them, but that was all. The Japanese commander was too good a soldier to show his hand.

As the day wore on, we crowded close and objects loomed very large ashore. You could see the coal-black strip of beach where our assault waves would land, and the sea broke on the rusting hulls of a few old wrecks. Above the beach were the gray terraces we had read about, mounting in gradual, uneven steps to the air strip. Beside the air strip there was a tangle of planes, smashed by our bombings and pushed carelessly aside, like rubbish on a city dump. To the north were the quarries which had been mentioned by the Intelligence. You could see caves to the south on Mount Suribachi. We were very close for a battle-ship and we knew the enemy had 8-inch coast defense guns.

We continued firing at pillboxes and at anti-aircraft emplacements, but there was no return fire and no trace of life upon the island. We stayed there until the light grew dim, and then we turned to leave the area until next morning. Twelve hours of standing on the bridge and the concussion of the guns left everyone very tired. We must have done some damage but not enough to hurt.

It was different the next morning—D-day minus two. When we returned to the dull work the island was waiting with the dawn. Today the sky was clearer and the sea was smoother, and the ships closed more confidently with the shore. The schedule showed that there was to be a diversion toward the middle of the morning, and the force was obviously moving into position.

"We're going to reconnoiter the beach with small craft," an officer explained. "And the LCI's will strafe the terraces with rockets."

It was hard to guess where the LCI's had come from, for they had not been with us yesterday—but there they were just behind us, on time and on order, like everything else in amphibious war. The sun had broken through the cloud ceiling and for once the sea was almost blue. The heavy ships had formed a line, firing methodically. Two destroyers edged their way past us and took positions nearer shore.

"Here come the LCI's," someone said. "You can see the small craft with them," and he gave the initials by which the small boats were identified. They were small open launches, manned by crews with kapok life jackets. They were twisting and turning nervously as they came to join the LCI's.

"Where are they going in those things?" I asked.

"They are going to see what there is along the beach," my friend answered. "Someone has to see." He spoke reprovingly, as though I should have known the routine that had been followed again and again in the Pacific.

Eight or ten LCI's—it was difficult to count them—were passing among the battleships, with their crews at their battle stations. They were small vessels that had never been designed for heavy combat. They had been built only to carry infantry ashore, but in the Pacific they were being put to all sorts of other uses—as messenger ships to do odd jobs for the fleet, as gunboats, and as rocket ships. Each had a round tower amidships where the commanding officer stood. Each had open platforms with light automatic guns, and now they were also fitted with brackets for the rockets. They were high and narrow, about a hundred feet overall, dabbed with orange and green paint in jungle camouflage. They were a long way from jungle shores, however, as they moved toward the beach of Iwo Jima.

Suddenly the scene took concrete shape. They would approach within a quarter of a mile of shore under the cover of our guns. Without any further protection their crews stood motionless at their stations.

Afterward a gunner from one of the LCI's spoke about it.

"If we looked so still," he said, "it was because we were scared to death. But then everyone had told us there was nothing to be scared of. They told us the Japs never bothered to fire at LCI's."

They were wrong this time, probably because the small craft that followed gave the maneuver the appearance of a landing. For minutes the LCI's moved in and nothing happened. They had turned broadside to the beach, with small boats circling around them like water beetles, before the enemy tipped his hand and opened up his batteries. Then it became clear that nothing we had done so far had contributed materially to softening Iwo Jima. The LCI's were surrounded with spurts of water, and spray and smoke. They twisted and backed to avoid the fire, but they could not get away. It all seemed only a few yards off, directly beneath our guns. Then splashes appeared off our own bows. The big ships themselves were under fire.

"The so-and-so has taken a hit," someone said. "There are casualties on the such-and-such." He was referring to the big ships, but at the moment it did not seem important. All you thought of were the LCI's just off the beach. We were inching into line with the destroyers.

It appeared later that when we had been ordered to withdraw we had disregarded the order, and thus all at once we were in a war of our own, slugging it out with the shore. There had been a great deal of talk about our gunnery and the training of our crews. There was no doubt that they knew their business when they began firing with everything that could bear. The 14-inch guns and the 5-inch batteries were firing as fast as they could load. The breeze from the shore blew the smoke up to the bridge in bilious clouds. The shore line of Iwo Jima became cloaked in white smoke as we threw in phosphorus. Even our 40-millimeters began to fire. It was hard to judge the lapse of time, but the LCI's must have let off their rockets according to the schedule while the Japanese were blinded by the smoke and counterfire. When the LCI's began to withdraw, we also moved off slowly. It was the first mistake the enemy had made, if it was a mistake—revealing those batteries, for the next day was mainly occupied in knocking them out.

The LCI's were limping back. One of them was listing and small boats were taking off her crew. Another was asking permission to come alongside. When she reached us the sun was beating on the shambles of her decks. There was blood on the main deck, making widening pools as she rolled on the sluggish sea. A dead man on a gun platform was covered by a blanket. The decks were littered with wounded. They were being strapped on wire stretchers and passed up to us over the side, since nothing as small as an LCI had facilities for wounded. The men who were unhurt were lighting cigarettes and talking quietly, but no one was smiling. The commanding officer was tall, bare-headed, and blond, and he looked very young. Occasionally he gave an order and then he, also, lighted a cigarette. When they began to hose off the blood on the deck, the crew must have asked for fresh water, because our men, gathered by the rail, began tossing down canteens. Then there was a call from our bridge.

"Can you proceed under your own power?"

The blond CO looked up. He evidently had not heard, because the question was repeated.

"Can you proceed under your own power?"

"We can't proceed anywhere for three days," the CO said.

They had passed up the wounded—seventeen of them—and then they passed up five stretchers with the dead—twenty-two out of a crew of about sixty.

"That officer ought to get a medal," I said to someone on the bridge.

"They don't give medals for things like that in the Navy," I was told.

It may be so, but I still hope he gets the medal.

That evening the Japanese reported that they had beaten off two landings on Iwo Jima and that they had sunk numerous craft, including a battleship and a destroyer. There was a certain basis of fact in this, since what had happened must have looked like a landing. One LCI was sinking, waiting for a demolition charge, as disregarded as a floating can.

After the reconnaissance of the beach had been accomplished, the pounding of Iwo Jima continued through the afternoon and through the whole next day. Planes dove in with bomb loads, while the ring of ships kept up their steady fire. At night the "cans," as the destroyers were called, continued a harassing fire. Incendiary bombs were dumped on the slopes of Suribachi. Rockets were thrown at it from the air. Fourteen-inch shells pounded into its batteries. The ship to starboard of us attacked the battery to the north on the lip of the quarry. The earth was blown away, exposing the naked concrete gun emplacements, but now that the novelty had worn off it was all a repetition of previous hours. The scene grew dull and very fatiguing, but the voices on the radio loudspeaker continued tirelessly.

"Dauntless reports a contact. . . . Bulldog is ready to give a drink to any of our pigeons that may need it. Audacity One to Tiger—I repeat: Did you get our message? Over. . . ."

The island lay still, taking it. No visible life appeared until the last day, when an installation was blown up and a few men staggered out from it. Some of us on the bridge saw them and some did not. One Japanese ran a few steps and seemed to stop and stoop to pick up something. Then he was gone. We had probably seen him dying.

The Japanese commander was playing his cards close to his chest, revealing no more targets by opening fire. It was clear that he also had his plan, less complicated than ours, but rational. He might damage our heavy ships, but he could not sink them, or conceivably prevent the inevitable landing. He had clearly concluded to wait and take his punishment, to keep his men and weapons under cover, until our assault waves were on the beach. Then he would do his best to drive them off, and everyone at Iwo knows it was not such a bad plan, either. He did not come so far from doing it when he opened up his crossfire on the beach. Some pessimists even admit that he might have succeeded if it had not been for that coarse, light sand which embedded the mortar shells as they struck, so that they only killed what was very near them.

At the end of D-day minus one our task force was still there, without many new additions, but it was different the next morning. At dawn on D-day the waters of Iwo looked like New York harbor on a busy morning. The transports were there with three divisions of Marines—a semicircle of gray shipping seven miles out. Inside that gray arc the sea, turned choppy by the unsettled weather, was dotted by an alphabet soup of ships.

There were fleets of LST's filled with amphibious tanks and alligators; there were LSM's; there were the smaller LCT's, and packs of LCI's gathering about the kill. The ring of warships was drawing tighter. Small boats were moving out bearing flags to mark the rallying points from which the landing waves would leave. It looked like a Hollywood production, except that it was a three-billion- , not a three-million-dollar extravaganza. There must have been as many as eight hundred ships clustered off Iwo Jima, not counting the small boats being lowered. The officers and crew faced it without surprise. Instead they pointed out small incidents and made critical remarks.

"See the LCVP's," someone said. He was pointing out the tiny dots around the transports where the landing craft were loading. "They'll be moving into position. Here come the planes." It was all working without a hitch, with H-hour not so far away. At nine o'clock exactly the first assault wave was due to hit the beach, but before that Iwo Jima was due to receive its final polishing. Its eight square miles were waiting to take everything we could pour into them, and they must have already received a heavier weight of fire than any navy in the world had previously concentrated upon so small an area.

Anyone who has been there can shut his eyes and see the place again. It never looked more aesthetically ugly than on D-day morning, or more completely Japanese. Its silhouette was like a sea monster with the little dead volcano for the head, and the beach area for the neck, and all the rest of it with its scrubby, brown cliffs for the body. It also had the minute, fussy compactness of those miniature Japanese gardens. Its stones and rocks were like those contorted, wind-scoured, water-worn boulders which the Japanese love to collect as landscape decorations. "I hope to God," a wounded Marine said later, "that we don't get to go on any more of those screwy islands."

An hour before H-hour it shook and winced as it took what was being dished out to it. In fact, the whole surface of the island was in motion as its soil was churned by our shells and by the bombs from the carrier planes that were swooping down across its back. Every ship was firing with a rising tempo, salvo after salvo, with no more waiting for the shellburst to subside. Finally Iwo Jima was concealing itself in its own debris and dust. The haze of battle had become palpable, and the island was temporarily lost in a gray fog.

"The LST's are letting down their ramps," someone said.

There could not have been a better place to observe the whole spectacle than from the air lookout station above the bridge, but there was too much to see. Only an observer familiar with the art and theory of amphibious warfare could possibly have unraveled all the threads, and an ordinary witness could only give as inaccurate an account as the innocent bystander gives to circumstances surrounding a killing on the street. There was no time any longer to ask questions or to digest kindly professional explanations. All the facts that one had learned from the secret documents were confused by the reality.

The LST's had let down their ramps and the amphibious vehicles which they had carried were splashing through the water, like machines from a production line. Watching them, I found myself speaking to a chief petty officer who was standing next to me.

"It's like all the cats in the world having kittens," I said, and the idea appeared to interest him.

The amphibious vehicles, churning up the sea into foaming circles, organized themselves in lines, each line following its leader. Then the leaders moved out to the floating flags, around which they gathered in circling groups, waiting for their signal to move ashore. The gray landing craft with the Marines had left the transports some time before for their own fixed areas and they also were circling, like runners testing their muscles before the race. The barrage which had been working over the beach area had lifted, and the beach, with the smoldering terraces above it, was visible again. It was time for the first wave to be starting.

It was hard to pick the first wave out in that sea of milling craft, but suddenly a group of the barges broke loose from its circle, following its leader in a dash toward shore. Close to land the leader turned parallel to the beach, and kept on until the whole line was parallel. Then the boats turned individually and made a dash for it. The Navy had landed the first wave on Iwo Jima—at nine o'clock on the dot—or, at least, not more than a few seconds after nine.

NOTE ON WAR MEMORIALS

(MAY 1945)

Thomas Hornsby Ferril

AM I ARGUING for hero busts all over town? Only if you're interested in reminding others of who these particular boys were and what they did. But take comfort. You're not so interested. You only think you are. It's only a pretext for exercising your reverence, your love, your sense of fitness. You have good taste. You are, in a word, less devoted to honoring them than pleasing yourself. You conveniently forget your sports-page attitude toward battle. You're unaware of the quirks of your own ego by which the soldier became your vicar, how he gave you access to your own nobility, and how the sordidness of his daily routine was washed away in your own high virtues. And now that it's over, you do the right thing. In the names of specific men, or groups of men, you transfer your emotion to sculptured abstraction, architectural beauty, or humanitarianism in which they are lost and you are glorified. Then soon, through this vicious alchemy of the spirit, war itself is exalted. Again we'll follow the grisly pattern of glorifying war in the name of those who were trapped by it and loathed it.

War memorials will be as beautiful as men can make them—in America, Britain, Russia, Germany, Japan—and a beautiful war memorial betrays every man who ever fought and always has. We can't outgrow the impulses of the Greeks and Egyptians, who, after disemboweling their fellows, gave beautification to butchery by erecting in its name the most luminous structures ever created, temples to swear by and die for—emotional catalysts to make the elements of war combine all the more readily the next time. And any man will die for the temples of his fathers without thinking twice how sordid were the pretexts that summoned the temples into being. It seems to be an ineluctable pattern, blundering into war, then calling it beautiful, and no spiritual mutation is indicated by which it may ever be otherwise. Perhaps its a physical defect. Anton J. Carlson, the distinguished physiologist-philosopher of the University of Chicago, quietly reminds us that the hypothalamus still dominates the cerebrum.

If we loved our fallen sons more than ourselves, if we would protect their children, then would we demand that war memorials in every land be foul, disgusting, stinking things recalling stupidity and pus, the chant of fevers and wistful questionings . . . *Why? Why? Why?* It is, I know, too much to ask. We love war too well and love ourselves too well. We can't break the emotional pattern of the ages because we don't even know it is a pattern. But if we can't have repulsive reminders of war, thank heaven we shall have a good many boring ones. Bad taste works a little in our favor. Equestrian statues, unfortunately, are no more: they were useful because they were foolish. But we can at least hope that in their places, here in our own country and all over the world, parks and plazas may be cluttered to overflowing with tanks, landing craft, wrecked planes, and marble-mounted bazookas—all so stubbornly anchored in concrete that they will be hard to get rid of when people begin to feel sheepish for having them around.

HOW THE RUSSIANS TRY
NAZI CRIMINALS

(JUNE 1945)

Richard E. Lauterbach

IT IS EXTREMELY difficult for us to feel as strongly as the Russians do about the Germans. Our country has not been ravaged. We have been taught to be skeptical, even cynical, about atrocities. We remember the debunking of such stories which followed the last war. Some of us suspect that these atrocities are exaggerated or even made up to play on our sympathies. Nothing could be further from the truth.

I belong to the post-war generation, a very cynical generation. I also belong to a cynical profession. Almost every day that I spent in the Soviet Union there were fresh atrocity stories in the newspapers. We rarely went on a trip toward the front that we didn't hear about Nazi barbarities or see the results of German viciousness. After a while, like other correspondents, I became calloused to such things. We even had the feeling that no matter how many people were massacred the story was "old," or not "news." But after I attended the Kharkov trials I began to understand the Russian attitude toward the Germans.

We flew down from Moscow to Kharkov. It was a gray day with a

245

low ceiling and the plane went above church-steeple level only to avoid church steeples. When we arrived it was still only midmorning. We went straight from the airport to the Ukrainian Musical Comedy Theater on Rymarskaya Street, where the trial was being held.

The theater was old and smelly. The central auditorium was packed with a thousand spectators, many of them standing. Tickets to the proceedings went to wounded Red Army men, front-line heroes on leave, outstanding production workers, and families of Kharkov citizens who had been slaughtered by the Germans during the occupation. The design of the theater was baroque, and white-sculptured nymphs arched against the upper boxes like so many little daughters of Atlas supporting the world. Despite the seriousness of the occasion, the setting seemed like a Hollywood premiere—klieg lights, microphones, cameras, celebrities, and photographers. Perhaps the courtroom of the Hauptmann trial in Flemington, New Jersey, would offer a more accurate comparison.

We were ushered into a box at the left, just opposite the prisoners' box. Prominent Soviet writers had boxes behind ours. On one door was a printed sign which read simply, "TOLSTOI." That rotund writer appeared presently. When a photographer shot off a flash bulb in his face he cursed him out just as a grand duke might have done thirty years before. Only the photographer talked right back—a big difference.

"Death in battle is too easy a death for their crimes," Tolstoi wrote in *Pravda* when the trial of three Nazis and one traitor opened. "Hitler freed the Germans from moral feelings of pity, nobleness, honor, and respect for man, but we haven't freed the Germans from their obligation to be men. . . . Today Kharkov began the first trial which opens a whole epoch of great and dreadful judgment for the Germans who have overstepped the laws of humanity. Today three Germans are being tried among the ruins of the town, surrounded by the tombs of their victims. They have behaved not like soldiers, but like bandits, torturers, licentious half-men. . . ."

The "licentious half-men" took their seats in their box. The trial was resuming. There were sneezes in the audience. Girls focused opera glasses and others craned their necks to see the four accused men. The Germans were all in uniform. Captain Wilhelm Langheld, fifty-two, a Nazi counterespionage officer, sat straight and correct. He was clean-shaven with a long, puffy-pink face, thin lips, and slick red hair. Reinhard Retslau, a member of the German secret police, had a bored expression, a chinless face, and spectacles. He sat very calmly and seemed to be listening to the testimony in Russian as well as the translation into German. He was thirty-six years old and wore a medal which Hitler had given him two years before. Lieutenant Hans Ritz, twenty-four, had a gnomelike head with a large skull, a sharp German nose, a caved-in chest, and a silly mustache. He was an assistant commander of an S.S. company; he had beaten people with canes and rubber hoses, and in June, 1943, he had taken part in a mass shooting of Soviet civilians near Kharkov. Mikhail Bulanov, called by one of the Russian writers "the black lining of the blue German uniform," was a Russian traitor. His black eyebrows had grown together over his closely set, black sneaky eyes. He looked like a jackal.

The trials were being run by the military tribunal of the Fourth Ukrainian Front. The chief judge was Major General Miasnikov. The defense counsel, appointed by the judge, was N. V. Kommodov, who is the Soviet Union's Samuel Liebowitz with a bit of Clarence Darrow thrown in. He had two assistants, S. K. Krasnacheyev and N. P. Belov. Both lawyers were well known. The prosecutor was N. K. Dounaev, a young Red Army colonel. The accused made no objections to the judges or the defense lawyers.

The testimony thus far had been incredible. The Germans, pretty sure that they were going to die, took the long chance that they might get only life imprisonment if they made a clean breast of things. They knew, too, that there was not much point in hiding facts. The Soviets had volumes of proof, cemeteries full of evidence. The accused had only to look into the eyes of the crowd at the trial to realize the hopelessness of claiming innocence. Langheld, a veteran of World War I, had related in his cold, expressionless voice how he beat women and starved prisoners without thinking of good or bad. He was almost the dramatic monologist or raconteur telling how he flogged an innocent young Soviet woman while her small son cringed in a corner watching his mother being tortured. Langheld said he beat the woman until she was covered with blood. She fainted. Next day she died. And what happened to the child? Oh, Langheld had forgotten that part momentarily. The child refused to be torn away from the dead body of the mother. That's why they shot him.

The audience listened in quiet horror. It was like a page from Wanda Wasilewska's *Rainbow*. Langheld was businesslike, accurate, choosing his words as if he were talking about a grocery store where certain foods had spoiled. They asked him, "How many innocent people have you personally killed or tortured?" He lifted his piggish little eyes to the ceiling, mentally counting. Then he replied like a bank clerk. To his regret he could not say definitely at the moment, but approximately he had shot, tortured, or otherwise destroyed, say, a hundred people.

The Soviet writers hated Langheld more than they did the others. They couldn't forget that he had been a British prisoner of war in 1917 and had been allowed to return home to resume his career all over again. The sharp-tongued David Zaslavsky wrote about him, "Langheld is Hitler reduced to the scale of one torture chamber."

The prosecutor was making his long summation. The newsreelmen took their pictures. Retslau kept staring at the speaker. Bulanov, in his black turtleneck sweater, looked terribly uneasy. Ritz had the manner of an Austrian provincial dandy. But he shivered occasionally as he felt the vindictiveness in the prosecutor's voice. Langheld seemed completely unmoved as if he were at a lecture on the weaving methods of the Navajo Indians and not at a trial where his life was in the balance. Often he closed his eyes or stifled a yawn.

The prosecutor paused to drink some hot tea. Then he continued, "The men who are in the dock are not responsible; we know who they are and they will have to answer. We try these three for their personal crimes, for what they have done with their own hands. . . ." He began to picture their crimes. He re-created scenes in which little children, thinking they were going for a joy ride, hopped into German vans.

They turned out to be the notorious gas wagons, or *doushagoopkas*. In them the children, with or without their parents, were asphyxiated by carbon monoxide while the van was already on its way toward some dumping ground. There was sniffling among the spectators. Handkerchiefs appeared. Even the tough Red Army men had to keep clearing lumps from their throats. "Retslau," charged the prosecutor, "is a professional killer. The Red Army stopped his career. You judges must decide his future. . . ."

Next he delved into the triumphs of Ritz. "He wanted to get into the Gestapo because it was nice and comfortable and the first outfit to run away when there's danger." Ritz was the type who liked to have his picture taken hanging innocent women and children and then send it back to his mother and sweetheart.

For Bulanov, the prosecutor reserved his special scorn. He was a deserter from the Red Army. He had helped repair *doushagoopkas*. He had even driven them.

Near the end of the summation, the prosecutor struck a Tom Dewey pose. "The crimes are proved not only of those sitting in the dock but of all those who will be!" he shouted. "For our mothers, wives, daughters, sisters—in their names, the state demands that you send these men to their death. . . . " There was a storm of applause.

We had lunch with Tolstoi, Konstantin Simonov, Ehrenburg, and Dmitri Kudriavtsev, Secretary of the Soviet Union's Atrocity Commission. When it was over we returned to hear Defense Attorney Kommodov make his final plea. He is the man who defended the Trotskyist bloc in the 1936–37 treason trials.

Kommodov began talking slowly, analyzing the specific structure of fascism. He showed how its very nature breeds war and brutality. In all epochs there are atrocities, he pointed out, but none can compare with this planned, regular annihilation of a peaceful people. "I shall not recount all the terrors committed by the Germans, having respect for your nerves." He spoke without notes, a glass of tea held in his left hand. Once, when he read a quotation from Stalin, he put on his glasses. The burden of his plea resembled the one the defense lawyer made in Richard Wright's *Native Son:* That the crimes were committed because of the society in which the defendants lived. When he had finished, a translator began reading the speech in German. Ritz sobbed as he listened to it. The others seemed unmoved.

Then, one by one, the accused made their last pleas. They sang echoes of Kommodov's tune, but with less effect. Retslau said it was useless to hide his crimes. He blamed German propaganda, which said the Russians were torturing German prisoners, cutting off their hands. "I can say the opposite is true. We were well treated in prison." He asked the judges to consider his background and training under the Nazi system. Langheld dozed as Retslau asked to be spared. He wanted to return to Germany and prove himself by his deeds.

Shortly after six all the Red Army guards were changed, and the court announced that the curfew was being suspended for the evening, so the crowd could stay. The next to speak was the hopeless Bulanov. When the Germans had taken him prisoner he had had the choice of death or transgression. Of course, most of the brave Soviet people preferred heroic death. But he, Bulanov, had no such high moral character. He asked the judges to imagine his feelings among the "German cannibals." He got only ninety occupation marks per month for his work. He said his guilt was tremendous, but he certainly hoped he could be used by the Soviets in some way; he would prove himself by hard work and good intentions.

When Langheld stood in front of the microphone the crowd stirred noisily and the judge rapped for order. The Prussian kept his hands behind his back. The klieg lights were switched on. Langheld blinked, faltered as he tried to speak. "I have nothing to add to the formal accusation," he said. "I beat prisoners; they were beaten under my orders; they were shot by my orders. I ask only one consideration. I am not alone. The entire German army is like that, too. I do not mean to cover up my own guilt. The reasons for my guilt lie in the German government. The Hitler regime has managed to suppress the generous feelings of the German people and to bring out the beastly instincts. This is especially true in the Wehrmacht. This evil has shown itself particularly during this war. To contradict or not to fulfill the orders we were given meant to sentence ourselves to death. And I was a victim of these orders. I ask consideration for my old age, and because I told the truth in the preliminary hearings."

I looked at the audience. There was no sympathy, only hatred. Ritz swayed as he stood up. He sounded like a whining boy. "I don't want to implore you, I don't want to blot out my crimes," he said. "It's unworthy of me as a man and a soldier. I wish to speak with frankness. . . . I want you to know that I did not relish killings. If so, I would have taken part in many more crimes, as I had plenty of chances. I acted on orders. The system of our army forced me to do it. . . . I was under orders when I committed crimes, under the sentence of death myself if I did not carry out these orders." He sighed. Then he began again, "The Hitler system is directed not only against other nations but against German people who do not obey him. Consider my life. I was a child of thirteen when the Hitler regime came to power. Since then I have been systematically educated." Ritz was something of an orator, and used his hands for gestures. I could not get all his testimony, but this is approximately correct: "I am young and I have my life before me. I want to live so I can testify against the other S.S. men who ordered these atrocities. . . . "

The court recessed at 9:15 P.M. We drove back to the hotel and had supper. About 11:30 a telephone call came that the judges were ready to announce their decision. We entered the packed hall. The prisoners were led in, under guard. The judges walked in from the wings. As they appeared on the stage everyone stood up, the Red Army men rigidly at attention. For the first time I noticed the light blue velvet curtain behind the judges, and the pretty Red Army girl court clerks.

At exactly 11:55 General Masnikov read the findings of the court and the verdict: "Death by hanging." The audience applauded. Then a Red Army lieutenant read the same thing in German. Bulanov ducked his head down. Ritz looked incredulous. Retslau tapped his thick fingers against the frames of his horn-rimmed glasses. Langheld betrayed nothing. The guards led them out.

I asked Ehrenburg when they would be hanged.

"Sunday morning," he snapped back. "What better time? Tomorrow."

On the way out of the theater I stopped to read a big billboard. It said, literally, "NEXT WEEK—ROSE MARIE."

Sunday morning was overcast but not too cold. Naturally one of the Americans, taking a deep breath of air, said, "A good day for a hanging." Nobody laughed. We piled into cars and went to see the end.

If the scene had been in a movie it would have jarred me by its savagery and unreality. Fitted into the context of time and place it had a stark but entirely believable reality. Around us Kharkov kids were scampering high on the snowy rooftops of shattered, windowless buildings. Nearby the great Kharkov cathedral, damaged by Nazi bombs, stood empty. About fifty thousand people dressed in their shabby Sunday best shoved into the enormous open market square. They were held in check by Red Army guards with fixed bayonets and low-slung tommy guns. In the dismal gray light of that chilly December morning loomed four gaunt fifteen-foot gallows—stout wooden beams with strong, thin nooses drooping from crossbars. Beneath the rigid nooses four open Chevrolet trucks were backed up. On each truck were three flimsy unpainted wooden tables.

Overhead two trim Lend-Lease Airacobras and a pair of ugly Russian U-2's hovered like vultures. Behind us a half-demolished office building still bore a German signpost on its crumbling façade. Its uncertain rafters were black with spectators. Photographers fought for vantage points. One newsreel crew was located on a platform twenty feet high opposite the gallows.

At 11:15 A.M. two cars plowed through the dense crowd. The first contained military and judicial officials. The second was a closed gray-green truck with guards and the condemned. The door was opened. The crowd stirred impatiently. With their hands tied behind them the Germans, Hans Ritz, Wilhelm Langheld, and Reinhard Retslau, were led out, followed by the Russian traitor, Mikhail Bulanov. The crowd surged forward, straining against the cordon of guards, despite whose efforts the circle around the gallows tightened.

Red Army men helped each of the condemned onto a truck beneath the coiled rope. Then they assisted each man's reluctant feet onto the center table while two guards flanked him on the side tables. The necks of the condemned reached the empty nooses. The Germans were in full uniform with epaulets and ribbons. They wore forage caps. Langheld had on a good pair of boots, high boots.

Suddenly the motors of the four one-ton trucks coughed, then roared. Major General Miasnikov, chairman of the military tribunal, mounted the rostrum improvised from packing cases. His voice over the loudspeaker system seemed to come from far off as he repeated the court's sentence. Then the General paused dramatically before he barked out the order:

"Lieutenant Colonel, fulfill the verdict."

The trucks lurched forward several yards.

The gathering let out an involuntary screech like the escape valve of an overheated boiler. Momentarily they broke forward. Four bodies, three in the dirty gray-green Nazi field uniform, swayed slightly. Death was surprisingly quick and simple.

As I threaded through the throng I could see no expression of horror, no remorse on their faces. After witnessing the courtroom trial and watching the spectators I had not really expected to find horror and remorse. The people of Kharkov had lived with terror and tragedy for so long under the Germans that the sight of three Nazi barbarians and one traitor hanging cold and dead on a Sunday morning in their snow-covered, cobblestoned public square carried no shock. For the people of Kharkov it was only the prologue of a new drama, not the climactic scene of an old one. This was one of the small moments of justice, their first satisfaction under law for months of unlawful brutality.

I asked a Red Army lieutenant how long the bodies would hang.

"Three days and three nights," he said. "Let Hitler shake and tremble in his bomb shelter."

Examining the strong-lined faces of these Ukrainians, you knew instinctively that they would never put down their arms until total victory was won; that they would never forget the one hundred thousand Kharkov citizens who starved to death under the Nazis. Talking with them about "what it was like," I realized that in every head there is a kind of projector constantly throwing slides on memory's screen: scenes of thousands of women and children being tortured, their lives snuffed out in the gas wagons . . . of rubber hosing and machine guns cutting down defiant old men like a scythe cutting through a wheat field . . . of digging graves and being shoved in, sometimes alive . . . of the mass slaughter of the Jews . . . of barbed wire and bayonets ripping a tattoo on honest flesh.

And if these scenes ever faded, the people only had to gaze about them. There was always their beloved Kharkov, a living tableau of Nazi artistic achievement—the once handsome, thriving Kharkov which they had built with their own labor, now broken, twisted, wrecked.

The Red Army lieutenant followed me back to the car. The crowd was scattering, slowly. The officer said to me, echoing the prosecutor at the trial: "Their names are Langheld, Ritz, and Retslau. But in our hearts it is Hitler, Himmler, and Goering who are hanging there today."

Before I could find suitable words for a reply, a red-faced old *babushka* who had overheard the Lieutenant's declaration mumbled what all of us were thinking. She said, *"Skoro budyet—soon it will be."*

After we had written our stories at the hotel, several of us walked around the town. Eventually we went back to the market square, where little booths and stalls were open and doing a flourishing trade. I stopped and bought a second-hand *chainik* (teapot) for forty rubles. It wasn't worth more than twenty cents at Woolworth's, but there is no Woolworth's in Kharkov or anywhere else in Russia. And it was the first teapot I'd seen for sale anywhere at any price in the Soviet Union. Five minutes after I had bought it another correspondent came along looking for one. There weren't any more. He offered me sixty rubles for mine. Despite my capitalist instincts I resisted the profit.

The four bodies were still hanging in the center of the square. Only a few late-comers were looking at the bluish corpses. The three Germans had lost their forage caps. And Langheld was already minus his fine high boots. In Russia boots are boots whether they belong to dead Germans or anyone else. You take them where you find them and consider yourself lucky.

A kid with a cruel sense of humor was trying to stick a lighted cigarette into Bulanov's mouth. When a Red Army man shouted something at him he sprinted away.

We continued walking around the market. Somebody bought an old map in German. There were also German oil paints for sale, and German textbooks, and a sorry collection of Christmas ornaments, including some frayed silver tinsel and a few large red balls. An old woman at another stall was selling empty German bottles with strange and wonderful labels—champagne from France, port from Spain, cognac from Poland.

About fifteen minutes later we left the market place. It was still crowded with Sunday strollers and shoppers and buyers. But nobody was paying any attention to the four bodies. A Russian photographer for *Pravda* who was with our sightseeing group said: "This must be very hard for you to understand." Then he went on quickly, "It's not that people have no feelings; it's because they *have* feelings. The business of death is every day. The business of trade, the chance to buy things—can you imagine what that means to them? When the Germans were here they didn't dare to sell anything for fear the Germans would grab it. Of course there isn't much here, but it seems like much to them. Do you think this is bad? What is your opinion?"

I said I understood. "I have bought a *chainik*," I said, tapping the bulge in my coat pocket.

The cameraman sighed. "It cannot be a very good *chainik*. The Germans would not have left it behind."

As we neared the hotel he asked again, "Are you sure you understand how the people feel?"

"Yes." Then I said, "This is a nice hotel."

"Not very," he said. "You should have been here before the war."

"I was. I was here in 1935."

He brightened considerably. "Then you *do* understand," he said heartily. "You do understand." But as we went up the stairs toward our rooms he had another thought and he said to me, "But your home is in America. It is safe. Have you perhaps lost someone in the war?"

I said no.

"Then you only understand a little, just a drop." Then he seemed to be afraid he had hurt my feelings and he squeezed my arm. "You will forgive me. Even if you are very sensitive—just a drop."

I thought he was wrong then. It wasn't until months later, when I saw the Maidanek "murder camp" in Poland that I thought of him again and realized that he was quite right. People like me could understand only "just a drop."

ANOTHER MAN'S POISON:

V-E DAY

(JULY 1945)

Rebecca West

THE MORNING BEFORE V-E Day my husband, with the farm and garden staff, hauled tree trunks and brushwood up from the strips of woodland that fringe our property and piled them up on the village green outside our house. In the afternoon he went on a trip that would have been hard to justify to the petrol controller and brought back two barrels of beer. On V-E Day we were completely isolated—the two hundred and fifty people who make up this village—because the busses which are our only means of transport were cut off and we felt that was appropriate, for all through the war isolation has been the hallmark of our lot. Other people have come to us from the cities but we have stayed here. If we have sometimes gone up to town it was in such discomfort that when we returned and found our accumulated duties lying in wait for us we resolved not to go again so long as we could help it. In consequence of this concentration of interests we know each other to the last eyelash and we like each other greatly.

On the evening of V-E Day we went to our church—all of us, Dissenters as well as Episcopalians—and filled it so that even the gallery, in which nobody has sat within living memory, groaned under the weight. We walked back to the schoolhouse and stood in the garden. On the table I set a portable radio and was amazed to reflect that it had been given to me years ago as a bread-and-butter letter by a man whose name I cannot remember, who had spent the weekend with my husband and myself in a furnished house we had taken one summer in Sussex.

Had I ever really known so many people that I could not remember their names? Had people really ever given each other such expensive and casual presents? Had my husband and I really gone about the country spending money on taking other people's houses, and when we got there had we really just sat about having people to stay with us without endlessly working and fretting about machines and fertilizers and seeds and permits? I remembered what peace had been like and dreaded being asked to undertake that kind of life again. I have not forgotten the words "Let me not deny that world which had many achievements"; I am only saying that if it were re-created I would be unable to take part in it.

After the King's good and gentle speech we cheered and walked through an exquisite evening to the bonfire. There was sunshine but much moisture in the air, so that the white hawthorn trees and the green-gold beechwoods shone as if the paint on them were still wet. As we touched off the brushwood, curiosity rather than concern was expressed lest the heat of the flames should melt the telegraph wires.

Placidly we went ahead. Our farm bailiff, wearing a top hat draped with a Union Jack, appeared at a table under the beech boughs and dealt out the beer. The bonfire blazed up and others answered it from the Buckinghamshire ridges about us. Through the damp but unraining night we stood round the fire, sometimes listening to Pete, the gardener's boy, whose gift for lewd song shows that the village if decorous is not naïve, and sometimes joining hands and dancing. And people said over and over again, "Well, at least nobody's being killed at the moment." That was all they hoped for from this peace. They knew that these bonfires that had been lit to commemorate the defeat of the German army were pinpoints in a night that had not yet lifted. My sudden moment of fear lest the careless 'twenties and 'thirties should return was not justified.

An automobile drew softly up. The flames disclosed a high-ranking R.A.F. officer getting out, one of the most beloved personalities of the village, anxious to keep his tryst with his home on this evening. He had just come from Rheims. Of what he had been doing there he could not speak. Our governors do not pretend to believe any more that it is best for as many people as possible to know as much as possible of the truth, and the secret they keep most jealously is the reason for this change of belief. He talked, instead, of champagne. There was any amount of champagne in Rheims for three and a half dollars a bottle, but there weren't any bottles. You had to bring an empty one if you were to get a full one. It was fantastic, this shortage of containers.

Someone was reminded that it was difficult to handle the wheat which was being sent to starving Holland because there were no sacks. We shuddered to remember the amount of horror in the world, and the R.A.F. officer mentioned that before he had gone to Rheims he had visited Buchenwald. It grieves us here that Buchenwald means beechwood, for our beechwoods are our special glory. He had been there on a ghastly errand: to take an important and gallant soldier belonging to one of the United Nations which has no special reason to feel confidence in its post-war state to recognize the corpses of his wife, his father, his brother, and his sister-in-law who had been killed in the last few days before the camp fell. The wretched man had been left by victory without a past or a future, but what had disgusted our R.A.F. friend was not these or any other of the murders of which he had seen the traces; it was the cleanliness of the place. The cellar under the crematorium, where the people who were to be burned were hanged, had been white-washed daily. Such efficient precautions had been taken against venereal disease that there was none at all. The horror of Buchenwald came not from sluttishness but from deliberation. Of such stuff is humanity made. Of such iniquities we can all be capable if we say no to the world instead of yes, and God forgive us.

For years we intellectuals have derided those who made black and white answers. "What are we to do with Germany?" somebody asked, and the R.A.F. officer answered, "There is no Germany. There are Germans—when we flew low over the country I saw them looking up and shaking their fists at us—but there is no Germany, the towns are gone. If, here and there, factories and offices and dwelling houses are still standing, too much is flat to let what remains work as an organism. For the moment, Germany is gone."

It was at that moment that the first discordant note of the evening, which was to be the only discordant note, whined and rasped through the flame-lit darkness. We all of us recognized it for what it was. Ethel was complaining, with complete injustice, that somebody had ill-treated her child. Even on this night of all nights Ethel could not behave.

We have all had Ethel. Her husband is a skilled laborer doing essential government work in the district and he and his family have to be housed. There is not a vacant house for miles. This country lies on chalk and could not be farmed intensively until modern engineering brought it a piped water supply, but when the water arrived there was an agricultural slump and farming stayed as it was without increase in population or in houses. (This situation existed in many parts of Europe.) There was also the further complication that this valley, unspoiled as it is, is only fifty miles from London; therefore the larger farms were bought by prosperous business or professional people, who lived in the farmhouses and played at farming, or let the land go derelict, while many of the smaller farms and the laborers' dwellings were turned into weekend cottages for the slightly less prosperous. (This has happened all over England and, indeed, all over western Europe in the neighborhood of larger towns.) But now we are farming intensively to the very limit of the power brought us by the water supply.

This means that we were bound to be short of houses anyway, even had London and the South Coast not sent us their evacuees. What the situation meant was murmured through the darkness.

"Such a dirty slut! I shan't forget the smell of the child's bedding."
I shuddered reminiscently. Neither could I.

"They had Dad's workshop fitted up as a sitting room and we
kept to the kitchen, but she would keep right after us, picking a
quarrel. Say what you like it's wrong to have to share a home with
anybody but your own flesh and blood." "It's wrong," said the
voice of one of the most intelligent of the younger women, sharp
with conviction, "to have to share a home with anybody but your
husband and your children. Four years we have been with Aunt
Lou and Uncle Bernard up on the common, and they couldn't
have been kinder, but it's been hell, hell, hell because there wasn't
room." "It's always so, not having your home to yourself," the
agreeing voices chorused softly and bitterly, until Pete set us off
with the song which laments

> She's took the table and the old arm chair,
> The three-legged sofa that we used to share,
> She's took the kettle and the old coffeepot,
> The cups and saucers and the old whatnot.

That was one that recalled the worst that war had done to us.
Everybody there had been bombed. Our woods are scarred with
craters left by thousand-pounders. We have all in our time pulled
back the curtains and seen our fields and gardens gay with incendi-
aries. Many of us went through the London blitz as well. *That* we
endured with fortitude, and it left no burdens on our minds, but
sharing our houses—whether we were hosts or guests—drained us
of vitality and peace. This does not mean that we were disagreeable, either in the way of being ungenerous or ungrateful. It does
not mean at all that we were moved by class feelings at a time
when we should have forgotten them. This was rarely so, even in
the cases when the class difference was so marked that it involved
environmental disadvantages resulting in uncivilized habits. We in
England have got down to fundamentals in this matter and,
believe us, it is much better to share your house with somebody
who is kind and dirty than with somebody who is mean and clean.

261

It is easier to introduce soap and water into a life hitherto destitute of it than the milk of human kindness. The reasons for not sharing houses are not material at all. In the root of them lies the plain fact that a man must have his own home as he must have his own head, his own spine, his own intestines. We need to work out our personal dramas with the people to whom we are bound in the fundamental relationships of life.

It is not easy for us with that experience behind us to understand how life can maintain itself on any civilized level among those who are unlucky; who squat together in the pit of rubble marking the obliteration of the city. Surely we were unique in history as we danced round the bonfire on V-E Day, for after no other great war have the victors celebrated their victory in full knowledge that their celebrations might be ironical, since maybe the argument had gone too far before it was terminated for it to be possible to terminate it.

We sang, we danced until midnight, but we knew that we were on the edge of doom unless the whole of humanity walked carefully. We knew we could not survive unless we rebuilt in the flash of a decade the solid framework which had been built up through the centuries to shelter man and is now destroyed. Society needs more food and more houses. The test of good government after the war will be the satisfaction of these necessities combined with the preservation of our liberties, without which bread becomes poison, houses prisons, and a beechwood Buchenwald. If any claim another test and create a state of disorder in which it will be difficult to attack these technical problems and maintain freedom, let them be accursed; for they are careless of such good people as sang and danced about our camp fire in exhaustion not to be dispelled, and in full consciousness of deep awards in their spiritual life.

ANYTHING BOTHERING YOU, SOLDIER?

(NOVEMBER 1945)

John Bartlow Martin

I AM MAD because we were all supposed to be in this together. Were we? The educators, the historians, the politicians, the generals said that we were fighting for our way of life. Were we? What, as a matter of fact, were we fighting for? Does anybody really know? "I am fighting for my draft board volunteered me," said a soldier. In August, 1945, I was reading Frederick Jackson Turner, the historian of the frontier, who said, in a dedicatory address in 1918:

"In time of war, when all that this nation has stood for, all the things in which it passionately believes, are at stake, we have met to dedicate this beautiful home for history. There is a fitness in the occasion . . . we are fighting for the historic ideals of the United States, for the continued existence of the type of society in which we believe. . . . We are at war that the history of the United States, rich with the record of high human purpose, and of faith in the destiny of the common man under freedom, filled with the promises of a better world, may not become the lost and tragic story of a futile dream."

That was in 1918. Remember the 'twenties, the bigness, the lords of creation, the corruption and betrayals, D. C. Stephenson, Warren Harding, and the lost generation? And then the dynasty of death, the road to war, the veterans of future wars? Remember the early 'thirties, those who sold apples? And now remember the words of the leaders of the early 'forties? For all we hold dear, the last best hope of earth. And look about us in 1945. In August, 1945, a month not to be forgotten, I was on furlough in New York and in the Midwest, my home.

I am mad because the headlines are all on reconversion, no more gas rationing, new cars. When you can get a refrigerator is as big a news story as unemployment, and both are bigger than demobilization. How did the "Autos Released" headline look to the boy with the tense face, walking down Michigan Avenue swinging an iron claw at his side? Everybody is worried about the war workers who are out of jobs. Good; the country can't stand too much unemployment. But what of the soldiers still overseas? Why not employ the war workers in the Army for a while and let the soldiers come home and hammer at the doors of the U.S. Employment Service? The soldiers have made sacrifices; aside from death or wounds in combat, they have been miserable, they have given up their homes or jobs. What have the war workers given up? Selective Service won't draft anybody over twenty-six but the Army keeps soldiers in their thirties. If they want a young Army, one of men under twenty-six, why don't they discharge everybody over twenty-six? The newspaper headlines say that former war workers under twenty-six face draft. Why don't former war workers over twenty-six face draft too? They will say the war is over, they have done their part in the factories, now let them alone. Very well; let the soldiers over twenty-six alone too.

I am mad because the cities went on a binge when peace was declared. All the people went downtown and drank all night and stood in crowds. (I will bet that the civilians who had lost sons or brothers or husbands stayed home that night.) What were the civilians celebrating? A friend of mine who has fought it out in a brokerage house, gambling on war babies, was in the Loop drinking till 6:00

A.M. What was he celebrating? He stood to lose money in the market.
I know this is not fair to him. Poor man, he went to the blood bank
and saved tin cans. And he is in his forties. But he talks about no
more gasoline rationing, about the cigarette shortage and meat
rationing, about the tightness of travel. (And in all conscience he is
respectful in the presence of a soldier, and I love him.) But—how
soon will he forget the war? People should never be allowed to forget.
They should never be allowed to forget the mud and the boredom and
the uncertainty and the nervousness—"nervous in the service," they
say—and the broken homes and the good-bys, the anticlimactic good-
bys, and the manifold indignities. But they are forgetting already. If
they ever knew. Some of them must never have known.

A woman asked me if I thought I would be out of the Army soon
and I told her no and she said, "Oh. You don't want to get out?" They
must never have known, never have known anything about it at all. The
advertising agencies, the cheerful radio announcers, sold them a bill of
goods. In Scarsdale, while we were waiting for Washington's answer to
Japan's offer of peace-but-the-emperor, we heard a radio broadcast from
a rehabilitation center for blind veterans. The prepared script was jolly,
the veterans had few cares in the world, the announcer sounded won-
derfully healthy and he had a hearty booming voice. "Has it made any
difference to you, being blind?" Anybody listening who did not know
would have been reassured. "There. I knew they didn't mind so much.
Everything's being done for them. It's all right." And so he could have
forgotten about the blind boys. He should never be able to forget.
Doesn't he know that they once were just like him, that all the guys in
all the holes and all the guys in all the dreary training camps were just
like him? Why do civilians so quickly forget that a man in uniform is
still really, in his heart, a civilian too? A man's friends can adjust themselves to his entry into the Army a lot faster than he can.

I am mad because the ad in *Life* (full page, in color; and plenty
expensive) showed pictures of tanks in a river in the jungle and said,
"Roughest, toughest test oil ever faced!" Nothing about the men who
had to sit inside the tanks. It was very heroic about the oil.

265

What kind of a world are the soldiers coming back to? I know of one city in the Midwest which plans an enormous program of public works. Good. Jobs for the boys. But the politicians are taking a dollar a yard on every yard of concrete that is to be poured. They are the same old spoilsmen who have had their snouts in the public trough for years. What kind of a world is this? Again, labor still is scarce. I know of one union leader who refused to send workmen to a job until the boss agreed to give the workmen ten hours' pay for eight hours' work. The records would show they worked ten hours, two of them overtime. But actually they would work only eight. Cozy. Again, on the train through the cornfields I sat in a bar car and talked to an elderly man and a woman. The conversation stopped the gin rummy game and nearly induced apoplexy. They suspected the British, the French; they hated the New Deal; they hated labor unions; they hated the Attlee platform and feared it; above all they hated the Russians. They argued for free enterprise with all the shibboleths to which there are no answers. "Look at Henry Ford." "Do you think it is wrong to make money?" "Don't you think this is the best country in the world?" "Look at Henry Kaiser." What kind of a world is this anyway?

I am mad because Joe Curran of the National Maritime Union warns Congress that the return of soldiers from overseas may be delayed unless wartime danger-pay is restored to merchant seamen. Poor mariners. Their pay has been cut. Joe Curran says some seamen have already left the ships, which may lie idle. Is this true? If it is, is it a matter of wages or of draft boards? Also, is Curran voicing a fact or a threat? Is he really saying that Congress had better raise the mariners' pay back to wartime levels or by God he won't bring the boys home? You can expect the local labor bosses, the local spoilsmen, to cheat. But here we are in the big time. Joe Curran might argue the long view, that he is working for the Rights of Labor. That by playing politics with the return of soldiers, he is only fighting fire with fire. (The ends and the means: a moral problem.) He ought not to do that. Until the last soldier is home, dare a single seaman leave his ship?

On seeing a news report that the Secretary of War was considering revising his demobilization plans, a G.I. overseas is quoted: "He damn better." That is good. Somebody had damn better find out what we were fighting for. A dollar a yard for the ward heelers? Featherbedding? Free enterprise advertised to duck the tax on free enterprise's excess wartime profits? Senator Bilbo? The others who attacked the Fair Employment Practices Commission?

I wonder how many other soldiers are good and mad. Plenty, proba-bly. (What ever became of the angry Populists?) One soldier at the PX said, "They'd better straighten up and fly right." The trouble is, get the soldiers out of those brown suits and they're not mad any more.

I am mad because the civilians never learned much about the war. Civilians think war means battle. But combat involves a minority of soldiers for a minority of their time of service. Civilians think you are lucky if you do not get shot. You are. But there are other matters. There is the enormity of the indignity to man. Many soldiers have never been in combat. Yet they have not been happy in the Army. They do not like that type of work. They have given up their homes. They have abandoned their careers. Their wives and children have gone to live with their mothers. They have stored their furniture, sold their clothes and car. And so on, endlessly. ("They Gave Him a Mop"—you can have it free, Warner Bros.) And they, confronted by a legless veteran of Iwo Jima, stand mute and awed, ashamed at the pal-triness of their own sacrifice. (He might read this and think, not say, "I bleed for you, Corporal.") This is one reason they do not answer when an examining officer asks them periodically the Army's ultimate ironic question: "Anything bothering you, soldier?" They do not talk about these matters very often. When they are on furlough their friends think, "He has seen such terrible things he does not like to talk about them, about the Army at all." Not so. He is ashamed, afraid of sympathy. Nor does he talk about these matters to other soldiers. They have a ready answer: "Your story is very touching. Would you like to see the chaplain? Or use the crying room for one hour?" Or, "Go on sick call." It is a shameful thing to talk about at all, especially in public. People do what they have to do. But by God somebody ought to talk about it. We were all in this together. (But some of us are still in it. My aching back!) We were all in this together, so none of us should ever forget it. So somebody has got to talk about it. Yet this is futile, for the gap between soldiers and civilians is unbridgeable. What little civilians knew about the war they have forgotten. They should have been taught more. The Army, instead of characteristically restricting the sale of *Yank* to military personnel, should have sold it on the newsstands. It's too late now.

A cynical friend of mine wants to start an organization. It would be a pressure group. Its slogan would be, "Let's Make It Up to the Boys." He probably would make a lot of money out of it. The politicians hope the veterans splinter and never wield their strength together. This probably will happen. It really is best for the country that it happen. But—is there not temptation in "Let's Make It Up to the Boys"? A sinister temptation.

The war is over, labor can strike, the boss can gouge, the mayor can steal. What can the soldier do? Stand retreat.

For so long the ads and the radio and the editorialists have promised the post-war world, that when we awoke one morning we had to tell ourselves a number of times, *"This* is the post-war world. Here we are." It looked no different. The Atomic Age had been announced. There were no more helicopters, no more soybeans, no more plastics, than yesterday. You still were in uniform too. That was the point. You still say, "After the war I am going to do thus and so." Soldiers say "after the war" all the time but what they mean is, "after I am out of the Army." They still say "after the war," though the war is over.

My wife and I heard the news at 6:00 P.M. It was flat. That was on a Tuesday. We had begun listening constantly to the radio on the preceding Saturday, in Scarsdale. Then it had seemed wonderful and . . . But back a couple of days earlier, I was walking down Fifth Avenue from Rockefeller Center when a captain stopped me on the street and said, "Have you heard the news, Corporal?" I didn't know what he was talking about. He told me Russia had come in. It was the most incredibly wonderful news I ever had heard, I think, possibly excepting that night downtown in San Antonio last spring when my wife and baby and I were house-hunting and we saw a crowd around a newsboy on Houston Street and we bought a paper and it said Germany had surrendered. We wept, and a Mexican girl cried and patted our baby and said that now maybe her baby's daddy could come home; he had been in the Bulge. (Ah, how the Texans hate the Mexicans!) Next day the news turned out to have been premature, but Germany was finished. Well, on Fifth Avenue, the captain said, "I think it'll be over within two months," and I thought he was too optimistic but for a few minutes, walking by his side (on the wrong side; I should have been on his left, and in step, but suddenly it didn't matter), it seemed as though it might be over in a very few months.

Then came the atomic bomb, and then the Japanese asked for peace and we sweated it out at Scarsdale with some friends. (Was the radio ever sillier? "We interrupt this program." "After another long, trying day." How the correspondents suffered! What makes a man imagine that because he is covering an event he becomes more fascinating than the event itself?) That was Saturday and Sunday, August 11 and 12, 1945; then Monday we lunched with a writer in New York and he was against a peace that kept the emperor. A publisher had said on Friday he thought maybe we ought to drop an atomic bomb on the palace, that quitting now was like asking the dentist not to drill the last sixty seconds and then, because he didn't, having to go back to him in two years. The end of the war had seemed wonderful, of itself; unquestionable. Now the New York intellectuals questioned it. Did they know about the mud and the cold, about how you march fifteen miles with full field pack, starting hours before dawn, and arrive dripping with sweat, then shiver, chilled through your body, all the rest of the day in the drizzle? This is an unfair basis to put it on; they did not know, how could they? And it shouldn't make any difference anyway. But it did. The peace came, in Chicago, on Tuesday, and it didn't seem like so much, it was such a peculiar peace, almost a civilian peace, somehow. And everybody talked of "the end of the war," not of "victory."

It got worse deeper in the Midwest. People asked how you like it in the Army. What can you tell them? If you do not know them well you say you like it all right except that there are certain disadvantages to working for a large organization. If you know them pretty well you tell them really how you like it in the Army. You do this partly because you think they ought to be made to know and they ought never to be allowed to forget it. But it makes them uncomfortable, and they think you complain without cause. This is due partly, of course, to the fact that people have been sold a bill of goods. They think the Army gets the best of everything, the best food ("YOU get butter all the time, don't you?"), the best weapons, best medical care; that it is efficient, expert, unbeatable. Unbeatable, probably; but efficient and expert, never. It is always fouled up, always and hopelessly, so hopelessly that it is funny. Your friends also are uncomfortable because when you tell them of your wife's travels as she followed you from camp to camp they are reminded of their own comfort—and of yours, which matched it, before you started tucking your tie in—and they think you are accusing them. You are not, really. But you are good and mad about the way other civilians have treated you. And you think your friends should not be so complacent.

In the South your wife and daughter have had to live in tourist cabins because private homes will not accept children. Tourist cabins are all right but they charge nearly $100 a month for one room and a tin shower. You are mad because the railroads won't honor furlough coach tickets on their crack trains which they are sure to fill at regular rates. (Something for the boys—why didn't somebody blow that one out of water a long time ago?) You are mad because when you buy beer by the case in San Antonio they knock the caps off all the bottles; they do this so they can charge you twenty cents a bottle and cheat on the Office of Price Administration. You are mad at all the cheap rackets like that on which the Southerners, poor heretofore, are trying feverishly to get rich. You are so mad you hope there is a hell of a depression after the war and everybody south of the Ohio River goes on relief. In the Army one is never rational. One is just mad. While the war is going on you keep your mouth shut, because so many are suffering so much. After the war the civilians suddenly let themselves go. So you do too. Hurray.

I am especially mad because I know better. Know better than this. I knew, when I was a journalist, that the corruptionists always sat smoking in their hotel rooms, that you played the game according to the house rules. I am mad now because this thing I am writing is naïve; like digging a foxhole, it is beneath me, beneath any rational man. I am mad because I am confused and because the old sophistication is somehow wrong. (Remember 1939 when you laughed at a Negro jazz man, Stuff Smith, when he said, "Stop that war—them cats is killin' theirselfs"?) Why should a man whose skin is black die for something that isn't there? (I have heard them say they are good enough to be buried side by side in Italy but not good enough to sit side by side on a bus in Texas.) And why should the old folks in Iowa hang out the golden star and give thanks that the other boy got home? Home to what? And why should the Arkansas sharecropper—God save us, he smelled and never wore shoes—go back to his acre and his mule when his father cannot sit in the Willard because the old man hasn't got a coat? And what of the boy whose friends were burned in Germany, the boy whose bride, like him, cannot gain entrance to the hotel by the sea because it is "restricted"?

And what of the general who awards the medal (posthumously) in the name of our nation's ideals but is all the time himself considering rank and promotion and base pay and allowances? (Statement of charges for the soldier who burned his shoes warming his feet.) Shall we now vote a bonus for the soldier who hit the beach, lost his rifle, constructed another from parts, got seven days at hard labor for zeroing it in at an unauthorized spot, volunteered to hunt Japs, killed several valorously, returned to confinement and was told he would have to make up in the stockade the time that he spent killing Japs? The platoon is forgotten, forgotten the tech sergeant's name. Only the place names remain—Tarawa, Iwo Jima, Cassino. Soon they will be forgotten. Already nobody knows what the campaign ribbons signify, the ribbons with battle stars that meant so much.

There is a time to be born, and a time to die. A time of war, and a time of peace. The preacher Ecclesiastes has said so. It is a sophisticated view. My friends hold it. They are complacent. You got drafted, you got trained, you got killed, you didn't, you came back, here you are back, have a drink. A time for war, a time for peace.

I am mad because these things should not bother me, they are included in the game, and I know the rules.

But how can they sit there like that?

THE BOMB AND THE OPPORTUNITY

(MARCH 1946)

Henry L. Stimson

THE ADVENT OF the atomic bomb has created a profound impression in all quarters of the globe. Bidden or unbidden, the atomic bomb sits in on all the councils of nations; in its light all other problems of international relations are dwarfed. This is so not because these other problems are no longer important in themselves, but because the question of the control of the atomic bomb towers above all else. No other problem has been so constantly in my thoughts as this one.

If the atomic bomb were merely another—though more devastating—military weapon, which could be assimilated into the customary pattern of international relations, conceivably we could then follow the old pattern of secrecy and sole reliance upon national military superiority, and depend upon international caution to stay the future use of the weapon. But, to my view, the recent unlocking of atomic energy constitutes a first step—and only a first step—in a new control by man over the primal forces of nature too revolutionary and dangerous to fit into the old patterns. The military application of this discovery underscores most sharply the divergence between man's growing technical power for destructiveness and his psychological power of self-control and group control—his moral power. If this is so, how this problem is approached in the sphere of the relations among the nations is a question of the most vital importance in the evolution of human progress.

The chief lesson I have learned in a long life is that the only way to make a man trustworthy is to trust him; and the surest way to make him untrustworthy is to distrust him and show your distrust. And it is from this lesson that I draw the conviction that only a direct and open dealing with other nations on this, the most pressing problem of our time, can bring us enduring co-operation and an effective community of purpose among the nations of the earth. It is the first step on the path of unreserved co-operation among nations which is the most important. Once the course of national conviction and action is set in this direction by the example of the major powers of the world, petty differences will be recognized for what they are, and the way toward a real fraternity of nations will be open.

We must not delay. The poisons of the past are persistent and cannot be purged by timid treatment. By its sole possession of the bomb, at least for the present, the United States finds itself in a position of world leadership. But this solitary possession is most certainly very transient. It must recognize this and act swiftly. It must take the lead by holding out an open hand to other nations in a spirit of genuine trust and with a real desire for a thoroughgoing co-operative effort in meeting and solving this problem. Truly this is a time for greatness of heart and of purpose, and unless we demonstrate these qualities now other nations cannot be expected to do so.

The development of atomic energy holds great, but as yet unexploited, promise for the well-being of civilization. Whether this promise will be realized depends on whether the danger of swift and unprecedented destruction can be removed from the earth. Whether it is removed depends on whether we and other nations move firmly, quickly, and with frank transparency of purpose toward the goal of uniting all men of good will against the appalling threat to man's very existence. The focus of the problem does not lie in the atom; it resides in the hearts of men.

ABOUT THE AUTHORS

The following biographical information is presented here as it originally appeared in Harper's Magazine.

John Gunther, of the London bureau of the Chicago *Daily News*, is of course familiar to our readers. Some of our best articles on European affairs have come from him. "Hitler" is the second of a series of portraits of European dictators. The others are "Stalin" and "Mussolini."

Elmer Davis was a news analyst for WABC during wartime. He has been a contributing editor to *Harper's* for many years.

C. Hartley Grattan is a regular correspondent of this magazine. He is the author of *Why We Fought* (1929), a book about the First World War.

J. B. Priestley is one of the best-known English novelists. In all he has written more than twenty volumes—novels, essays, travel, and plays. His works include *The Good Companions, English Journey*, and *Midnight on the Desert*.

E. B. White was responsible for the "One Man's Meat" section of *Harper's* from 1938 to 1943.

Hans Schmidt is a pseudonym. He is a well-known German who recently made his way to this country.

Ida Treat, the American wife of a French naval officer, has taught languages at the Flora Mather College in Cleveland. With a grant from the Paleontological Institute of Paris, she conducted excavations among the primitive ruins of the Pyrenees and uncovered the first complete skeleton of an early Stone Age man. She was on the staff of *Vu*, the French equivalent of *Life*.

Dorothy Thompson has been, for more than twenty years, the tornado reporter who must get there or else, and latterly the tornado columnist whose work is syndicated in more than 150 papers. Her books include *I Saw Hitler, Refugees, The New Russia*, and *Let the Record Speak*.

Bernard DeVoto has filled "The Easy Chair" of *Harper's* since 1935. He wrote the three-volume study of the American West *The Year of Decision: 1846* (1943).

Margaret Bourke-White is one of the best-known American photographers. Early in 1941 she went to Russia with her husband, Erskine Caldwell, and they were there when war between Germany and Russia broke out. Since 1929 she has been on the staff of *Fortune* and *Life*.

Willard Price has traveled extensively in his capacities as staff writer for *The Survey* and as editorial secretary of the Methodist Board of Foreign Missions. His books include *Ancient Peoples at New Tasks, The Negro Around the World, Children of the Rising Sun*, and *Barbarian*.

Bella Fromm was the society reporter for the German newspaper *Vossische Zeitung*. She left Germany for the United States in 1938. After her arrival she was for some time in danger of her life from Gestapo agents who came from Mexico for the express purpose of murdering her and destroying her papers.

Patrick Maitland is a correspondent for the London *News Chronicle*. "I'm sorry to say," says [his] agent, "that even after talking to Mrs. Maitland, all we can give you is the fact that since last Christmas he has been covering the war in the Pacific." Previously, Mr. Maitland was in Czechoslovakia when Hitler entered in March 1939, and was in Poland when war broke out.

C. J. Fernand-Laurent was introduced to us in New York at the beginning of April as "the last man out of France to reach America." By the time the article appeared this may no longer be strictly true—hence the quotation marks in the subtitle. Yet M. Fernand-Laurent's report is unique in that he is both a recent arrival and a man of position in France. He did not escape till December, when he managed to make his way out of the Pyrenees into Portugal. For many years he has been a member of the Chamber of Deputies, representing a Paris consituency.

Virginia Snow Wilkinson will only say about herself that she was born in Utah, married in California, has three children, and divides her time between home, writing, and, very recently, building ships.

Frederick Lewis Allen is editor of *Harper's Magazine*. The British Ministry of Information recently invited a number of American editors to visit England and see conditions there for themselves. Mr. Allen received one of the invitations and accepted it. He wrote his impressions on the return voyage.

D. W. Brogan, a Scotsman, is a Cambridge professor, an adviser to the BBC, and an authority on both French and American history.

One of Them. This article, by a captain in our Army Air Force in England, was written not for publication but in letters to the Captain's family. He agreed to publication only if we made it anonymous.

William L. Shirer, CBS commentator and former European correspondent, is the author of *Berlin Diary.*

William Fifield was formerly a radio director at CBS, New York, and then went to Hollywood, where he wrote scripts for the major networks. His classification as a Consciencious Objector under Selective Service is based on religious conviction.

Oscar Williams is the author of several books of poetry, *The Golden Darkness* (1921), *The Man Coming Toward You* (1940), and *That's All That Matters* (1945).

Geoffrey Grigson is an English critic and poet. He is also the founder and editor of the magazine *New Verse*.

E. E. Cummings is the author of many volumes of verse and of *The Enormous Room*, one of the few surviving novels of World War I.

Henry Treece, a Flight Lieutenant in the Royal Air Force, is now stationed in London. He is the author of four volumes of verse.

John Berryman is a short story writer, critic, and author of a single volume of verse. He is now an instructor at Princeton.

C. Lester Walker's article has been fraught with difficulties. Commissioned in July, the first draft was dispatched to the Pentagon for clearance on September 30th with publication scheduled for December. It was on January 17th, three months and two-thirds after the original submission of the manuscript, that at last we had an O.K. from the War Department, the Navy Department, the British Army, and the Royal Air Force!

John P. Marquand is *Harper's* correspondent with the Pacific Fleet.

Thomas Hornsby Ferril has been a regular contributor to *Harper's* since 1942. He is a publicist for the Great Western Sugar Company. His published poetry collections include *High Passage* and *Westering*.

Richard E. Lauterbach was *Time-Life* correspondent in Moscow, 1943–44, and chief of *Time's* Moscow Bureau. He is now an associate editor of *Life*. His book, *These Are the Russians*, will shortly be published by Harper and Brothers.

Rebecca West is a well-known English novelist, critic, and political journalist. Among her works are *The Judge* (1922) and *The Thinking Reed* (1936).

John Bartlow Martin, having passed through basic training and orientation, is now careering temporarily in the Army. *Harper's* readers will remember him as the author of a number of excellent narratives of crime and of a widely quoted and hotly debated article called "Is Muncie Still Middletown?"

Henry L. Stimson was Secretary of War under President Taft (1910–1911) and again under Presidents Roosevelt and Truman from 1940–1945. He was also Governor General of the Philippines (1927–1929) and Secretary of State under President Hoover (1929–1933).

Paul Fussell is an author and educator. His many works include *The Great War and Modern Memory* (1975), for which he won the National Book Critics Circle Award in 1975 and the National Book Award in 1976, *The Boy Scout Handbook & Other Observations* (1982), and *Wartime: Understanding and Behavior in the Second World War* (1989). He served in the United States Army from 1943 to 1946, and was in action in France. He received two Purple Hearts and a Bronze Star. He is currently professor of literature at the University of Pennsylvania. He lives in Philadelphia.

Katharine Whittemore, editor of the *Harper's Magazine* American Retrospective Series, is a writer and editor living in Cambridge, Massachusetts.

ACKNOWLEDGEMENTS

"Hitler," from *Inside Europe Today,* by John Gunther. Copyright © 1961 by John Gunther. Reprinted by permission of HarperCollins Publishers, Inc.

"No More Excursions!," by C. Hartley Grattan. Reprinted by permission of Jacqueline Snitkin.

"Where England Stands," by J. B. Priestley. Reprinted by permission of Sterling Lord Literistic, Inc.

"One Man's Meat: On 'Secret' Information," from "Freedom" from *One Man's Meat,* by E. B. White. Copyright © 1940 by E. B. White. Reprinted by permission of HarperCollins Publishers, Inc.

"One Man's Meat: Following Fashion," from "Intimations" from *One Man's Meat,* by E. B. White. Copyright © 1941 by E. B. White. Reprinted by permission of HarperCollins Publishers, Inc.

"Who Goes Nazi," by Dorothy Thompson. Copyright © 1941. Reprinted by permission of McIntosh and Otis, Inc.

"The Easy Chair: Toward Chancellorsville," by Bernard DeVoto. Reprinted by permission of the Avis M. DeVoto Trust.

"America's Enemy No. 2: Yamamoto," by Willard Price. Reprinted by permission of Mary Virginia Price.

"The Easy Chair: Commencement Address," by Bernard DeVoto. Reprinted by permission of the Avis M. DeVoto Trust.

"What the Germans Told the Prisoners," by William L. Shirer. Reprinted by permission of Don Congdon & Associates.

"Another Man's Poison: Note on War Memorials," from *I Hate Thursday,* by Thomas Hornsby Ferril. Copyright © 1944, 1945 by Harper & Row, Publishers, Inc. Reprinted by permission of HarperCollins Publishers, Inc.

"How the Russians Try Nazi Criminals," from *These Are the Russians,* by Richard E. Lauterbach. Copyright 1944, 1945 by Richard Edward Lauterbach. Reprinted by permission of HarperCollins, Publishers, Inc.

"Another Man's Poison: V-E Day," by Rebecca West. Reprinted by permission of Sterling Lord Literistic, Inc.

"Anything Bothering You, Soldier?," by John Bartlow Martin. Reprinted by permission of Harold Ober Associates, Inc.

THE AMERICAN RETROSPECTIVE SERIES

VOICES IN BLACK & WHITE:
Writings on Race in America from *Harper's Magazine*

TURNING TOWARD HOME:
Reflections on the Family from *Harper's Magazine*

THE WORLD WAR TWO ERA:
Perspectives on All Fronts from *Harper's Magazine*